"This is a wise, generous, and beautiful book. David Tacey is one of our most important academic and cultural commentators on the state of contemporary religiousness and spirituality, especially in relation to the work of C. G. Jung, and in *Jung and Spirituality* he distils his insights from several decades of comprehensive inquiry. Passionate yet clear-minded, Tacey conveys in always-accessible prose the seriousness, complexity, and depth of Jung's influential contributions to this area of perennial as well as pressing concern in our lives."

Professor Roderick Main, Department of Psychosocial and Psychoanalytic Studies, University of Essex

"A powerful addition to the canon of David's life work exploring the depths of Jung's work and its relevance to our modern spiritual crisis. Full of thought-provoking insights and revelations, it is an important work in the crowded field of Jung studies with urgent relevance to these times of great unravelling."

Edward Watts, BAFTA and Emmy award-winning filmmaker

JUNG AND SPIRITUALITY

JUNG AND SPIRITUALITY

David Tacey

AEON

First published in 2025 by
Aeon Books

Copyright © 2025 by David Tacey

The right of David Tacey to be identified as the author of this work has been asserted in accordance with §§ 77 and 78 of the Copyright Design and Patents Act 1988.

British Library Cataloguing in Publication Data

A C.I.P. for this book is available from the British Library

ISBN-13: 978-1-80152-164-2

Typeset by Medlar Publishing Solutions Pvt Ltd, India

www.aeonbooks.co.uk

CONTENTS

CHAPTER 1

The nature of spirituality

We moderns are faced with the necessity of rediscovering the life of the
spirit; we must experience it anew for ourselves.

—Jung (1929a)

Spirituality arising from the collapse of religion

The most important fact about contemporary spirituality is that it emerges as a global phenomenon at a time of transition and upheaval. It arises as one epoch closes and another opens. It is doubtful, for instance, that we'd be talking about spirituality at all if the established religions were still effective in capturing the imagination of the majority. The world religions are containers of spirituality, but in our time the traditions and their symbols have become what T. S. Eliot called a "a heap of broken images" (1922, p. 63). According to Robert Frost, the grail cup is "hidden" and "under a spell so the wrong ones can't find it". The task, he says, is to find living water so we can "be whole again beyond confusion" (1947, p. 1245, lines 58, 62).

The spirituality revolution, as I called it years ago (2003), is designed to enable us to do what Frost indicates: find the water of life and be whole again. Undoubtedly a new hybrid religion will emerge as a result of the spirituality phenomenon, although it most likely won't be entirely new, but composed, I believe, of a blend of Christianity and Buddhism, with elements of Hinduism, Islam, Judaism, and indigenous traditions. It seems to me that the mystical traditions of all religions have much to offer a future religious dispensation. No religion is ever fully new, but is based on what is best and most enduring in the traditions before it. Usually it wells up from the grassroots and flourishes across vast areas until a great teacher or teachers come along to build it into a cohesive religious structure. Then the philosophers and theologians begin to craft it into a system until we eventually end up with a fossilised set of precepts and dogmas that have to be broken down again.

The history of religions is the story of one attempt after another to capture and express the secrets of spirituality in a current language or cultural epoch. It is captured for a while, but over time the essence is lost and the container is broken. This is heartbreaking for many, because the container becomes identified with the essence. But as religions becomes systematised they lose touch with experience and hence lose their spiritual life. There is no such thing as an absolute revelation of the sacred that can remain eternally true. Jung put the problem in para-doxical terms: "Eternal truth needs a human language that alters with the spirit of the times," (1946, § 396) and even more emphatically: "All the true things must change and only that which changes remain true" (1955–56, § 503).

Jung wrote much about the rise and decline of cosmologies, since we are in the middle of the passing of the Christian aeon: "The gods of Greece and Rome perished from the same disease as did our Christian symbols: people discovered then, as today, that they had no thoughts whatever on the subject" (1934a, § 26). The religions decline because all passion is spent; the once-powerful symbols lose their vigour and people are no longer gripped. When this happens the core of religion, which is spirituality, emerges from its formal containment, and like a butterfly from a cocoon it takes flight into a new horizon. It is an auspi-cious event, and extremely dangerous because many people not only lose their faith but also their orientation and grounding in life.

In its free-form flight from traditions, spirit moves towards the mys-tical, because mysticism is based on the experience of the sacred, and predates any formulation in dogma. Thus we are finding today that it is the mystical sub-traditions of the religions (Sufism, Kabbalah, Christian meditation, esoteric Buddhism, shamanism) that are flourishing, with great appeal to a broad range of people. Often people flit from one form of mysticism to another, sampling the kinds of nourishment that are available during the decline of the mainline religion. The collapse of a fossilised religious system can take place in a relatively short time, often a couple of hundred years, while the whole cycle from beginning to end can take thousands. Throughout it all, spirituality remains the constant, the living water, that is always threatened with extinction by the dry and sometimes oppressive religious structures.

The most spiritual poets of the modern era have turned to mysticism to regenerate their lives and poetry. This has been spectacularly successful in the case of T. S. Eliot, whose *Four Quartets* is one of the great masterpieces of all time. Also, Ted Hughes, Gary Snyder, Robert Bly, Les Murray, and Mary Oliver have been nourished by the sources of mysticism available to them. There is often a recognition that the most creative poets need to turn away from fashionable issues and intellectual debates to find the deeper connections that lead them to the sacred. Mary Oliver is a stunning example:

> Knowledge has entertained me and it has shaped me and it has failed me. Something in me still starves. In what is probably the most serious inquiry of my life, I have begun to look past reason, past the provable, in other directions. Now I think there is only one subject worth my attention and that is the precognition of the spiritual side of the world and, within this recognition, the condition of my own spiritual state. (1999, p. 153)

For Mary Oliver, spirituality is not an intellectual matter, not a debate about reality, or an academic exploration. Spirituality is an immediate apprehension of the world around and within us. That is why she goes on to say:

> What I mean by spirituality is not theology, but attitude. Such interest nourishes me beyond the finest compendium of facts. In my mind now, in any comparison of demonstrated truths and unproven but vivid intuitions, the truths lose. (Ibid.)

Spirituality is not theology, as the religious often claim. It is a mental and psychological attitude to reality, an openness to the depths of our experience. This is why some say that Buddhism, for instance, is not a religion, in the sense of a collection of propositional beliefs that have to be followed, but a philosophical mode or form of consciousness. The sense of rivalry between spirituality and religion is due to the fact that spirituality is increasingly unaligned with any existing tradition, but a movement beyond traditions, although sometimes borrowing from them all. As Mary Oliver says, spirituality is attitude, a way of perceiving things and a way of looking at the world. It is the unproven but vivid intuitions that command her attention as she approaches old age.

What is spirituality?

Because of the freewheeling nature of contemporary spirituality and divergent views and understandings, spirituality is especially difficult to define. But if I were to offer a definition it would be something like this: "Spirituality is that aspect of humanity that refers to the way individuals seek and express meaning and purpose, and experience their connectedness to the world." Or else: "Spirituality is the discovery of connectedness at various levels of experience." In seeking spirituality we touch on at least four domains: we seek to connect to the soul or interior self; to other humans; to the world of nature; and to the cosmos and creator of life.

I say we seek to discover connections but perhaps I should say we uncover or even recover them. My sense is that such connections already exist, and antedate any attempt to discover or formulate them. This is why Mary Oliver refers to spirituality as "precognition", not an act of cognition, because it apprehends what exists prior to our knowing. She writes of a "spiritual ecology" in which:

> ... there exist a thousand unbreakable links between each of us and everything else, and our dignity and our changes are one. The farthest star and the mud at our feet are a family; and there is no decency or sense in honoring one thing, or a few things, and then closing the list. The pine tree, the leopard, the Platte River, and ourselves—we are at risk together, or we are on our way to a sustainable world together. We are each other's destiny. (Ibid.)

If we strive too hard to forge these links we might miss them, since what is needed is receptivity to a pre-existing mystery, not a wilful enterprise.

Mystics emphasise that spirituality is about discovering what is already there; for them it involves no special technique or craft to reveal these links. Those of a sceptical bent say we "make" these connections, and they were never there before we fabricated them. But this is a humanist fallacy which attributes too much agency to the human will. The mystics argue that we don't manufacture these connections, but recover a pre-existing order. It is an order we could not see before, the order of the One World or Unified Field, because our consciousness was too constrained to bear witness to the larger whole. In my view spirituality restores the world to the unitary field it was before the ego split the world into subject and object, inner and outer, self and other.

Although it is common today to see spirituality as a lifelong quest or search, in ancient traditions it is seen not so much as a heroic accomplishment as an awakening to a reality close at hand. Spirit is not conceived as far off, a result of great striving, but closer than your own breath. "You cannot get there, you can only be there" is a saying I once heard about spirituality. If spirituality is the search for sacred connections, mysticism is the awareness that sacred connections are searching for us.

Another definition suggests itself: "Spirituality is an innate human capacity to experience transcendent reality." In this definition, the transcendent is emphasised. Why do we hunger for transcendent reality? Jung says it is because we are not only made in the image of God but the soul is made of God. The divine is an essential aspect of our nature. When this aspect is thwarted, it makes the spiritual desire within us even more desperate to seek expression.

What transcendent reality is, we don't know. If we did know, it wouldn't be transcendent. I just know that we live better lives if we acknowledge the transcendent and act as if it were real and close at hand. I feel it is healthy if we adopt an attitude of humility; we should not attempt to know this reality too fully. An attitude of observance, matched with the art of not-knowing, is the best attitude with which to approach the sacred.

If we get too rational about spirit and its substantive reality, chances are we will lose the plot and head into a kind of fanaticism. As Jung put it, it is not possible for our finite minds to grasp the infinite (1931b, § 283). When we think we know the divine, we can be sure, at that moment, we are far from grasping it. As Rudolf Otto said in *The Idea of the Holy*, "A God comprehended is no God" (1917, p. 25).

Religion and spirituality aim for the same goal: reconnection or binding back to the primal unity of being, regardless of what we might name this unity. It is no accident that the etymology of the word "religion" places us conceptually in the same field as spirituality. Religion derives from the Latin *religio*, meaning to "reconnect" or "bind back to". In late antiquity religion meant to "bind fast" or "place a bond between humans and gods". In a separate etymology, relevant to the study of scripture, religion derives from *relegere* meaning to "read again" or "careful consideration" of sacred texts.[1] Both Jung and Derrida employ these two etymologies in their studies of comparative religion and the religious function of the psyche.

In Jungian terms, spirituality is the encounter with archetypes. When we meet the archetypes we connect with another world, because archetypes are the organs of a universal mind, our means of contact with the world beyond. Every meeting with an archetype is a meeting with the mystical domain, because every archetype brings with it an experience of the pleroma from which the archetypes emerge, as if from the mind of God. When we meet an archetype we are brought into relation to the Ideas (eidos) in the Platonic sense. These are the non-physical, timeless, absolute, and unchangeable essences of things, of which natural objects are the imitations. In Wordsworth's poetic language, the archetypes come to us "not in utter nakedness, /But trailing clouds of glory .../From God who is our Home" (1807, lines 58–65). At the heart of every complex is an archetype, and contact with our complexes leads us back to the archetypal core of our experience.

The interiority of the world

There is "a motion and a spirit that rolls through all things", as Wordsworth put it in "Tintern Abbey", and once this interior spiritual reality is uncovered we can readily fall in love with the world (1798). When the interiority of the world is uncovered it becomes a cosmos; no longer a collection of things it becomes a field in which we can participate by virtue of intuitive vision. Spirituality cannot be experienced by those who only look at the world externally, as an assortment of objects. It comes when we engage feeling and intuition, and sense that what is in the world is also within us. Our subjectivity is not private or personal, but is part of the inwardness of everything, the soul of the world. This is how indigenous people experience the world, through belonging to what may appear external but is experientially part of their soulful interiority.

Western people need to learn this skill from indigenous cultures and poets. We in the West live in a world that is viewed as spiritually dead or inert. If we feel a spiritual life within the world we are told by intellectuals that this is "nothing but" the projection of our interiority onto the world. This has been the modern outlook at least since Descartes. We look at the world, but do not feel ourselves to be part of it. We remain outsiders, and do not share the indigenous experience of belonging.

But when spirit is uncovered we become entranced by the world, and everything changes. We are no longer observers, but lovers of and participants in the world. As Wordsworth wrote: "Therefore am I still/A lover of the meadows and the woods/And mountains; and of all that we behold/From this green earth" (ibid.). His word "therefore" is pivotal; once we see its spirit we are impelled to fall in love with the world. The presence of spirit changes a collection of objects into a communion of subjects. Spirituality enables the world to reveal its hidden order, and love or eros enables the world to take new shape and become a cosmos. The nature of spirituality is to induct us into the spirituality of nature.

This is how spirituality transforms the world and ourselves. Spirituality transforms the world into a cosmos through connectedness and love. It is intimacy or eros that enables the world to reveal its hidden order. We open our eyes to the web of meaning and aliveness that binds the various attributes and dimensions of the world. Through spirituality, synchronicities and links are brought to our awareness as never before. With this perceived unity comes a sense of ourselves as relational; we are no longer fragmented persons in a broken world.

Spirituality transforms our longing into belonging. We might catch glimpses of cosmic order through meditation, contemplation, or spiritual exercises. But eventually cosmic awareness can enter our daily lives and grant us a vision of life as it was meant to be. Thus spirituality is not so much a matter of introducing something new, but unpacking the acquired and conditioned layers that block a deeper reality. As William Blake put it: "If the doors of perception were cleansed, every thing would appear to man as it is, infinite" (1793).

It follows from this that experiences of connectedness, however fleeting or minor, can give rise to a sustained commitment to the pursuit of such experiences throughout the entirety of our lives. It is then that we are able to announce to others and to ourselves that we are on a spiritual journey. We might say we are "hooked" at such times, and the sense of relief and homecoming is such that we are prepared to alter our lives to create conditions that are favourable to the further pursuit of such experiences. Spirituality is not a chore but an attempt to recover our original belonging.

Michel Foucault, one of the great philosophers of modern times, is hardly known for his advocacy of spirituality. But in one of the last interviews he gave before his death in 1985, he said:

> By spirituality, I understand that which precisely refers to a sub-
> ject acceding to a certain mode of being and to the transformations
> which the subject must make of himself in order to accede to this
> mode of being. (1984, p. 14)

Spirituality involves identifying a non-normative mode of being, and generating the changes and adjustments that must be made to realise our goal. In the New Testament this is *metanoia*, which means to begin again, think again, start over. In the English Bible this word is mistranslated (in my opinion) as "repentance", but it means far more than this, and points to a psycho-spiritual transformation that effectively acts as an initiation into another dimension of being. But the churches generally fail to bring about the transformation that Jesus called for, and the best they can aspire to is repentance.[2]

If the neo-Marxist Michel Foucault can see this, why can't others, in particular the churches, who hide from these wider challenges? The churches don't want to become experiential or mystical, but want to revert to business as usual, which means supporting the status quo and supplying a moral code which does not require any real change. Or else, we notice that some churches have engaged in a rebranding exercise: they call themselves centres of spirituality without changing their structure or offerings. They sense the change of mood in the public, and that spirituality is in fashion and religion out, but still cannot cater to it. They try to make themselves postsecular by subterfuge, but the public are not convinced.

At the heart of religion, as I have said, is the pursuit of connectedness, but when religion is routinised and systemised to such an extent that it no longer delivers experiences of that connectedness, we can say it is spiritually dead. The heartbeat of connectedness no longer throbs at its core and we are impelled to look elsewhere for our heightened experiences. It is significant that the climactic moment of the religious ritual in the Christian West is "holy communion", that is, a moment in which the distance been us and the holy is annulled and we are held by the divine embrace. The Catholic mass includes the experience of holy communion at every service, which is one reason why the Catholic tradition endures. However, the Protestant service replaces the sacrament of communion with the reading of the word or scripture, thus foreshadowing the end of Christianity as an intellectual approach replaces the emotional sacrament.

Spirituality has certain features in common with political ideologies. Like conservative politics, it believes that concentration on a transpersonal goal brings stability and contentment to personality and society. Like radical politics, it believes alienation needs to be overcome before life can be lived with dignity and freedom. Marxist theory, as distinct from its barbarous practical applications, emphasises that the source of human suffering is alienation, and this is accentuated in the modern world, where there is much change, speed, and uprootedness.

Left politics attempts to overcome alienation through social and political revolution and spirituality through psychological transformation. Unlike radical politics, spirituality does not advocate violence to achieve its goals, but rather a quiet interior revolution in which individuals feel connected to the world and others. Spirituality is the art of transformation, in which people are shown how to overcome their encapsulation within the confines of the ego. With authentic spirituality, egotism is overcome and we are invited to experience our birthright: a sense of belonging and kinship with creation.

Response to a call

Spirituality requires that we find a quiet place in our heart to allow spirit to come to us, rather than go in search of it. When spirituality comes to us, we have transcended the ego-driven search, a desire to fill the hollowness inside, and allow the effulgence of the divine to emerge. Then we have found the ground upon which mysticism takes place. Mystical experience occurs when we feel ravaged by the divine, entering our lives like the beloved. This is the experience that is described in erotic terms in "The Song of Songs" or "Song of Solomon", in the Hebrew Bible.

In theological terms, spirituality is a response to a call, a call from the creator to us. We only go in search of spirit because it first came to us. In biblical terms, we can only love because we were first loved.

I John 4: "We love because he first loved us" (1 John 4:19). The biblical injunction is insistent that our love and compassion must flow horizontally towards others, and not only vertically to the Most High: "Whoever claims to love God yet hates a brother or sister is a liar. For whoever does not love their brother and sister, whom they have seen, cannot love God, whom they have not seen." The spiritual mission is not fulfilled unless we direct our love towards the world, as well as to the heavenly sphere.

Spirituality requires receptivity and attentiveness to soul, nature, others, and God. It requires an aptitude for listening deeply, seeing deeply, and intuiting deeply. Spirituality is the intuition that there is a larger background to our lives, that something other than ourselves is close at hand, and this makes life meaningful and gives us a sense of belonging. We live, but something greater lives its life through us. Again, there are biblical parallels: "I live; yet not I, but Christ lives in me" (Galatians 2:20).

Christianity provides a culturally specific manifestation of this experience, but today, in a pluralistic and multifaith world, which forces us out of a narrowly Christian frame, we need to distil the religious example to find the archetypal pattern inside. We need to go beyond the specifically Christian case, to find the universal process that is found in all cultural and religious contexts. In this way we move beyond the tribal and denominational outlook to the global or archetypal pattern which will form the basis of a new religious sensibility.

Spirituality is not possible without intuition. This might account for the fact that spirituality is more accessible to women than men. Innumerable surveys and reports have shown that intuition is more prevalent in women, and large numbers of men do not understand intuition or else feel threatened by it. It is a function of consciousness that attends the feminine principle. Spirituality is about receiving, listening, greeting. We intuit another world in this one, but it is a world we cannot see or touch. This does not mean it is imaginary or make-believe, but it is a world that is not readily available to scientific scrutiny or academic study.

The French poet Paul Eluard wrote: "There is another world, but it is in this one."[3] Intuiting the reality of another world is the primary spiritual impulse; it is what kick-starts the spiritual journey. Cultural materialism says this awareness of a second world is deluded, but spirituality reverses this charge and argues that materialism is deluded, in the sense that it blocks out much reality. Thus we have to do with a battle of world views, and it is difficult to see how this battle can be resolved. People often fall on one side of the divide or the other. Is this world of appearances the only world, or is there an even greater world within and beyond this one?

Spirituality as counter-cultural

In a world of increasing fragmentation, the spiritual longing is a desire to heal the gaps and rifts that have opened in modernity. Spirituality is and has always been a countercultural enterprise. In the Gospel of Matthew, Jesus says: "For what will it profit a man if he gains the whole world, but loses his soul?"[4] This is another definition of spirituality, seen as the task of keeping the inner life going while not succumbing to the glamours and attractions of the world. This doesn't mean we should spurn the world, or strive to live outside it, but as we live our lives, we have to be mindful that a greater life is living us. Our human will is not the only force in play. Life is a balancing act between our will and a greater will. "Thy will be done on earth, as it is in heaven." All these ancient sayings and aphorisms provide glimpses into how to live the spiritual life.

Naturally enough, spirituality is not and cannot be supported by mainstream culture. The mainstream is ego-based and invites us to view life as a personal quest to gain wealth, comfort, and material security. The mainstream invites us to wrap ourselves up in egocentric cocoons. Do governments, nations, and societies understand the need to have an inward experience of the spirit? No, and the churches don't either. The secular and religious see no need for it, and don't even see inward experience as reasonable or real—hence it is negatively viewed as escapism. In *The Meaning of Psychology for Modern Man*, Jung wrote:

> Small and hidden is the door that leads inward, and the entrance is barred by countless prejudices, mistaken assumptions, and fears. Always one wishes to hear of grand political and economic schemes, the very things that have landed every nation in a morass. Therefore it sounds grotesque when anyone speaks of hidden doors, dreams, and a world within. What has this vapid idealism got to do with gigantic economic programmes, with the so-called problems of reality? (1934c, § 328)

Spirituality is a recognition that society is incomplete, and needs to be supplemented by a deeper longing for wholeness and connection. Spirituality is the drive of the spirit for transcendence, for more than what society offers. It is a reaction against secularism, but as yet this increase of interest in spiritual enquiry has not resulted in a boost to the religious organisations. This could change if the religious organisations could reshape themselves as places of spiritual enquiry. Some do this in name only, but if they can do something more than change their name or self-description, there is a hope that some of them will survive.

Spiritual desire is felt everywhere today, and people often look for transcendence in a range of different forms and expressions. Many try drugs, as a way of breaking the egocentric cocoon and experiencing other planes of reality or states of mind. Others use sex as an expression of the search for transcendence and release from the mundane. Still others become obsessed with individual or team sports and treat them as religious devotions, investing all the affinity, trust, and belief in sports that was once entrusted to institutional religions. Nature, forests, groves, glades, and landscapes can give people connectedness to the earth as well as detachment from the enclosures of cities and suburbs.

Explorations of foreign cultures and countries, unfamiliar terrains, and different languages and accents can foster altered states of consciousness, especially if the foreign places are immersive, exotic, and beckoning. Others are attracted to foreign cuisines, foods, diets, and beverages as ways of breaking boundaries and the sense of entrapment. Naturally food, travel, and hospitality industries are aware that consumers are looking for more than material pleasures as they explore these activities and pastimes. We aren't just wanting food, scenery, or physical exercise, but are wanting to break the chains that bind us, break from the familiar, and enter other worlds. When we recall that ecstasy is defined as "removal to elsewhere", we can see the enticements of travel and exploration. Advertisements make it clear that we are seeking spiritual release as well as pleasure or indulgence. There is an awareness among copywriters and advertising agencies that clients are prepared to pay money to appease the spirit and find a sense of release.

Spirituality can lead to conflict between people, within families, marriages, and relationships, as one person decides to risk the beckoning of spirit, and another says: "No, not for me; this represents a parting of ways." I have known many relationships that have come to grief over this. Often the resistant partner wants proof of the existence of spirit or

God, and says if there is no proof, they are not going to risk it. They then accuse their partner who responds to spirit of escapism, avoidance of reality, eccentricity, or madness. It is often the male who says this to the female who has set out on a journey.

To start a spiritual journey is often to feel isolated and alone in the secular world, and so finding like minds and compatible others is a major consideration. The larger world to which spirit points can lead a person to a deeper connection with nature and the environment. This is sometimes called "creation spirituality", and much of the grassroots support for environmentalism and ecological concern is motivated by spiritual, not just environmental interests. People often experience spirit in nature, a sense of presence or depth or hidden life that gives them a sense of renewal and enlargement of soul.

But just as spirituality leads a person into the natural world, so it leads him or her into their own interiority. A person discovers there is much more to the self than the ego and its motivations. There is a larger reality within, which has traditionally been called the soul. This is what the religions ought to have connected people with, but alas, part of the reason for the demise of the religions is because they construct the divine as far above, distantly removed from the self. The mystical dimension, which means the activation of soul, has been missing.

Spirituality challenges our understanding of normality and sanity. Insofar as we are conditioned by society to accept "normality" as presented to us, spiritual desire threatens the status quo and fills us with a restlessness that others may condemn as eccentric or mad. A person who develops an interest in God in secular society might be ridiculed and viewed as abnormal. Hence schools, universities, and governments prefer to ignore or berate the new interest in spirituality, viewing it as a fashion which is destined to die out as people come to their senses.

But spiritual desire will not die out; studies indicate it will most likely increase exponentially. There are figures on this by social researchers.[5] David Hay (2006) argues that the spiritual need is "ineradicable". It would seem that, despite what secular authorities believe, spirituality is normal although made to appear abnormal by our entrenched outlook. Secularism leaves too much out of the picture. It would seem that seeing through the limitations of secularism is the first sign of spiritual longing.

The soul challenges the ego to seek something beyond itself. This can lead to conflict with ourselves and our social conditioning. There is a desire to break out, to run contrary to rules, to seek more than what is sanctioned. Our egoic selves long for stability and security, whereas the spirit leads us out of our cocoons into an encounter with a greater reality. The spirit or soul beckons us out of our shells, and sometimes our first response to this beckoning is refusal. "I am happy with who I am, and do not wish to change."

If our resistance continues and the spirit is insistent, it can bring about circumstances that destroy our cocoons, forcing the ego into submission. If we do not learn the lesson of humility before a power greater than ourselves we may be forced to be humiliated. Spirituality is a call to transformation and if this is greeted with fear and resistance, the consequences can be dire. The avoidance of the call to spirituality is often a source of psychological disturbance and neurosis. As Jung put it: "A psychoneurosis must be understood, ultimately, as the suffering of a soul which has not discovered its meaning" (1932, § 509).

In his memoirs, Jung says he suffered a great deal of isolation throughout his life, especially in his early years. For him the intuition of a second reality or greater world was an intuition that brought isolation and loneliness. It also drove him towards nature, to find the solace and comfort he could not feel in the human world. I will discuss this in a later chapter, but the larger world to which spirit points can lead a person to a deep connection with nature and the environment.

Living with a secret

The spiritual life gives the sense that one is living with a secret, which cannot easily be shared with others. One would like to share it, but a sense of fear and self-protection generates a sense that the secret should be hidden, lest others try to steal or destroy it. The secret is a blessing in many ways, because it represents one's connection to a larger reality, but it is also a burden, insofar as it represents something that cannot be shared or communicated without difficulty.

At the approach of puberty, Jung felt the need to give expression to the secret life inside him. He tells how, in his tenth year, he took hold of a school ruler, and carved from it "a little manikin about two inches long, with a frock coat, top hat, and shiny black boots" (1961a, p. 36). He put this little figure in a pencil case, with a "smooth, oblong blackish stone" that he had taken from the Rhine river. He had painted the stone and carried it around in his trouser pocket. The stone, he felt, belonged to the manikin and he hid both in a secret place:

> This was his stone. All this was a great secret. I took the case to the forbidden attic at the top of the house and hid it with great satisfaction on one of the beams under the roof—for no one must ever see it! I knew that not a soul would ever find it there. No one could discover my secret and destroy it. I felt safe, and the tormenting sense of being at odds with myself was gone. This possession of a secret had a very powerful formative influence on my character; I consider it the essential factor of my boyhood. (Ibid.)

All through Jung's life he had a fear that there were others who might want to destroy his secret life, his sacred self, due to resentment, malice, or envy. He felt that society, religion, and science knew little about the secret self, from which everything arises, and in which truth is found. At times it seems that Jung was paranoid about society's capacity to destroy his secret. Why people would be so opposed to the spiritual self, Jung could never understand, because it is the essential nature of our being. He believed the ego is threatened by the secret, and tried to defend against it by attacking it.

Jung was often plagued by fears of chaos and inundation, by threats of despair, and it was all the more important for him to fashion images of the inner self that brought meaning and stability to the personality. He tells how he was led to create the manikin because of a sense of "disunion with myself and uncertainty in the world at large" (ibid.). This symbolic act of creating a new self gave him "a feeling of newly-won security" and the satisfaction that he now "possessed something that no one knew and no one could get at" (ibid., p. 37). By implication, we all need to fashion symbols of the inner self, so we can transcend egotism and aspire to a security that the ordinary ego cannot provide.

In religious terms, Jung had fallen out of church religion and moved back in time to ancient animism, where manikins, symbolic stones, and tokens held enormous significance, were treated with the greatest respect, and surrounded by taboo. He says that, in later life, the rounded pebble reminded him of the cache of soul-stones discovered at Arlesheim, Germany, and further back in time, of the "Australian churingas" (ibid., p. 38). In Australian Aboriginal ceremonies of male initiation,[6] the young male is given a sacred stone or *churinga*, to symbolise the "second body" or new life from which he must now live. At the climax of the ritual, the elder holds out the stone, and says: "Here is your body, here is your second self" (cited in Neumann, 1949a, p. 289).

There are parallels to this in all the world's religions, where the profane and self-centred life of the ego is terminated, and a new self is put in its place. St Paul speaks to the Ephesians about "putting on the new self that has been created in God's way" (Ephesians 4:24). In tribal societies, the time for laying aside the old and putting on the new self is about the age of twelve or thirteen, when the boy is leaving childhood and finding a new centre or basis for the adult personality. In Jung's story the second self is not passed to him by tradition or by an elder. His story is "modern" and outside tradition, and he invents a personal symbolism consisting of manikin, stone, and hiding place. The modern person has ancient longings for this archetypal process of rebirth, but he or she has fallen out of tradition, and personal symbols become important in the absence of a shared public symbolism. The creativity of the psyche must now take the burden of responsibility, and show the way towards rebirth, security, and meaning.

We see in this narrative several elements that were to become foundational to Jung's approach to psychotherapy. One is the importance of imagination and artistic expression to the inner life. Without imaginative expression, the inner life can be dulled, and never allowed to find its voice. Another point is the importance of ritual to the well-being of the soul: the carving of the manikin, the hiding of it in the attic, the placing of scrolls of paper on which secret words had been written, are acts in which "care of the soul" is being enacted. Third, we see the importance of a secret as a way of affirming the reality of the soul. "The little wooden figure with the stone was a first attempt, still unconscious and childish, to give shape to the secret" (1961a, p. 37).

Ceremony, solemnity, secrecy—these must not be dismissed as esoterica or superstition, but are needed to help us transcend the flatness of the mundane, and to give verticality and form to the spirit. Late in his memoirs, Jung elaborates on the idea of a necessary secret.

> It is important to have a secret, a premonition of things unknown. It fills life with something impersonal, a *numinosum*. A man who has never experienced that has missed something important. He must sense that he lives in a world which in some respects is mysterious;

that things happen and can be experienced which remain inexplicable; that not everything which happens can be anticipated. The unexpected and the incredible belong in this world. Only then is life whole. For me the world has from the beginning been infinite and ungraspable. (Ibid., p. 390)

Living with the idea of a secret self is synonymous with isolation. This is a new isolation imposed by our secular conditions. In tribal societies, the secret of one's identity was given by elders and tradition. In modern society, the secret no longer inducts us into public ritual, but rather excludes us from the secular order.

In an interesting passage, Jung says that to possess a secret that connects one to a spiritual life is to "become a deviant from the collectivity" (ibid., p. 377). He continues:

Like the initiate of a secret society who has broken free from the undifferentiated collectivity, the individual on his lonely path needs a secret which for various reasons he may not or cannot reveal. Such a secret reinforces him in the isolation of his individual aims. A great many individuals cannot bear this isolation. (Ibid., p. 76)

He surmises that many are called to a spiritual life, but end up shunning it because it isolates them from the social environment in which they live. To remain true to the spiritual life, one must gather inner strength and resolve, and not bow to external pressures. But if people falter and cannot summon the strength:

As a rule they end by surrendering their individual goal to their craving for collective conformity—a procedure which all the opinions, beliefs, and ideals of their environment encourage. Only a secret which the individual cannot betray—one which he fears to give away, or which he cannot formulate in words, and which therefore seems to belong to the category of crazy ideas—can prevent the otherwise inevitable retrogression. (Ibid., pp. 376–377)

He says that many of his patients could not make the sacrifice required; they did not want to appear "different" from their families or peers.

They were forced to betray the secret and join the group. But anyone "who attempts to do both, to adjust to his group and at the same time pursue his individual goal, becomes neurotic". Such people "play hide-and-seek with others as well as themselves"; they "do not take the game of life really seriously". They are saddled with a neurosis which represents the split between the call to transformation versus the call to conformity.

Jung is not saying that the spiritual journey should be the main occupation of life, and the world must be set aside. He is saying that one should not compromise the spiritual life for the sake of conforming to society's standards. Naturally one has to be in the world, but not necessarily of the world. Do not allow the world to dictate its values to you, because the chances are that its values are wrong. He is saying that to have your soul and be in the world at the same time, one needs to be a little crazy.[7]

The secret, he says, "belongs to the category of crazy ideas", because the notion of an interior self is "crazy" to a world that seeks only material security and social adjustment. An element of craziness or eccentricity keeps us sane and enables us to maintain the integrity of the personality. Most psychiatry advocates social adjustment at all costs, and Jung was an anti-psychiatrist opposed to a conditioning that leads to a betrayal of soul. He recommended that the values of society should be critiqued rather than replicated, and that we cultivate a secret space so that the soul can flourish.

The beckoning horizon

A person on a spiritual journey discovers there is more to the self than the ego and its motivations. There is a larger reality, which has been called the soul. This is what the religions ought to have connected us with, but alas, part of the reason for their demise is that they have constructed the divine as outside, up there, and removed from the self. This is another way of saying that Western religions have been too external and historical, not connected with mystical sources. When a person realises that the spirit is found in the inner world as well as the outer, they often look upon religion with scorn. Why has religion pretended that spirit is outside, when spirituality makes us aware that there is a kingdom within?

One of the best descriptions of the spiritual life is found in the writings of Rabbi Abraham Joshua Heschel. He writes in *Man Is Not Alone*:

> The search for reason ends at the known; on the immense expanse beyond it only the sense of the ineffable can glide. It alone knows the route to that which is remote from experience and understanding. Neither of them is amphibious: reason cannot go beyond the shore, and the sense of the ineffable is out of place where we measure, where we weigh.

He speaks of our longing for the far horizon:

> We do not leave the shore of the known in search of adventure or suspense or because of the failure of reason to answer our questions. We sail because our mind is like a fantastic sea shell, and when applying our ear to its lips we hear a perpetual murmur from the waves beyond the shore. Citizens of two realms, we all must sustain a dual allegiance. (1976, p. 24)

This is a wonderful and evocative passage. He affirms that we do not leave the shore of the known only because reason has failed us. We leave the field of reason because something larger than reason calls us to itself. This is infinitely greater than reason can comprehend, let alone describe. We have to get used to the idea that we live in the presence of a tremendous mystery, and the intellect cannot get a handle on it, but only allow us to use metaphorical terms and symbolic expressions to convey it to ourselves and others.

In *Trauma and the Soul*, Jungian analyst Donald Kalsched argues that the human soul needs to be drawn out of its hiding place, and requires some stimulus, even a shock or trauma, to inspire it to become activated. He says the victims of early trauma

> … often report having been "saved" by an inner world full of preternatural presences. Often they report synchronous experiences that defy rational understanding. And many of them describe a blurring of boundaries between ordinary and non-ordinary reality, which allows them uncanny access to an immaterial reality that is inaccessible to better adapted people. (2013, p. 3)

Trauma appears to rupture the psyche so that spiritual (but also demonic) forces are allowed to rise up from the depths and play a healing role in the experience of suffering. He says it is often the case that the "better angels of our nature" are activated by adverse circumstances, and that is a reason why spirituality and psychotherapy are often found together in the works of many writers. He says: "This is the way it is with the human soul. It seems to need a resonant image from the human or non-human environment if it is to come forward, something it recognizes" (ibid., p. 21). When a fascinating or shocking event occurs in a life, the soul is awoken from its resting place and comes to life in a way that might otherwise not have happened. This reminds us of the words of poet Friedrich Hölderlin: "But where the danger is, there grows as well that which saves" (1802, quoted in Bambach, 2016, p. 473).

Commenting on these words of Hölderlin, the philosopher Heidegger writes that "The world is being emptied of what is whole and heals." There is not much in today's world that acts to facilitate the awakening of the soul. In such a world, he says, we have lost our spiritual bearings and have no compass. Heidegger despairs that

> ... not only is the holy lost as the track to the godhead, but even the traces leading to that lost track are well-nigh obliterated. The more obscure the traces become the less can a single mortal, reaching into the abyss, attend there to intimations and signs. (1936, pp. 94–95)

What Heidegger could not see at the time was that psychotherapy would reveal the lost track to the godhead. The track would be discerned through the depths of painful suffering, in which the autonomous healing powers would be constellated. Unsupported by religion or culture, the psyche is seemingly able to activate healing powers in the absence of sacred rites or ceremonies. As Kalsched explains:

> Ironically, trauma survivors are in a unique position to claim this larger vision, because they are often forced prematurely into "non-ordinary reality"—a spiritual and often mentalized world that helps them survive the unbearable pain of their early affect-relationships. They become what James Grotstein calls "orphans of the Real", but simultaneously they become avatars of the Ultra-Real. (2013, p. 4)

Hence through the fractured place in their psyches where trauma shattered their worlds, survivors of trauma often get a glimpse into another world of psychic reality. Jung would have referred to this as the archetypal or daimonic world where numinous powers latent in the deep strata of the unconscious suddenly come into view—especially in dreams. Kalsched concludes: "There are few, if any, atheists among trauma survivors" (ibid., p. 5).

Compulsions and addictions

The craving for spiritual experience was correctly diagnosed by Jung as the essential driver of many of the popular addictions, whether alcoholism, drugs, sex, or whatever our option to achieve release. Sex in particular holds out the possibility of connectedness and the idea of achieving relief from egoic confinement by ecstatic union with the Other. The Greek root of ecstasy is *ek-stasis*, meaning to be outside (*ek*) the usual or habitual place (*stasis*).

In popular language we talk about being "beside ourselves" with joy, or "off our tree" or "transported", and all these terms relate to the experience of *ek-stasis*. This is now viewed in an entirely secular and physical sense, but ecstasy was traditionally associated with mystical writings, the state of rapture in which the soul was engaged in the contemplation of divine things. Through loss of ego and merging with the beloved other, the mystic hopes to enter a state of swoon, trance, or stupor which will transport him or her to the divine.

Needless to say, with such transformative expectation unconsciously present in sex, the experience often falls short of what is anticipated. Sex can be "good" but the transformation for which we crave is withheld. It inevitably falls short of the desired end because we are looking for a fulfilment that sex alone cannot deliver. Only love can take us beyond the ego that separates us to the spiritual experience that unites us with the other. This, it seems to me, is the wisdom in the old adage that we should not have sex without love, or as it became domesticated over time, no sex outside marriage. The experience of love is the only thing that can satisfy our primal urges, and as tradition says: God is Love. Hence whichever way we look at it, the experience of the divine is the answer to our desires. St Augustine put it best when he said in his *Confessions*: "You have made us for yourself, O Lord, and our hearts are ever restless, until they can find their rest in you." This might sound strange in today's world, but I believe it to be true.

Jung claimed that the desire for alcohol is an ersatz form of spiritual hunger. He told his alcoholic patients, some of whom formed Alcoholics Anonymous, that they were seeking God and making the category error of assuming that it can be had through alcoholic intoxication. Again, it was a form of ecstasy that was being sought. Jung said he never had any luck weaning anyone off alcohol unless he could encourage them to find God; that was the only way of resolving the addiction. He said these addictions are not resolved by overcoming the desires that fuel them, but by channelling these desires into spiritual forms.

The addiction is a false substitute for what the soul really wants. Jung's teachings on alcohol were so successful that today we have a worldwide network which is indebted to his original inspiration (McCabe, 2015). Jung told the founders of AA that the winning formula for alcoholism is *spiritus contra spiritum*, a seemingly arcane dictum, but it has been proved right time and again throughout the globe. Spiritus (the living Spirit) can counteract (*contra*) alcoholic spirits, which is a cheap and destructive version of Spirit. The only way to satisfy and quench the desires that possess them is to connect (*religio*) with the living Spirit, although not necessarily in the form of joining a church or religious organisation. To break free from the power of alcohol only the spirit can set you free. This is a pointed example of what he would write in the *The Red Book*: "You are a slave to what you need in your soul" (2009, p. 263).

But this dictum is true for every addiction and compulsion. We are all enslaved by what we don't understand about ourselves. W. H. Auden, who was influenced by Jung, put a different spin on this: "We are lived by powers we pretend to understand" (1939). The more unconscious we are of our spiritual desires, the more addicted we will be to the ersatz products that stand in as substitutes. Because society does not and cannot avail us of the means of satisfying the soul, we are all victims of the allure of consumerism; sitting ducks for the enticing commodities the consumer economy makes available to us.

It is our barely comprehensible desires for spirit that keeps the capitalist economy afloat and moving forward. To adapt Jung's slogan to a political context: we are slaves to consumer capitalism because of the unassuaged needs of the soul. If we could find the key to spirit, capitalism would fall on its face. To put it more clearly, it is to the advantage of the consumer society to ensure that we do not find our way to spirit (Carrette & King, 2005).

The global turn to spirituality

It would be a mistake to assume that the spiritual turn I have described is found only in Western societies. Although my focus is mainly on the West, with the nearly spectacular defection from the established churches to other styles of spiritual expression, the spiritual revolution is a global phenomenon.

In the rest of the world it is possible to discern an equally spectacular turn away from the formal structures of church religion in favour of a less dogmatic and scriptural, and a more mystical kind of spiritual life. But outside the West, this shift has often happened within the existing religious structures (mosques, temples, churches) rather than against or outside them.

Julia Day Howell's work on religion in Indonesia shows how Muslim-majority Indonesia has moved to a spiritualisation of the mainstream religion that is characteristically postmodern. She shows how Islam has shifted, since the 1980s, away from rationalised and cerebral forms towards more personalised and experiential ones. This includes the remarkable comeback of formerly suppressed Sufism, Islam's mystical tradition, in both popular and middle-class forms. Sufism is commonly cast as antithetical to Salafi Islam. In the past, the Sufis have been viewed as heretics propagating practices wrongly introduced into Islam centuries after the time of the pious ancestors.

Howell concludes that the shifts in Islamic culture in Indonesia bespeak a country that is now more interested in spirituality than in religion per se. The instrumental rationalism and sober or dry scripturalism is no longer paramount in the lived expression of Islam. Indeed, Francois Gauthier writes that the situation in the Middle East is similar. Gauthier argues that in the Islamic Middle East we can observe the same shifts, where "a spiritualised brand of Islam has spread massively" in recent years.

China has been described in the past as "a society without religion". But Fenggang Yang claims that "In the last three decades or so, unbeknown to most sociologists in China and the West, a quiet spiritual revolution has swept the vast land" (2014, pp. 562–578). A lot of research has been done recently on Shenzhen, a new Chinese metropolis of 13 million inhabitants. It is a designated Special Economic Zone, where one would imagine that the rationality, utilitarianism, and secularism inherited from the communist era has survived. But this is far from being the case.

According to Lizhu Fan and James Whitehead, the Special Economic Zone is spiritually thirsty and follows many non-traditional patterns. The extreme modernisation and rapid urban growth of Shenzhen has catalysed the emergence of "new questions of meaning and purpose" (2005, p. 15). Yet, rather than turning to the approved religious institutions, urbanites give "very personal expression to their spiritual search in the age-old idiom of China's common spiritual heritage".

The rise of Christianity in China is one of the sensational stories of our time. Academic sources suggest that "By 2030 there will be more Christians in China than in any other country on earth."[8] However, according to sociologist Jung Ha Kim, the large numbers of Chinese people who are turning to Christianity are not so much embracing the conventional forms of Christian worship as they are adapting them to their personal and often idiosyncratic uses:

> Chinese Christianity ... privatizes spiritual quests by cultivating the desired state of consciousness through personal meditation, indeed, through individually catered lists of how to sit still, empty one's mind, maintain a sense of tranquillity, and so forth. Chinese Christian spirituality is, then, made to be ultimately anti-institutional and highly individualistic. (1996, p. 66)

Although some reports suggest that the Chinese have appropriated Christianity uncritically, here is a suggestion that what is taking place in China is close to what Christianity might wish to develop, but has yet to develop, in the West. Jung Ha Kim indicates that Chinese experience is turning a Western religion into the "interiorised", "privatised" experience that might have flourished in the West had the churches had the foresight to adjust to what people wanted before the mass defection.

François Gauthier (2023) says that Chinese cities are home to a massive rise in "spiritual-not-religious" communities whose basic structures and the dynamics are akin to what is experienced in the West. The spirit of China is awakening from the blight of communist style atheism and turning to an expressive type of individualism, in which "The goal and meaning of life is to realise the unique self that we believe we have, and to express it publicly." Fenggang Yang says, "Chinese Christianity empowers people to go against some of the traditional beliefs and practices that have become obstacles to change. So it's an empowering force for modernization" (2014, p. 576).

It seems as if the stronger the political efforts are to attempt to eradicate religions, the more intense are the reactions from resurgent populations, who practice spirituality under the radar of atheist regimes. As Hugh Mackay put it: "Prohibition and persecution inevitably stimulate and reinforce the very attitudes, beliefs and practices they seek to suppress" (2016, p. 5). Fenggang Yang writes:

> The lack of sufficient attention to spirituality [in China and other Asian countries] by many intellectuals and writers today is not because of the lack of spirituality in these societies per se, but because spirituality is either invisible or incomprehensible to them. It is a blind spot in the kind of modernist mentality that has become mainstream in academia, which has sanctioned ignorance and negligence of spirituality in cultural research. (2014, p. 576)

Endnotes

1. For an accessible and reliable etymology see: https://etymonline.com/search?q=religion
2. Jesus begins his ministry by calling for *metanoia*, a transformative change of heart; Matthew 3:2.
3. I have not been able to find a reliable source for this quote, which is widely attributed to French poet, Paul Eluard.
4. Matthew 16:26; and Mark 8:36.
5. See for instance, 'Understanding the Spirituality of People Who Don't Go to Church: A report on the findings of the Adults' Spirituality Project at the University of Nottingham', August 2000. https://spiritualjourneys.org.uk/pdf/look_understanding_the_spirituality_of_people.pdf
6. In deference to Aboriginal sensitivity to gender, and the separation of men's and women's secret business, I, as a male writer living on Aboriginal land, am unable to comment on women's business. For more on tribal initiation, see my chapter "Rites and Wrongs of Passage", in *Remaking Men* (London: Routledge, 1997a).
7. I think of the lyrics of the 1991 popular song "Crazy" by Seal and Guy Sigsworth: "But we're never gonna survive, unless we get a little crazy."
8. Report of Purdue University's Center on Religion and Chinese Society. Quoted by Anderlini, J.,The rise of Christianity in China. *Financial Times*, February 7, 2014.

CHAPTER 2

Jung, spirituality, religion

> *The creative principle has its home no longer in the symbolism of a*
> *cultural canon, but in the individual. It has almost ceased to live in*
> *favoured holy places, in sites or at times dedicated to it, or in men con-*
> *secrated to it, but may live everywhere, anywhere, in any way and any*
> *time, that is to say, anonymously.*
>
> —Erich Neumann (1954, p. 168)

The phenomenon of spirituality

Jung died in 1961 and did not live to see the ascendancy of spirituality that he had predicted and the world witnessed from the 1960s to
the present. He said modern men and women no longer want belief,
but experience, and that is what spirituality claims to offer. We live
in a time in which popular opinion is privileging "spirituality" above
"religion" and where the latter is regarded with a good deal of suspicion. "Religion" as the term is used in popular discourse refers
to practices that are viewed as institutional and external to the self,
whereas "spirituality" refers to the personal pursuit of the sacred, often
expressed in untraditional ways.

27

The separation of these terms, and the construction of spirituality and religion as opposites, is anomalous from an historical perspective. In the past, and still today in theological and monastic communities, "spirituality" refers to the living core of religion and the personal appropriation of a lived faith. In the Catholic church there are, among others, Jesuit, Benedictine, Franciscan, and Dominican "spiritualities", and each refers to the disciplined pursuit of a life of devotion and prayer. But in the wider public domain "spirituality" has little or nothing to do with religion, and refers to all forms of human activity that concern the search for meaning.

Spirituality still exists as the inner life of religious traditions, but this use of the term now seems marginal, compared to the vast numbers who appropriate the term in a different way. Spirituality inside religions refers to the capacity to enter into the core of a tradition and to weld it to experience. Spirituality outside religions refers to the capacity to bear witness to a depth dimension of experience which has been lacking during the period of high secularism. In their popular usage, "spirituality" has expanded as a term and "religion" has contracted. In the past, spirituality was the core of faith and religion was the container that held the spiritual within itself; today they have changed places and their meanings have been reversed. Spirituality is now the broader term, and "religions" are optional pathways within the larger circle of spirituality. These changes and reversals are part of the "spirituality revolution" that I identified two decades ago (2003).

Hence today we often hear people describing themselves as "spiritual but not religious", but this would have made little sense in Jung's time. Arguably, Jung played a significant role in prying spirituality and religion apart. But to scapegoat him as a figure of evil, the Catholic church claims that it was Jung who established the new fashion for interior spirituality: "From Jung's time onwards there has been a stream of people professing belief in 'the god within'."[1] The bizarre element of this depiction of Jung is that every mystical tradition emphasises the presence of the god within, and such traditions go back long before Christianity. I have always felt the Catholic church despises Jung because he represents a considerable threat to its authority. If we can connect with a god within, and live according to its dictates, there is not a great need to show obeisance towards external sources of spiritual authority. Hence Jung is regarded as an embodiment of evil who radically relativises the authority of the churches.

Jung was not a supporter of any church or religious institution, but nor was he prepared to give church religion away. Although the way of institutional faith was not his chosen path, he displayed a certain respect for the traditions that had carried the spiritual life in the past. But like numerous mystical thinkers before him, he felt that modern humanity had outgrown the need for reliance on external sources of authority. The Catholic church has always discredited and demonised mystical thinkers who draw attention to an alternative source of authority.

One need only refer to the way in which the church has treated its own mystics and prophets throughout the last two thousand years. At the time the Christian church formed, there was an alternative parallel tradition often referred to as Gnosticism, and the early church was quick to debunk this tradition as heretical and even demonic. Gnosticism is still spoken about in church circles as a source of evil, and the church made several attempts to exterminate this rival tradition and assassinate its devotees and exponents. For instance, the massacre of the Cathars in the south of France is just one example of the murderous brutality displayed by the church in dealing with what it perceived to be a rival and dangerous tradition.

Therefore, Jung carries the burden of this Gnostic legacy, and is regarded with similar revulsion and distaste. However, it is true that until Jung's time, the spiritual and the religious were still aligned due to the power of persuasion that the churches held over people's lives. The majority of people saw "spirituality" as a practice reserved for those who were "very" religious, for whom prayerful devotions to a tradition exceeded those of the average practitioner. Today, however, in our increasingly secular conditions, those who are "not very" religious are claiming the mantle of spirituality for themselves. And as they do, they are often quoting Jung for cultural reinforcement and moral authority.

Spirituality as a "religious attitude"

Jung employed the term "spirituality" in his writings, but he championed the development of what he called the "religious attitude" or the "religious outlook" on life. This can create confusion for modern readers, because his use of these terms might suggest that he was promoting "religion", in the sense of being aligned with the traditions. Jung disliked organised religion and saw it as detrimental to the life of the soul and spirit. It might be said he suffered a complex about religion, related to his complicated relationship with his clergyman father, but this does not mean we have to be embroiled in that complex as well.

Jung strongly differentiated "the religious attitude" from institutional religion, or what he called "creedal faith" (1938, pp. 51–53). The religious attitude, also referred to as the "symbolic attitude", is one of reverence towards, and careful consideration of, the contents of the interior domain, in particular reference to fantasies, visions, dreams, and synchronicities. By referring to this as a *religious* attitude, he is thinking of the original meaning of the word religion (from the Latin, *religio*), namely, to "bind back" to the sacred. Jung wanted to rescue the original meaning of *religio*, and appropriate it for all experiences of the sacred, especially uncanonical ones.

In a much-quoted passage from his influential essay, "Psychotherapists or the Clergy", Jung writes:

> I have treated many hundreds of patients. Among those in the second half of life—that is to say, over thirty-five—there has not been one whose problem in the last resort was not that of finding a religious outlook on life. It is safe to say that every one of them fell ill because he had lost what the living religions of every age have given to their followers, and none of them has been really healed who did not regain his religious outlook. This of course has nothing whatever to do with a particular creed or membership of a church. (1932, § 509).

For years this important quote has puzzled and confused readers. On Facebook there is an amusing thread of comments that is telling. One commentator says: "I think Jung meant spirituality, not the dogma of religion." Another adds: "Remember that what he referred to as 'religion' is not what most people mean." Someone else says: "Carl, there are like four double negatives in that quote; what the hell are you saying buddy?" And so on, in a veritable torrent of comments trying to figure out what Jung was saying.[2]

I find it significant that religious writers quote the above passage approvingly but leave out the last line: "This of course has nothing whatever to do with a particular creed or membership of a church." Without that line, it might seem that Jung was advocating a return to the church. This is far from the truth: in his memoirs he said, "The farther away I was from the church, the better I felt" (1961a, p. 94). But the notion that a "religious outlook" has "nothing whatever to do with a particular creed or membership of a church" must have struck many as odd in 1932. Today, the strategic deletion of the last line, as found in a recent book by Jason Smith, *Religious but Not Religious*, makes Jung seem more conservative than he is (2020, p. 119). Smith is a Jungian analyst, but trained in the United States, where there is a penchant, in keeping with America's passion for religion, for presenting Jung as a religious revivalist.

Like many Americans, Smith uses Jung to support his religious view of the world. Such analyst-writers use only those bits of Jung that seem to support the propping up of collapsing religious structures. Smith attempts to summarise Jung's position as follows:

> We are desperately in need of some framework that organizes the chaos of life events and crises into a cohesive, meaningful whole, shoring up our resilience and endurance … (Ibid.)

In my opinion, this is Jung in reverse. Jung does not think we are "desperately in need of some framework that organises the chaos of life events and crises". On the contrary, Jung believes we need to find the courage to live without such crutches and supports. He urges us to face the chaos of the modern condition, to stare into the abyss, and accept that our present chaotic culture is one without suitable guiding symbols or frameworks.

I am astonished that the religious "defenders" of Jung get him so wrong. There are many writers of this kind, who provide wrong clues and misleading directions. In this context, I can mention the works of John Sanford, Morton Kelsey, and Wallace Clift. Also, some of the popular writings of Robert Johnson seem to misrepresent Jung's position, while ironically trying to promote him at the same time.

The American-Christian "journey into wholeness" movement seems to sentimentalise Jung and sees him as a kindly pastor who wants to protect the flock from too much reality. Jung is not interested in some kind of easy "journey into wholeness"; he wants people to experience the desperate ravages of our time, and the condition of being without religion, which for Jung is paradoxically the most holy position one can adopt today—in the sense that it seems to be the prerequisite before a new dispensation is revealed. More later about this intriguing point of view.

He speaks of the necessary nakedness of the modern condition. His essay, "The Spiritual Problem of Modern Man", extols an existential acceptance of our spiritual poverty, as the only legitimate position to adopt in these times (1931a, § 148–196). In his opinion we need to fall apart and suffer our brokenness before we can begin to consider any achievement of integration. No wholeness before falling apart, which is almost the opposite of the journey into wholeness movement. This movement supports the notion of clinging to the past to protect us from the present.

As such, they are perpetuating a falsity while parading as disseminators of the Jungian message to those looking for a way forward. This could be called the domestication of Jung for those who don't want to go outside their comfort zone; it has also been called the "auntification" of Jung for those who want to remain safe in their spiritual journeys (Shamdasani, 1998). The real message of Jung, however, is more radical than the assumptions of the "safety first" following:

> I do not expect any believing Christian to pursue these thoughts of mine any further, for they will probably seem to him absurd. I am not, however, addressing myself to the happy possessors of faith, but to those many people for whom the light has gone out, the mystery has faded, and God is dead. (1938, § 148)

This message of Jung is camouflaged, ignored, or denied by some of his religious supporters. He says he is addressing the modern man and woman who, in his view, have necessarily lost their faith in the wake of science and intellectual enlightenment.

Jung's post-Christian vision

In addressing a conference of Christian and Jewish clergy in London in 1939, Jung tried to make his position clear on the vexed subject of religion:

> What I have spoken of [in terms of the mystery of the Catholic faith] is, alas, to a great extent the past. We cannot turn the wheel backwards; we cannot go back to the symbolism that is gone. Doubt has killed it, has devoured it. I cannot go back to the Catholic Church, I cannot experience the miracle of the Mass; I know too

much about it. I know it is the truth, but it is the truth in a form in which I cannot accept it any more …. It is no more true to me; it does not express my psychological condition. My psychological condition wants something else. I must have a situation in which that thing becomes true once more. I need a new form …. [But] I am not going to found a religion, and I know nothing about a future religion. (1939b, § 632–633)

Despite Jung rejecting the idea that he is a prophet who is prophesying a future world religion, his works are prophetic to a high degree. It is as if Jung is embarrassed about his prophetic ministry, his prophetic calling. The prophets are often despised by the priestly classes, as they are at odds with each other. The priest wants to preserve the past at all costs, and perpetuate it in his or her own career, while the prophet says the past is no longer valid and there is "new wine" that cannot be placed in "old wineskins".

Jung is more like Jesus than those who follow him: he is a radical teacher who declares the past dead, and says the future requires a total commitment and radical turnaround. In the same way that Judaism could not embrace Jesus because he offered a vision too radical for it to accept, so Christianity cannot embrace Jung for the same reasons. Although he says he knows nothing about a future religion, this is a false lead, because in a sense every word he wrote is about the possibility and necessity of a new religion. It is not as if he was deliberately misleading the public, but he tried to preserve his reputation as a scientist; we must not forget that he was brutally rejected by the Freudian psychoanalytic movement precisely because they could detect spiritual aspects in his psychology. Jung was nursing his wounds with regard to his prophetic role.

But a clergyman in his 1939 London audience hit the mark when he asked Jung whether he thought

there would be a new revelation—as some would phrase it, a new incarnation of the World Teacher, a new collective fantasy? Or was there likely to be a reinterpretation and new appreciation of the esoteric meaning of Christianity—perhaps with the aid of psychology? Or would there be no collective expression, but a period in which each man had to make his own individual contact and live out his own personal expression? (Ibid., § 608)

The answer to these questions was yes, yes, and yes. Jung thought there would be a new collective dispensation; but not yet, it is too early. He believed there would be a new appreciation of the esoteric meaning of Christianity, and yes, he believed the modern period was a difficult one in which each person had to make their own individual contact with the sacred and live out their personal expression.

Jung believed that traditional Christianity was no longer suitable for the modern psyche and its questioning consciousness. It was not suitable for at least four major reasons. First and foremost, Christianity takes its stories, miracles, and myths literally, and this can no longer be supported by modern consciousness. According to Jung, the whole story has to be reinterpreted as metaphor and symbol, and not naively regarded as historical fact.[3] I take up this topic in a later chapter, "Returning Religion to Its Symbolic Roots". The new interpretation will indeed lead to a new appreciation of the esoteric or hidden meaning of Christianity.

Second, the cosmological system of Christianity is too patriarchal for our modern era, and the feminine is missing to such an extent that it calls into question the validity of the whole system. Jung found some hope in the 1951 declaration of the Assumption of Mary by the Vatican Council, seeing this as a long-awaited affirmation of the feminine in a patriarchal tradition. However, the Vatican saw the Assumption in literal terms, as an historical event, whereas Jung viewed it symbolically and said it could only be useful if regarded in non-literal terms. This topic is also pursued in greater depth in the aforementioned chapter.

Third, Jung dismissed out of hand the Christian doctrine that Christ is a universal saviour, and that the task of Christianity is to convert the whole world to the universality of the Christian message. This topic is taken up in a recent book by theologian Ilia Delio (2023). Jung rejected the doctrine of Christ as universal saviour because the revelation of Jesus is one example of the individuation process, inspiring to others, but in no way can it be reified as an absolute metaphysical event. For Jung, Christ was neither universal nor saviour; these are the claims of the tradition that purport to represent the significance of his life. Jung's is a double refutation of the Christian doctrine, which emphasises the universality of Jesus as saviour of the world.

For Jung the proper relation to the Jesus figure is not to worship him as God or his Son, but to be inspired in our lives by his courage and example. As Jung said to his audience at the Terry Lectures at Yale University:

> We all must do just what Christ did. We must make our experiment. We must make mistakes. We must live out our own vision of life. And there will be error. If you avoid error you do not live; in a sense even it may be said that every life is a mistake, for no one has found the truth. When we live like this we know Christ as a brother, and God indeed, becomes man. This sounds like a terrible blasphemy, but not so. For then only can we understand Christ as he would want to be understood, as a fellow man; then only does God become man in ourselves. (1937, pp. 108–109)

Jung is saying: Christ is not our saviour, but an exemplar of the individuation process. He is not God but our spiritual brother, and he urges us to do as he did, to "live out our own vision of life". Jung believed that the true meaning of Christ is that each of us must aspire to what he did, not copy him or assume that our own salvation is somehow secured because of what he did for us. We are on our own, just as he was on his own, because he thought the traditions of the past were no longer adequate.

Fourth, Jung believed Christianity did not give enough acknowledgement to the principle of evil and darkness; it lacked an awareness of the importance and reality of the shadow, in his terms. "The image of God has a shadow," he announces in *The Red Book* (2009, p. 230). Christianity downgraded evil from a cosmogonic principle to something seen only in terms of the Latin *privatio boni*, that is, the absence of good. Since Christianity regarded God as all good, perfect, and without blemish, there was no room for evil in the Christian conception of God.

Jung saw this as an error in Christian thinking, and spent much of his life trying to correct this shortcoming by giving evil the reality that he argued it deserved. This theme is taken up in the later chapter on "The Individuation of God". He wrote numerous essays on this problem, and the crowning achievement of this lifelong struggle was the magnificent *Answer to Job* (1952a). Jung argued that Satan and the devil were split-off aspects of the divine, and when Jesus struggled with the devil in the desert he was struggling with the demonic aspect of his own nature, not with an "entity" outside himself. The notion of the devil as something external to Jesus or God was regarded by Jung as an example of the projection of the dark side of the Godhead.

These four problems constitute much more than a fine-tuning of Christianity, as some Christian Jungians want us to believe. Taken seriously, Jung's four challenges to Christianity represent a deconstruction and radical reworking of the whole religion. Indeed, some believe that Christianity could not recover from the challenges that Jung posed to Christianity.[4]

Father Victor White was a disciple of Jung's work for decades, and saw Jung's psychology as a way forward for the Catholic faith. But he realised his discipleship was hopeless after the publication of *Answer to Job*. White turned away from Jung, acknowledging that Jung's critique of Christianity involved a dismantling of the religion. White was, in my view, one of the more honest religious followers of Jung, who was forced to admit that Jung was not merely tinkering with his religion or providing a psychological understanding of the dogmas of the faith. The defection of Victor White from the Jungian school (because Jung was not religious enough) was as inevitable as Freud's turning away from Jung for opposite reasons (Jung was not scientific enough).

Being rejected from both sides, religious and scientific, would have reduced a lesser man to a quivering wreck. But in his public and didactic moments, Jung took authority into his own hands, and stood up to the challenges of Freudians on one hand and clergymen on the other. If we return to his encounter with clergy in London in 1939, we see Jung confident in his "alternative" spiritual expression and sure-footed about where he stood in religious terms.

Jung's credo: start with the heart

As a way of illustrating this, Jung tells the story of an exchange with a Jesuit father, who asked him about the role of dreams in his psychology. The Catholic tradition has an ambivalent attitude to dreams. While it accepts that dreams played an important role in the distant past, for leaders such as Moses, Jacob, and King David, dreams are often viewed today as the voice of the devil, or as "temptations" to sexual expression in the manner of Freudian doctrine. Hence the strange fact that clergy often accept Freud's position regarding dreams, rather than side with Jung, who saw dreams as God's forgotten language. Jung's outlook was more threatening to them, because if God spoke to everyone through dreams, what would happen to the authority of the church and its ordained priesthood?

In Jung's view, the priesthood is not needed as an intermediary between ordinary people and God, because God speaks to everyone, if they care to listen and know how to listen to the symbolic language. Jung reports that the Jesuit father said that, with regard to dreams, the church expresses caution: "Well, there we have to be careful," said the priest, "as we are already a bit suspect. We have the means of grace of the Church." Jung remarked to the clergyman, sounding like a complete outsider:

> "Right you are," I said, "you don't need dreams. I can give no abso-
> lution, I have no means of grace; therefore I must listen to dreams.
> I am a primitive; you are a civilized man." In a way that clergyman
> is much more wonderful than I am. He can be a saint; I cannot be
> a saint—I can only be a nigger, very primitive, going by the next
> thing—quite superstitious. (1939b, § 682)

Jung adopts a typical countermove towards an opponent by elevating the priest and diminishing himself. Jung often alludes to the fact that he is outside the church and beyond its protections and ministrations. He says he is *extra ecclesiam* and cannot rely on any of the official means of salvation. Hence he remarks, quite defensively, that he is a "primitive", "quite superstitious", who must "listen to dreams" for the guidance they can offer. The church does not need to listen to dreams, he says, because the pathway to salvation has been laid out in its dogmas and teachings. The official adherence is to the clergy and the priests, not to the psyche.

In "Archetypes of the Collective Unconscious", Jung tries to dis-abuse his followers of any notion that the established Christian faith is a reliable source of revelation today:

> I am convinced that the growing impoverishment of symbols
> has a meaning. It is a development that has an inner consistency.
> (1934a, § 28)

He is saying there is meaning in our spiritual poverty. Here he sounds much like the spiritual poets I mentioned at the start of this book: T. S. Eliot and Robert Frost. He says we should embrace our lack of religion in order to discover a new revelation that is "at hand". He is not sure what it is, but says in a prophetic tone that it is coming.

In *The Red Book* he writes a section called, "The Way of What Is to Come" (2009, pp. 229–231). And what is to come is not a continuation of the old. Jung writes that "the way of what is to come" is a new pathway of increased and heightened interiority. He puts forward what amounts to a manifesto of the new:

> The way is within us, but not in Gods, nor in teachings, nor in laws.
> Within us is the way, the truth and the life. (Ibid., p. 231)

These words are carefully chosen to contrast John 14:6: "Jesus said unto him, 'I am the way, and the truth, and the life. No one comes to the Father except through me.'" Obviously the new dispensation is to replace the old dispensation of Jesus. Jung stresses the difficulty and challenge of the new: "The signposts have fallen, unblazed trails lie before us" (ibid.).

In his "Psychology and Religion" lectures at Yale University, Jung spells out his theology as well as his psychology. He argues that Western civilisation has approached the fourth stage in a fourfold process: from polytheism, to monotheism, to the Incarnation of Christ, to the new stage: the sanctification of the many:

> The gods at first lived in superhuman power and beauty on the top of snow-clad mountains or in the darkness of caves, woods, and seas. Later on they drew together into one god, and then that god became man. But in our day even the God-man seems to have descended from his throne and to be dissolving himself in the common man. (1938, § 141)

Again, he suggests to his audience that the Christian phase is over (at least for him), and a new phase, in which the individual has to carry the burden of God, has begun. In the fourth phase, the God-man has descended from his throne and is dissolving himself in the common man. This momentous act is happening right now.

Jung and the East

Jung says we should not try to prop up the old religion, and nor should we rush to India to "try to cover our nakedness with the gorgeous trappings of the East" (1934a, § 28). In *The Red Book* this thought becomes: "Do not be greedy to gobble up the fruits of foreign fields. Do you not know that you yourselves are the fertile acre which bears everything that avails you" (2009, p. 231). In Jung's time, people were already turning to the East for spiritual guidance, and Jung felt ambivalent about it. He kept saying if we run off to the East we will miss the spiritual opportunity of the present: the discovery of the emerging wisdom within:

> It seems to be quite true that the East is at the bottom of the spiritual change we are passing through today. Only, this East is not a Tibetan monastery full of Mahatmas, but lies essentially within us. It is our own psyche, constantly at work creating new spiritual forms and spiritual forces ... (1931a, § 190)

This is a fascinating perspective on our current situation, and one which only a mythic or metaphorical approach to human experience could divulge. In his essay on the *Tibetan Book of the Dead*, Jung wrote that instead of imitating the East,

> It would be far more to the point to find out whether there exists in the unconscious an introverted tendency similar to that which has become the guiding spiritual principle of the East. We should then be in a position to build on our own ground with our own methods. If we snatch these things directly from the East, we have merely indulged our Western acquisitiveness, confirming yet again that everything good is outside, whence it has to be fetched and pumped into our barren souls. (1939a, § 773)

We have to accept that we have lost our bearings and need to turn within to find an Ariadne's thread to lead us out of the impasse. We need to be persuaded that something good can come from within, and to find the courage to look into the unconscious with sensitivity, and not to be terrified by early impressions. But instead of displaying this courage, we seem to prefer to run off in other directions to avoid the confrontation with our souls. Many of us are keen to go East, pagan, Celtic, Wicca, occult or primitive—anywhere but within.

Jung has been criticised for being so sceptical of the turn to the East, but he does so for a reason: we need to focus on the new revelation emerging from the Western psyche. I am, however, sympathetic to those who argue that Jung is too negative about the turn to India, but he is concerned that such a movement might sabotage what is taking place in the Western soul.

I cannot see why we can't focus on both of these: the turn to the East can help us understand what is emerging in the Western soul. The East knows much more about interiority than the West, and there is absolutely no dichotomy here. Anyway, Jung is hypocritical about this matter: he turned to the East a great deal, and many of his major ideas and theories come directly from the East.

For instance, his key idea of the Self is lifted straight out of Hinduism, as the Indian concept of the Atman or Purusa is at the basis of Jung's concept of the Self. So I don't think we can believe his caution about turning to the East when he engages so much in this activity (Collins & Molchanov, 2013). There is in fact no parallel to Jung's concept of the Self in Western civilisation; it only makes sense if we consult Eastern sources.

Avowing spiritual poverty

But to return to Jung's argument about the Western crisis, we need to consider this memorable passage in which he speaks of our *symbol-lessness* (a curious term) and how to endure this condition:

> It seems to me that it would be far better stoutly to avow our spiritual poverty, our symbol-lessness, instead of feigning a legacy to which we are not the legitimate heirs at all. We are, surely, the rightful heirs of Christian symbolism, but somehow we have squandered this heritage. We have let the house our fathers built fall into decay, and now we try to break into Oriental palaces that our fathers never knew. Anyone who has lost the historical symbols and cannot be satisfied with substitutes is certainly in a very difficult position today: before him there yawns the void, and he turns away from it in horror. What is worse, the vacuum gets filled with absurd political and social ideas, which one and all are distinguished by their spiritual bleakness. (1934a, § 28)

What is evident throughout Jung's career is his belief that we will not stare into the "yawning void" forever. Something will come up to meet us, to guide and befriend us, and that is his consolation. This something is what many call the god within, the birth of the transcendent spirit in the human being, and not only in "special" or "ordained" human beings, but in everyone. In some of his essays he explains how the so-called "transcendent function" can be activated in such circumstances, and answers will emerge that point the way out of the present lack of direction.

Jung refers to this idea by using the mystical idea of the "sanctification of the many", an idea he borrowed from Meister Eckhart. I had a friend, now deceased, who once told me that the "God-shaped hole" is God. That seems to me to be what Jung is getting at here. He believes that the inner Self, once activated and given a chance to lead us out of the spiritual crisis, can and will come up with creative solutions to our collective and individual plight.

The reader needs to grasp the seriousness with which Jung puts forward his notion about the need to face the void. We need to lean into the emptiness, and tolerate it in the hope that we are transformed by something unexpected and miraculous. Jung's position is summarised soundly and poetically by his disciple Erich Neumann:

> The creative principle has its home no longer in the symbolism of a cultural canon, but in the individual. It has almost ceased to live in favoured holy places, in sites or at times dedicated to it, or in men consecrated to it, but may live everywhere, anywhere, in any way and any time, that is to say, anonymously.
>
> Because in our time the creative principle always hides in an anonymity that discloses its origin by no divine sign, no visible radiance, no demonstrable legitimacy, we have entered upon the spiritual poverty suggested in the Jewish legend about the Messiah in the guise of a beggar, sitting and waiting at the gates of Rome. (1954, p. 168)

This is a brilliant answer to those who claim that Jung seeks to preserve institutional religions at all costs. Neumann grasps with clarity Jung's idea that the sacred has abandoned its traditional containers and is, as it were, naked, without traditional dress. It "may live everywhere, anywhere, in any way and any time, that is to say, anonymously". This is not of our choosing but a decision of the sacred in our time. It disrobes itself, so it can dwell in our midst in radically democratic ways.

The journey involves not knowing too much about what this mystery might be. This describes what the poet John Keats called "negative capability", which he says is the ability to be "capable of being in uncertainties, mysteries, doubts, without any irritable reaching after fact and reason".[5] He means that we should trust the processes of creativity, and not allow the ego to dictate terms for us. We ought to dwell in a state of openness to all experience and allow what wants to emerge to emerge.

Religion is not what we do, but what is done to us

Jung did not want *religio*, the binding back to the sacred, to be impeded or blocked by the decline of religious organisations. In this regard, his work anticipates the writings of Jacques Derrida, the postmodern philosopher. Derrida argued in several important works that we need to rediscover *"religion without the religions"* (see Caputo, 1997). Like Jung, Derrida was moved to uphold sacred experience but distanced himself from the institutions that are referred to as "religious":

> What is religion? What is going on today with it, with what is designated thus? What is going on there? What is happening and so badly? What is happening under this old name? (1996, pp. 34–38)

Separating the activity of *religio* from the institutional religions was a concern of Derrida, but he never referred to Jung as Derrida was coming from a philosophical point of view, not depth psychology.

Derrida argues a case for religion, and for the return of religion, despite all the shocking associations with that word, including hypocrisy, moralism, racism, piety, clerical sexual abuse, and warmongering fundamentalism. These problems and accusations have damaged the credibility of the religions in our time. However, for Derrida the term *religion* remains a good one, despite these associations. He argues that "the enigmatic 're'" at the beginning of *re-ligio* ensures that this phenomenon will *re*-turn, *re*-vive, *re*-new (ibid., p. 37). "Religion [is] what succeeds in returning" (p. 39). He felt religion should be pursued in its original form of "binding back" to the Other, and he provides us with a memorable definition of religion:

> However little may be known of religion in the singular, we do know that it is always a response and a responsibility that is prescribed,

not chosen freely in an act of pure and abstractly autonomous will. There is no doubt that it implies freedom, will and responsibility, but let us try to think this: will and freedom without autonomy. Whether it is a question of sacredness, sacrificiality or of faith, the other makes the law, the law is other: to give oneself back, and up, to the other. To every other and to the utterly other (*tout autre* ...). (Ibid., p. 34)

This is a haunting passage which rewards reflection. There is more than a hint of Emmanuel Levinas (1975, p. 40) in Derrida's definition. But if we want to understand his concern with religion, we need go no further than this definition, which says it is "not chosen freely in an act of pure and abstractly autonomous will". Derrida emphasises that *religio* is not something we do, but *something that is done to us* (op. cit., p. 34). It happens to us from forces beyond the ego. The numinous approaches us, before we might think of approaching it.

At a personal level, Derrida was aware that the numinous was not a conscious interest of his for a long time, but it welled up from his unconscious and overtook him. Hence for him *religio* is seen as a verb which has great appeal, whereas formal religion is a noun which is static and distrusted. This separation of the active from the passive forms of the word "religion" is part of the deconstructive process that Derrida performed on religion, indicating that Jung anticipated developments in postmodern thinking long before postmodernism was even invented.[6]

Jung and Derrida were both sensitive to the enduring validity of *religio* in the present time, which is a time of religious decay.[7] Both thinkers were aware that *religio* must never pass away, since it is a vital part of human experience, and perhaps the most vital indicator that we are alive and responsive to mystery. Derrida defined *religio* as an act by which one "gives oneself back, and up, to the other. To every other and to the utterly other (*tout autre* ...)". This "act of religion", he said, is "not chosen freely in an act of pure and abstractly autonomous will" (ibid., p. 34).

In a parallel movement, Jung argued that *religio* is "a dynamic agency or effect not caused by an arbitrary act of will". "It seizes and controls the human subject, who is always rather its victim than its creator." "The *numinosum*—whatever its cause may be—is an experience of the subject independent of his will" (1938, § 6). But what makes Derrida's work hard to fit into the contemporary conversation is not only the difficulty of his writing but the fact that he clung steadfastly to the term "religion" to describe the experience of the sacred. However, he did make occasional concessions that religion is not a good enough term to hold what he was referring to:

> Distinctions are required: faith has not always been and will not always be identifiable with religion, nor, another point, with theology. All sacredness and all holiness are not necessarily, in the strict sense of the term, if there is one, religious. (Op. cit., pp. 8–9)

He mostly brushed the *religions* aside as irrelevant to the experience of the sacred, but contemporary society has preferred the term "spirituality" to describe the experience of being moved by the numinous. Despite my interest in this term, I am still not convinced that the term "spirituality" is a wise choice, due to the long historical association it has with a disembodied and non-corporeal experience of the sacred, as discussed in a later chapter, "Individuation as a Spiritual Journey".

The primacy of experience

Jung argued that his separation of spiritual experience from the religions was not an invention of his, but he was following a trend set in place by modernity. He claimed that the "exodus from the German Protestant Church", was "only one of many symptoms which should make it plain to the clergy that mere admonitions to believe, or to perform acts of charity, do not give modern man what he is looking for" (1932, § 507).

He noted "The wave of interest in psychology which at present is sweeping over the Protestant countries of Europe ... is coincident with the mass exodus from the Church." He saw that interest in psychology reflected a spiritual interest in the psyche and its symbolic productions, even if what passes for "psychology" in the universities bears no resemblance to anything approaching the spiritual. He was aware of the gravity of the present situation: "We have come to a serious pass," he said (ibid.), and in another essay: "We are only at the threshold of a new spiritual epoch" (1931a, § 190).

Jung said we should look to the arts, music, literature, and poetry to find the prophetic imagination that has been dead for so long in the churches. But above all he believed we should turn to the unconscious, to dreams, fantasies, and visions, to lead us out of our spiritual impasse. This, one might suggest, is an extremely introverted directive regarding the imminent spiritual renaissance, but Jung could not see any "external" source of spiritual leadership in his time, apart from that found "outside" the ego in the depths of human interiority. He kept emphasising that modern humanity is in an experimental mood, and such experiments might yield results if carried out in the right spirit:

> Modern man wants to break with tradition so that he can experiment with his life and determine what value and meaning things have in themselves, apart from traditional presuppositions. (1932, § 528)

In the modern context, experience is primary and tradition has been heavily discounted. As a psychotherapist, Jung was aware of the need for people to experience a spiritual life and not merely "believe" in an external faith system. If Jung placed priority on experience it was because most of his patients had grown up with an "inherited" faith which had proven ineffectual in providing an orientation for their spiritual lives. In other words, Christianity lacks a psychology, and that prevents it from being experienced as mysticism.

His emphasis on experience was compensatory to the historical emphasis in the churches on received belief and the "passing on" of faith through the family line. He saw that the new interest in psychology contained an element which was not entirely psychological, but also spiritual and philosophical:

> Modern man turns to the psyche with very great expectations, and does so without reference to any traditional creed but rather with a view to experience. Modern man seeks *knowledge* instead of *faith*, which is the essence of the Western forms of religion. Modern man abhors faith and the religions based upon it. He holds them valid only so far as their knowledge-content seems to accord with his own experience of the psychic background. He wants to *know*—to experience for himself. (1931a, § 171)

Whereas formal religion relied almost totally on belief, the new style of spiritual expression is hungry for knowledge of the interior life. Today a great many people are on spiritual journeys and the word "journey" has become inseparable from spirituality. Everyone's journey is different, and there is an acceptance in the secular community that this has to be so.

To religious traditions, however, such diversity looks chaotic and unsettled, and there is a lack of order to the idiosyncratic pathways of the modern individual. The post-traditional person is in an "experimental" mood, and wants to venture into the interior world, to see what is there and what might be understood about the depths of the self. In this fascination for experimentation, the scientific emphasis of Western culture might stand us in good stead.

The scientific approach to spirituality

The modern person's interest in the unconscious is partly the result of a scientific approach to reality, and in this case, to the reality within. Ever since the intellectual enlightenment, science and education have urged us to put inherited presuppositions and received beliefs to one side, and base our knowledge on what is empirically verifiable. This may have landed us for the time being in a spiritual wasteland, but it has at least instilled in us a spirit of enquiry that we can make use of in our spiritual crisis. It may have established the conditions for a deeper and more mystical form of religious engagement:

> We are now reaping the fruit of nineteenth-century education. Throughout that period the church preached to young people the merit of blind faith, while the universities inculcated an intellectual rationalism. Tired of this warfare of opinions, the modern man wishes to find out for himself how things are. And though this desire opens the door to the most dangerous possibilities, we cannot help seeing it as a courageous enterprise and giving it some measure of sympathy. It is no reckless adventure, but an effort inspired by deep spiritual distress to bring meaning once more into life on the basis of fresh and unprejudiced experience. (1932, § 529)

Instead of accepting the dictates of tradition in the manner of our forebears, there is in the modern individual a desire for direct, personal knowing. Although many of us have rejected the rationalism of science, we have nevertheless been informed by scientific methods. We may be applying a series of *ad hoc* scientific principles to our spiritual lives.

To combat the attacks of conservative religious critics, we might justify our behaviour by saying there is "scientific method" in our madness.

The method is as follows: tradition is set aside and we make our own observations of reality. We draw hypotheses based on individual experiences and experiment with our theories. In this process, we often draw on a number of religious traditions and styles, and do not confine ourselves to the traditions of our forebears. We regard ourselves as citizens of the world and explore the religions of the world.

We "pick and mix" from a variety of beliefs and practices, and are drawn to those elements of religions that most nearly correspond to our experiences, hunches, or intuitions. We test our theories against reality and draw conclusions about life, meaning, and truth. Finally, we may or may not decide to link our personal journey with the religious tradition of our family line. But if we do make this link, we will have to be prepared for some dissonance if we want to pursue our journey in the context of a traditional faith community.

What to religious tradition looks like waywardness and loss of faith, is from another perspective a desire to place faith on a sounder, more scientific footing. In this sense, secular waywardness may ironically serve the advancement of religion. The institutions of faith are astonished at this brash new attitude in the public, and wonder why it has taken hold and what can be done about it. They have not prepared themselves for this new interest in individual exploration, and find themselves in a crisis of relevance. The typical response of tradition is to ask people to believe and cast doubt aside.

Religious authorities asked in Jung's time and even more so in ours: Who do modern people think they are? What gives them the right to think they can demand more than the churches can give? How can they call for the spiritual understanding that was previously reserved for mystics, monastics, and saints? How can they ask for things that properly belong to the realm of God's grace? What has got into modern people? Is it the devil or a fallen angel? Why this unholy hunger for transcendence?

The new experimental or "scientific" spirituality looks unholy to religious tradition. It seems to it to be arrogant and insolent, and places too much emphasis on the interior self, which tradition has always distrusted. Religious tradition only knows the self as "ego", and not as the transcendental *Self* that Jung (following Eastern philosophies) has in mind. Since Western tradition sees the self only as ego, it sees our preoccupation with self as narcissistic and selfish.

The deeper aspect of the self, which is popularly known as the "inner" or "true" self, is almost unknown to established religion, which has tended to project the sacred outwards upon religious founders, messiahs, priests and clergy, saints and martyrs, and official rituals. The idea of the sacred within is seen as a modern heresy, an indulgence of fantasy or a justification for egotistic behaviour. Institutional religion seems not to have understood its own mystical traditions.

The meltdown of religious forms

The important point, for Jung, is that we make individual contact with the sources that have become petrified in dogmatic forms, and are now lost to modern consciousness. We have to throw off the dead weight of dogma and reach into the soul, even if much of what we discover in the soul is similar to the wisdom already enshrined in dogma. Jung uses alchemical imagery to explain his radical approach to religious matters and to his work as "alchemist" of the soul:

> To gain an understanding of religious matters, probably all that is left us today is the psychological approach. That is why I take these thought-forms that have become historically fixed, try to melt them down again and pour them into moulds of immediate experience. (1938, § 148)

This alchemical approach is what many of Jung's critics fail to understand. They see his role as destructive, as "reducing" sacred dogmas to psychological processes, almost as if they were being debased and profaned. However, as an alchemist in a new key, Jung is adopting a transformational approach to religious tradition. He argues that tradition has become useless in its present form and only by relating it to the soul can it become meaningful again. The way to revive religion is to deconstruct it, so that the energies can be released in a new way. His conservative critics note his deconstruction and breaking down, but not his second, revitalising process that reconstitutes the ideas of religion and invests them with new meaning.

To emphasise that Jung is not completely outside tradition, but working with a reformist zeal and a mystical concern for the living essence of religion, it is worth comparing his alchemical strategy with that of Thomas Merton, a Cistercian monk who sees himself as working within Christian tradition. According to Merton, the mystic who prepares to have a direct experience of the numinous has to throw out a lot of material to get down to the ground of being. The mystic who burns with the love of God has to burn away a lot of hackneyed understandings of the world, as well as worn-out religious understandings:

> What a holocaust takes place in this steady burning to ashes of old worn-out words, clichés, slogans, rationalizations! The worst of it is that even apparently *holy* conceptions are consumed along with all the rest. It is a terrible breaking and burning of idols, a purification of the sanctuary, so that no graven thing may occupy the place that God has commanded to be left empty: the center, the existential altar which simply is. (1961, p. 13)

If we compare Jung and Merton we see that they are preoccupied with the same religious urge, to clear away obsolete paraphernalia and dogmas and to ready oneself for the incursion of a living experience of the numinosum. Why are we so willing to grant that Merton is firmly within tradition whereas Jung is irredeemably outside it? Surely both take their context within the mystical tradition that is always at odds with the conventional religious norms.

Jung's approach to our transitional time is unsentimental. He is not concerned about the external forms, but is concerned about the forces of the sacred, which have to be drawn out of the alchemical fire, to see what new forms will emerge. Jung believes that modern men and women need a convincing encounter with God, and we must move away from religion as a *belief* in ideas about God to religion as an *experience* of God.

The trashing of the religious heritage by modernity has an unexpected deeper significance. We get rid of belief but we still find ourselves thirsting for experience. Belief is squandered and lost, but we are unable to lose our hunger for the sacred, for that is the essential nourishment of the soul. Modern atheistic humanity can overcome the forms of the sacred, but it cannot overcome the longing for the divine because that is an innate urge. Although modernity has dispensed with religion, it finds that what it has rejected comes up again as an existential longing. As Freud might say, the repressed returns, and it returns in a new way and with a different character.

The religions of the West have declined for various reasons, and for Jung they are good reasons, such as the inability to reconcile the statements of faith with the demands of science and reason. We cannot carry on as if this had never occurred. We have to accept that a rupture has happened, and to deny this is not only unhistorical but irresponsible. Jung never writes off the Judaeo-Christian tradition, and believes that a revitalisation may be possible. But he believes it is important for us to face the abyss that opens up before us. The way to be true to the West is to accept our nakedness and the apparent dissolution of our tradition.

The nakedness to which we are driven is a nakedness in which we might be able to remake ourselves in the encounter with reality:

> Modern man has become "unhistorical" in the deepest sense and has estranged himself from the mass of men who live entirely within the bounds of tradition. Indeed, he is completely modern only when he has come to the very edge of the world, leaving behind him all that has been discarded and outgrown, and acknowledging that he stands before the Nothing out of which the All may grow. (1931a, § 150)

Jung sees the loneliness of the modern condition as sacred. It is a negative capability or mystical aloneness which could give rise to a new experience of God. If we are in a state of darkness, it is holy darkness. If we are naked, it is holy. We are to reflect on our condition with gravity and seriousness. From such emptiness, Jung believed, something new might emerge. This is close to Heidegger's philosophy. Jung and Heidegger apparently disliked each other, but it may have been because they were too much alike. Instead of speaking of our nakedness and symbol-lessness, Heidegger says the prophetic need today is to plunge into the "abyss", so that we might come face to face with Being in a new way (1950, p. 117). Heidegger's Being is similar to Jung's Self or God. Both consider that a new encounter with ultimate reality is needed, without which humanity might die for want of an authentic life.

In the above passage, Jung is quoting Goethe's Faust, Part Two: "In this, your Nothing, I may find my All!"[8] Modern people have to be plunged into an existential abyss which may lead to the rebirth of religious consciousness at a new level. Depth psychology could act as a midwife to the birth of a new religious consciousness. The task is to turn to the unconscious with an attentive eye and careful ear, listening for the echoes and images that arise naturally from our inner core.

The challenge is to value the psyche more highly, and regard it as the ground from which new religious life can emerge. We must overcome the Freudian prejudice that views the unconscious as a rubbish dump into which the ego casts the unacceptable elements of the day. We have to re-educate ourselves about interior life, and understand that God can speak to us in the small and humble places of the soul. This means attuning ourselves to the interior dimension and recognising that the divine can emerge in the most unlikely places.

Endnotes

1. Pontifical Council for Culture and Pontifical Council for Interreligious Dialogue 2003: *Jesus Christ: The Bearer of the Water of Life: A Christian Reflection on the "New Age"*. Vatican, Rome. Located at: http://vatican.va/roman_curia/pontifical_councils/interelg/documents/rc_pc_interelg_doc_20030203_new-age_en.html

2. See Facebook page: https://m.facebook.com/carl.jung.gustav/photos/a.10153040847317083/10157014997297083/?type=3&source=57&__tn__=EH-R

3. This argument is forcefully put in the Preface to his *Answer to Job* (1952a), CW 11.

4. This is the view of Murray Stein in his book, *Jung's Treatment of Christianity: The Psychotherapy of a Religious Tradition*. Asheville, NC: Chiron, 2013.

5. John Keats, Letter to George and Tom Keats, December 21, 1817.

6. On Jung's anticipation of postmodernism, see Hauke, C., *Jung and the Postmodern*. London: Routledge, 2000.

7. See my brief comparative study in Tacey, D, "Imagining transcendence at the end of modernity: Jung and Derrida". In: L. Huskinson (Ed.), *Dreaming the Myth Onwards: New Directions in Jungian Therapy and Thought*. London: Routledge, 2008, pp. 58–68.

8. See Jung, "The Spiritual Problem of Modern Man", translator's footnote 2 (1931a, § 150).

CHAPTER 3

Descent of spirit[1]

*Our unconscious hides living water, spirit that has become nature, and
that is why it is disturbed.*

— Jung (1934a, § 50)

The buried life

Jung claimed that a spiritual life lies buried in the unconscious and could
be dug up and brought before consciousness with therapeutic results.
He used this method to heal suffering patients in his clinical practice, and
felt the same method could be applied to whole societies, to heal the neuroses of the modern age. His views were berated as mystical and implausible
by critics, and scientific colleagues found his ideas arcane and medieval.
He seemed to them like some kind of throwback to an ancient age of
alchemists and witch doctors. Even Jung was surprised at the abstruse
nature of his own ideas, which erupted spontaneously from a level below
his scientific thinking. In a telling statement, Jung admitted that he was
burdened by the rediscovery of what the ancients called "gods":

> All ages before ours believed in gods in some form or other. Only
> an unparalleled impoverishment in symbolism could enable us to

> rediscover the gods as psychic factors, which is to say, as archetypes
> of the unconscious. No doubt this discovery is hardly credible
> as yet. (Ibid.)

If his ideas seem "hardly credible" to him, imagine how they seemed
to others, especially critics and rivals. In this and other statements, he
apologises for being arcane in an age of science, which had its roots in
the intellectual enlightenment. The point of the enlightenment was to
chase away the mists of the past, to make way for an age of pure science
and clear perception of the observable world. Jung partly subscribed
to this ideal, but the deeper and stronger part of him subscribed to the
counter-modern ideal of preserving the wisdom of the past and making
it accessible to the modern era. He was a complicated figure, neither
progressive nor conservative in the usual meaning of those terms.
He sat in the middle, wanting the best of both worlds, while also in
danger of losing both.

Obviously what Jung meant by "gods" had nothing to do with
archaic figures of gods as objective, outside realities or beings. Zeus
with his thunderbolt, or Poseidon with his trident, and so on. He is
speaking symbolically about the forces in the deep unconscious, which
he believes are usually personified in the figures of gods in various
religions and pantheons. Jung exposed himself to unnecessary ridicule
by opting to refer to the archetypes as gods, but in his defence he says
that the archetypal forces of the unconscious have been represented
thus in countless cosmologies. But his critics were not sympathetic, and
exploited Jung's decision to refer to archetypes as gods as a means of
undermining his credibility. They turned Jung into a laughing stock and
his collective unconscious into a Disneyland.

Jung's ideas contradicted the modern age and he was aware of this
as a personal and professional burden. He stuck to his views and paid a
price. He was relegated to the margins of respectability and ignored by
the psychological and medical mainstream, with only a small network
of supporters to promote his cause. In some respects it was a miracle his
work survived, given the great resistance to his spiritual findings. Jung
dug deep into the unconscious, where time and space are different from
life at the surface. In one sense he dug up an arcane world that seemed
to have passed with the progress of time, but another way of describing it is to say that the arcane world erupted like an explosion from
below, because he was open to its reality and receptive to its meaning.

In every era, there are some who remain true to sacred reality, and they are faced with a shamanic burden. To some, they like look like inspired visionaries and to others they are embarrassing.

In *The Red Book* (2009) Jung differentiates between two kinds of spirit, the intellectual "spirit of the times" and the non-rational or post-rational "spirit of the depths". It is from the depths that Jung's vision arises, although much of his energy was spent on the task of shaping the spirit of the depths to make it more acceptable to the spirit of the times. That is, he was trying to convert theology into psychology. He was trying to forge a bridge between these two kinds of spirit, in the hope that communications could be carried from the depths to the surface, and from the surface to the depths. Erich Neumann (1949a) referred to this as the ego-Self axis, and this is what Jung was attempting to build in his life and work.

Beyond the ego, but within the person, is a deeper Self which needs to be capitalised because it must not be confused with the ego. The East refers to this as the Atman or Purusha, and the Atman is the human approach to the transcendent. The West has never understood the inner reality, and has not been able to discern a greater Self behind the ego. So when Jung refers to this larger Self, most of his critics see him as advocating a form of narcissism. For them, there is nothing in the person apart from the greedy and selfish ego, and they see Jung indulging the ego and pretending it is sacred, a kind of fake religion for a narcissistic age. Jung learnt from his experience and from studying Eastern texts, that there is indeed a reality in the interior person, that is known to Western mysticism but not to Western philosophy or mainstream religion. Hence our philosophy and religion have no interest in Jung, whom they mostly despise as an obscurantist or manipulator. They see him promoting an ersatz religion, a kind of anti-religion that turns the mischievous ego into God.

It seems that only those who have intuited that a larger reality lives within their being are able to listen sensibly to what Jung has to say. Jung was aware that the old religions of the past no longer speak to the majority, and agreed that the old image of an external God had collapsed. In this regard, he conceded with Nietzsche that "God is dead". But Jung saw this as a provisional crisis, a phase that the West is passing through. The deeper wisdom suggests that the traditional image of God died so that a new experience of God could be born. Jung believed that the West is going through an atheistic phase for a mystical purpose: when the old God collapses a new God emerges from the depths of our being. Jung is the psychologist of this moment in history, which means he is a prophet of a new dispensation. Again, we can either accept this as a valid conjecture, or scorn it as a delusion of his followers.

I used to argue against the idea that Jung was a prophet and thought he was only a psychologist of our age. But having studied Jung and his works for the past fifty years, I realise that the prophetic aspect of his work is undeniable. No other major thinker of the last hundred years has come close to what his work announces and prepares us for: the collapse of old religious beliefs and the birth of a new religion of the soul. Jung provides the framework and understanding that enables us to make this transition.

Not progressive, not conservative

Jung provides an alternative to two of the major voices of our time that seem to be at odds: the progressive and the conservative. The voice of the educated intellect says we need an increasingly secular society with fewer beliefs and no vestiges of spiritual desire. This is the voice of our education system, found in schools and universities of the modern, and now postmodern, era. For this voice, religion and spirituality need to be replaced by science and knowledge. We don't need God or gods, as these are social constructions imposed on people by moribund traditions and outmoded beliefs.

The second voice is that of the established religions. They say atheism is a mistake, an error of society, and the way back is the way forward. We must revive the religions that we have lost or forsaken, in the interests of order, community, and sanity. To revive the old beliefs is good for us, and the only way to recover coherence and order in our time. This voice says tradition is calling us back to the past, to the security and shelter of the ancient canopy.

This conservative voice strives to present old beliefs in new ways, to make them more attractive to modern taste. It introduces rock music and youth festivals, changes the liturgy and offers meditation as a sign of its progressive ability, and may attempt to rebrand itself as "spirituality", since the term "religion" is on the nose for various reasons. But its appeal is sentimental and regressive, and it has no intention of changing the core beliefs and foundations of its traditions. There is new window dressing, but the basic features remain the same.

Jung was suspicious of revivalism, just as he was of the progressives who called for increased secularisation and disempowerment of the churches. He did not want to boost the secular left or the religious right, but called for the discovery of the psyche and in particular the capital "S" Self behind and beyond the ego. For Jung, the encounter with the "Undiscovered Self" (1957a) is the only way forward for individuals and society. Respect and reverence for the psyche, and its central archetype the Self, is the way to free individuals and humanity from the domination and authoritarianism of political ideologies and religious hegemonies. "The world today hangs by a thin thread," he said, "and that thread is the psyche of man." Jung asked us to look within for the salvific guidance that can help us survive the chaos of modernity, and overcome the spectres of political ideologies on the one hand and religious authorities on the other.

Jung disagreed with social progressives, who wanted us to ditch the traditional idea of the sacred and put our energy into the promotion of political causes. Modern politics asks us to ignore the old images of the sacred and view the political quest itself as sacred. Jung has something in common with the progressives: he asks us to turn away from traditional religions. But there is a big difference: we turn away from tradition not to become atheistic or to get rid of God, but to find God in new places, in the heart of experience, and in the utterings of dreams, visions, fantasies, synchronicities, and intuitive guidance. We can make use of discarded traditions, and Jung was a keen explorer of the sacred in creeds, ideas, and prayers, but for him the source of the sacred is no longer outside but inside. Not only inside the mind, but in the inwardness of everything, nature, tradition, and all human and natural reality. For Jung, a new sun was rising from the inward dimension of being, and this was overdue in the West, which had emphasised the external aspect of the sacred.

For social progressives, the sacred was a mere human construct of society and culture; for conservatives the sacred was outside in history, scripture, and tradition. But Jung emphasised that the sacred was not a stage in the history of consciousness, but an element in the structure of consciousness, a formulation adapted from Mircea Eliade (1969). This is the discovery that will revolutionise society and personality. We will find a new centre, an *axis mundi*, around which everything can be ordered and discovered anew, and he saw this as the next phase of Western civilisation. The first was the age of the Father, typified in Judaism, and then the age of the Son, in Christianity, and the next or third is the age of the Holy Spirit, which will be found in the psyche or soul. The guide and inspiration of the third phase would be found in mystics such as Meister Eckhart who emphasised the rebirth of God in the human soul, for which Eckhart was condemned by Catholic tradition. The search for God in the soul relativises the authority of the church, and it was sensed as an evil development and frowned on, just as the Gnostics had been condemned in earlier times.

In our time, the secular emphasis of progressives has received a considerable setback by the emergence of a hunger for spirituality in the community. This is puzzling both to the secular left and the religious right, since it does not play into either of their courts. But Jung could foresee this development after the Second World War, when it became apparent to him that people had a hunger for sacred experience in a new key. It was no longer sought in traditions or institutions, but in the depths of personal experience, where it manifested as a hunger for numinous, life-changing encounters. Intellectuals believed God was dead, and atheism would be the keynote of a future society. Religious traditions prayed for a return to the old faiths and hoped for a global conversion. Both groups were wrong and yet Jung's prediction that the spirit of the depths would come to the surface was coming true in the new revolution which has been dubbed the "spiritual but not religious" movement.

The new hunger, Jung said, points to a gnostic revival, where the emphasis is not to rid ourselves of spirits and gods, but to modernise them by making them psychologically comprehensible to an educated audience. People will come to appreciate that there are eternal forces at work in this apparently secular age, but they will not respond to the old forms in which these forces were contained. New spirit requires new containers, or to use a biblical metaphor, new wine requires new wineskins. We have the new wine but not yet the new wineskins, which Jung predicted could take hundreds of years to develop, given the slow-turning wheels of institutions.

Throughout this book we will be asking time and again: what is spirituality? It's a question that has to be asked repeatedly, because we need to get a better understanding of it. The hunger of the soul must be fed, and we cannot begin to feed it unless we discover what this hunger entails, what drives it. What do we long for when we say we long for spirituality? Contrary to the beliefs of some intellectuals, spirituality is not an escape from the world and its problems, but a deep dive into the world and the energies that drive it from the inside. Spirituality attempts to reach into the life forces and energies more fully, rather than confine ourselves to the surface. Spirituality is not an abstract act, but a practical attitude we adopt toward reality.

Descent of spirit

In thinking about Jung's psychology and what is has to say about spirituality and the search for soul, the phrase "descent of spirit" comes to mind. I put this phrase in a search engine, and 40 million results came up. None of them, as far I could see, related to Jung, but almost all were concerned with the Pentecost, the descent of the holy spirit upon the apostles, as described in the Bible (Acts 2:1–11). These passages describe the way in which the fiery spirit showered upon the apostles, with magical effects and transformations in their lives. It is counted as one of the major miracles of the New Testament. I wondered if this phenomenon had any relation to Jung's psychology and I concluded that it did.

In Jung's cosmology, spirit has fallen from its heavenly heights into the human psyche, having extraordinary and far-reaching effects on human beings. This fate has happened to everyone, not simply to a handful of apostles or believers. I don't know if Jung had the Pentecost in mind when he wrote of the fall of spirit from heaven to earth, but even if he didn't it doesn't matter, as the analogy holds. Jung believed spirit fell to earth by default, not by design, because with the collapse of religious beliefs and institutions the spiritual impulse is now found in the human psyche rather than heaven. Jung saw the spirit falling out of theology into psychology. One book that helped me clarify aspects of Jung's idea of the fall of spirit was *Descent of Spirit* by Grant Watson (1990). Watson was a field scientist influenced by Jung, whose writings made him conscious of the spiritual aspects of human biology.

In his essay "Archetypes of the Collective Unconscious", Jung provides a memorable description of our spiritual condition:

> Since the stars have fallen from heaven and our highest symbols have paled, a secret life holds sway in the unconscious. That is why we have a psychology today, and why we speak of the unconscious. All this would be quite superfluous in an age or culture that

possessed symbols. Symbols are spirit from above, and under those conditions the spirit is above too ... Our unconscious, on the other hand, hides living water, spirit that has become nature, and that is why it is disturbed ... The "heart glows", and a secret unrest gnaws at the roots of our being. (1934a, § 50)

Spirit has fallen to earth and "become nature", and "that is why it is disturbed". In the New Testament the spirit is symbolised by fire, but in Jung the symbol has changed to water, as the spirit has become what he calls "living water", that is, water turbocharged with spirit from above. Religious fire has dissolved into psychological water. The unconscious, which would normally be a natural structure of the psyche, is no longer merely natural. The things of the world have been infected with the eerie glow of the sacred. As the poet Theodore Roethke put it: "All natural shapes are blazing with unnatural light" (1964, p. 1502, line 17). Spirit has contaminated nature and there is a ghostly disturbance in the world that refuses to allow us to rest. Jung writes:

When our natural inheritance has been dissipated, then the spirit too, as Heraclitus says, has descended from its fiery heights. But when the spirit becomes heavy it turns to water .... This water is no figure of speech, but a living symbol of the dark psyche. (1934a, § 32–33)

Although Jung tried to assume the stance of a scientific empiricist, such statements read as mythological imaginings or poetic metaphors for the life of the spirit. He tries to explain: "Psychologically, water means spirit that has become unconscious," (ibid., § 40). but the force of his argument is in the poetry, not in the interpretation. Whenever we talk about the fate of the spirit we are automatically in the realm of poetry or myth, whether we like it or not. Spirit and soul exist in a poetic realm and can only be accessed by literary figures of speech, not science or reason. That is why I have discovered more about spirit from poets than psychologists, apart from Jung himself.

The impact of the collapse

Jung's notion that "spirit has become nature" is his explanation as to why the world is in a chaotic condition. The two poles of our existence, spirit and nature, which in other times are kept in a complementary relationship, have collapsed into one world, and this has led to confusion, where we cannot tell one from the other. The polarity between spirit and nature has been subverted by our failure to attend to the sacred order as a social and personal duty. Just as electricity requires the tension between polarities to function properly, so our minds work best when spirit and nature are held in dynamic tension. When we live between the two poles of spirit and matter, heaven and earth, we find a yin/yang balance and live correctly.

But when spirit collapses, our base instincts and higher desires become entangled and confused, and we are unable to tell them apart. A sacred impulse, such as the desire to unite with God or gods, can no longer be distinguished from the desires of the flesh, or even from criminal desires such as rape, incest, or child abuse, all of which are epidemics of our time. The desires of the spirit fall into the body, contaminating it with longings that can never be realised at the physical level. The sacred becomes profaned by this downward movement, and the body thrashes around trying to realise desires that belong to the realm of the spirit. This could be why the divorce rate is so high; we expect a human being to be a god, and invariably we are disappointed.

What many see in the world today is increasing secularisation and the diminishment of the religious institutions. But whereas sociologists of Jung's time believed that the secular turn of society would lead to the complete loss of spiritual feeling, Jung's argument worked in reverse. It is precisely the absence of religious feeling in society which led, he argued, to the intensification of the religious impulse in the psyche. Jung's paradoxical argument is that society alienates us so radically from religious forms that the psyche gives rise to compensatory yearnings for the sacred. "If anything of importance is devalued in our conscious life, and perishes—so runs the law—there arises a compensation in the unconscious" (1931a, § 175). By way of the process of compensation, the longings of spirit are intensified and what would otherwise remain silent is pushed to the fore, affecting our thoughts and behaviour.

The intensification of the inner light

The leading sociologist of Jung's time, Max Weber, predicted a pattern of increasing secularisation along with a process of disenchantment, loss of spirit, or "demagicalisation", as he called it (1918, p. 16). Weber was describing what was happening at the surface, but he was not reckoning on the existence of Jung's subterranean impulse towards transcendental meaning. Few people saw that the principle of compensation would generate a new compulsion towards meaning. However, Zen Buddhism had pre-empted the situation that Jung would describe. This Zen saying helps us understand Jung's paradoxical thinking:

> There are two suns, one in the sky and one inside the heart. When the sun in the sky becomes weak and the world darkens, the sun inside us blazes more strongly.

When God "out there" in the heavens or worshipped in institutions grows weaker through lack of belief, the God "in here" becomes stronger. Jung said "When all visible lights are extinguished one finds the light of the self" (1943, p. 301). Using the same metaphor as Zen, he said when religion declines the inner world lights up with spirit because there is "a life-producing sun in the depths of the unconscious" (1938, § 100). This life-producing sun is what drives many to seek ultimate meaning. What this means in historical terms is that religion is weaker institutionally but stronger psychologically.

This produces a curious turn of events, where the world looks divided against itself: public interest in "spirituality" rises at the same time as interest in "religion" declines. The new wine cannot be poured into old wineskins. Contradictory things can be said about the contemporary world and its relation to the sacred. The intensity of our relationship with the sacred increases informally and decreases formally. The Chinese curse, "May you live in interesting times", suggests itself as we attempt to negotiate this troubled time of transition.

The idea of heaven falling to earth is a constant one in Jung's work, impacting his thinking at several levels. In *Psychology and Religion* he imagines the evolution of religion in the West as a movement from above to below:

> The gods at first lived in superhuman power and beauty on the top of snow-clad mountains or in the darkness of caves, woods and seas. Later on they drew together into one god, and then that god became man. But in our day even the God-man seems to have descended from his throne and to be dissolving himself in the common man. (Ibid., § 141)

In this reading, the religious impulse is continually being taken further into the common realm. Religion evolves by a devolution, a movement from above to below. Jung seems to think that this is a natural and necessary process, although at the same time he laments this devolution because we human beings don't really know what is happening to our world. God falling to earth, becoming man in Christ and then dissolving into the "common man" is a process Jung understands but fears and worries about at the same time.

He speaks of the same process in a talk delivered after his Terry Lectures at Yale. Jung says the pagan gods of Greece had been concentrated into one God, the great god Pan. Then, as paganism was dying in Greece to make way for the Christian revelation, the captain of a ship in the Aegean Sea heard a sound of lamentation and a loud voice crying: "The Great God Pan is dead." On this matter, Jung comments:

> Great Pan, who is God, is dead. Only man remains alive. After that
> the one God became one man, and this was Christ; one man for
> all. But now that too is gone, now every man has to carry God.
> The descent of spirit into matter is complete. (1937, p. 108)

The demise of the God above is a tragedy, a loss of the transcendent dimension and the hallowed otherness of the sacred. But this (con) fusion of sacredness and humanity is also a great opportunity, a chance for the human being to glimpse and grasp the transcendence within him- or herself. This is a story of the increasing intimacy between divine and human, and the abolition of the chasm between these realities.

If humanity is able to respond correctly to this descent of spirit into matter, we might be able to experience the sacred potentials of life at close hand. However, Jung insists that the descent of spirit ought not result in a contamination of the ego with the sacred energies. Instead, we have to recognise that the sacred has relocated into what Jung calls the Self, as distinct from the ego. The Atman, or God Within, is what Jung thinks of as the result of this process of continuing incarnation.

Gods and diseases

The spiritual stirrings we experience today are welling up from the unconscious, hidden from sight and barely discernible. The collapsed spirit disturbs the psychological peace and puts us in a state of anxiety. We know things do not feel right, but we don't know why. We are suffering a metaphysical implosion, a religious neurosis. It is astonishing that the gods or archetypes of which Jung speaks, normally obscured from view, come into the horizon of awareness when we are gripped by ill health.

It seems that, in our time, suffering is the royal road to the sacred. Perhaps it was always so, but in our society, where talk of the gods has been banished and those who discuss the subject are thought to be crazy, the breaking apart of the personality that occasions illness or suffering is a requirement for such an encounter. When the normal self is displaced by illness or suffering, we have to engage in dialogue with forces that are stronger than ourselves. Our inner world is mystical to a surprising degree, especially where illnesses are concerned.

In an earlier book (2011) I explored the role of archetypal forces in a range of pathological formations, including neurosis, sexual dysfunction, incest and child abuse, and cancer phobia. I also looked at alcoholism, depression, self-harm, and suicidal impulses from the point of view of psychospiritual factors. In my view, many of these pathologies are primarily *diseases of the spirit* and secondarily diseases of the body. This is why the medical model as it stands can do little to heal these problems. It can reduce symptoms in some cases and alleviate some of our sufferings, but it cannot transform these pathologies unless it introduces the dimension of spirit or soul into the equation.

In some areas of medicine, this change is already underway, as found for instance in the *Oxford Textbook of Spirituality in Healthcare* (Cobb, Puchalski, & Bruce Rumbold, 2012) and in the *International Handbook of Education for Spirituality, Care and Wellbeing* (De Souza et al., 2009). Seemingly oblivious to the spiritual dimension of health since the Enlightenment, our medical world is now, reluctantly, being drawn into this discourse. Archetypal medicine is not Jung's personal inven- tion, but is a persistent and age-old tradition, found wherever the spirit is recognised as a potent ingredient in human health and well-being (Ziegler, 1983). In a history of archetypal medicine we would have to include every ancient and pre-modern culture, from the late medieval period, back to the classical period, further back to the Stone Age and beyond. Every spiritual culture has recognised the role of hidden forces in disease, including the shamanistic practices of indigenous cultures and the god-centred healing arts of Greece and Rome. Only our civilisation has decided to throw out the spiritual factor because it cannot see or test it in a laboratory.

In ancient Greece, a defiled god would turn wrathful and fierce, and further back, in the Stone Age, a friendly spirit would turn demonic and hostile. Not much has changed in this regard. Since we make no room for the gods and do not respect them or invest energy or interest in their well-being, the situation we face is difficult. In 1929 Jung announced "The gods have become diseases" (1929b, § 54). because they seem to have no other option in our lives than to become factors of disturbance. They are shunned by our intellects and reason. Since our minds ignore them, the only place they have left to make themselves felt and draw our attention is in our bodies, sufferings, and sexual disturbances. Then we might listen, but then, we might not. Some of us seem more prepared to suffer blindly than have to admit that the world might be enchanted by forces beyond ourselves. Our culture has become "pneumaphobic", as sociologist John Carroll put it (2001, p. 53). We are fearful of the spirit and will do anything to avoid it.

Many people would sooner die than have to come to terms with a divine presence. Our conditioning has made us enemies of spirit, and the present situation makes us less likely to turn towards spirit with interest because it has become wrathful at our neglect. We do not feel like opening the doors of our perception to forces that have turned against us, and yet we must. This is the odd predicament we face: the savage gods have to be befriended. Jung's original announcement about the gods becoming diseases needs to be set in this context. In an essay written to introduce the Chinese text, "The Secret of the Golden Flower", Jung wrote this remarkable passage:

> We think we can congratulate ourselves on having already reached such a pinnacle of clarity, imagining that we have left these phantasmal gods far behind. But what we have left behind are only verbal spectres, not the psychic facts that were responsible for the birth of the gods. We are still as much possessed by autonomous psychic contents as if they were Olympians. Today they are called phobias, obsessions, and so forth; in a word, neurotic symptoms. The gods have become diseases; Zeus no longer rules Olympus but rather the solar plexus, and produces curious specimens for the doctor's consulting room, or disorders the brains of politicians and journalists who unwittingly let loose psychic epidemics on the world. (1929b, § 54)

Jung contrasts the "phantasmal gods" of the past with the "psychic factors" that were responsible for their original formation. We live in a time where the old forms and names are dead, and yet the eternal and ongoing spirits themselves have not been recognised or given new names. A sense of dread hangs over civilisation and this anxiety is related to our failure to name or appease the gods. At least some of our modern diseases can be converted back into gods, but each person has to make this spiritual journey in his or her own way. Society at large is not going to help us.

It is hard to imagine that readers at the time this was written (1929) would have greeted this with anything other than perplexity or indifference. In the 1920s, a time of belief in scientific progress, Jung is contradicting everything that most took for granted. Readers must have said: The gods still alive and to be taken seriously? And somehow they have transformed into diseases? It would have been too much for most to have digested, yet nevertheless uttered by Jung with the surety and tenor of an Old Testament prophet. With the abundant scepticism of early twentieth-century thought, Jung must have seemed an odd figure. Freud must have thought: Just as well we offloaded him years ago.

The fallen gods disturb the stability of the psyche, and express themselves in symptoms, phobias, diseases, and epidemics. In my book *Gods and Diseases* (2011), I explore clinical and medical expressions of repressed spirit. But such expressions are also found in social upheavals, civic violence, and disruptive political movements, such as attacks on the democratic process, the rise of tyrants, aggressive fundamentalisms, and religious terrorism (see Tacey, 2019). When spirit is lost sight of, civilisation puts itself in grave danger and can be destroyed by the return of the repressed.

The explosive return of spirit

This is a theme of the work of postmodern philosopher Jacques Derrida, who is still referred to as a nihilist and yet is probably the most spiritual of philosophers since Nietzsche. Derrida wrote of the "return of the religious" and defined it as the "coming of the other" (1998, pp. 2, 18), where the "other" is a term for everything that is different from the ordinary ego. The "explosive force" of the religious, he said, can "interrupt history" and "tear history apart". In this interruption to "the ordinary course of history", we have to "be prepared for the best as for the worst, the one never coming without the possibility of the other" (ibid., p. 18).

It is astonishing to think that spirit, which played a vital role in the civilising process, has fallen to such ill repute, violence, and pathology. What was celebrated as the pinnacle of cultural achievement is now in a state of decline and threatens the well-being and health of humanity and the world. The highest values thrash around in the darkness, looking for expression. They have become "shades" of the psychic underworld and are contaminated with unsavoury elements of our psychology, such as complexes, instincts, and impulses. Spirit is like an angel that has fallen from heaven, having lost its lofty abode after being rejected by humanity.

When Nietzsche said "God is dead", he did not mean that God had died of old age or natural causes, but that we had killed him. "We are all his murderers," cries Nietzsche's madman in the marketplace, his lantern held aloft (1887b, aphorism 125, pp. 167–169). The immortal ones cannot die, but we can destroy their health and turn them into demons. As the novelist Christopher Koch put it in *The Year of Living Dangerously*, "The spirit does not die, of course; it turns into a monster" (1978, p. 236). When we stop believing in the gods they disappear from our conscious awareness. This is registered in mythological terms as the "death" or murder of the gods. They become dead to us, because we have died to them.

Darkness has given rise to a new kind of light

The spirit of the holy has been eclipsed, and we can no longer find this light by the official means, but only by arduous and difficult dialogue with the psyche. To put this paradoxically, we could say that the light can only be discovered in the dark. The light has been reduced but not extinguished by its radical descent. It has become weaker, softer, more diffuse. It has become harder to see but is still possible to discern. It is as if the sun had been extinguished and instead of the gleam of Apollo or Phoebus, we have a new kind of radiance, a galaxy of little lights, a night sky of stars. To see these lights we must learn to see in the dark, discern glimmers of myth in dreams and moments of grace in the ordinariness of our lives. The divine light has been humbled and we have to humble ourselves to recover it.

But at the same time the interior landscape has been lit up as never before. Our unconscious has been illuminated by the descent of archetypal powers that were upheld and revered in religious symbols. Parts of the mind that have never seen the light of day have become accessible to our experience and are discovered in therapy and analysis. The interior landscape has been lit up by fallen lights, and it is not by our doing that we have such access to the unconscious. Some imagine we carry lanterns into the cavernous reaches of the mind, but these areas have been illuminated for us by changes in the spirit of the depths. We become explorers of the interior because we have been forced into it by shifts in the collective psyche.

It is the collapse of spirit that has forced the birth of depth psychology as a discipline. We only discover the psyche as an immediate reality when culture breaks down and no longer honours the yearning of spirit. Jung put it this way:

> The very fact that we have such a psychology is to me symptomatic of a profound convulsion of the collective psyche. A spiritual need has produced in our time the "discovery" of psychology. (1931a, § 159)

Only in dark times, when we ignore the sacred, do spiritual problems loom large and religious contents disguised as complexes call for attention, forcing us to deal with the inner life. The suffering of the spirit forces us to become aware of the unconscious and seek ways to free the inner man or woman from bondage. What culture fails to achieve we must achieve as individuals, even if this means contradicting society and living against the grain. But no matter what modernity thinks, or what the state prescribes, we still have to contend with the problems of the soul, even if the soul is declared non-existent by the currency of the day.

The notion that the interiority of the self is deepened by the loss of religious belief is not unique to Jung. He knew he was giving a psychological interpretation to insights already articulated by German poets and philosophers. Jung's spiritual psychology finds its cultural background in German Romanticism. Goethe, Schiller, and Schlegel established the literary and aesthetic groundwork upon which Jung built his psychology of the sacred (Bishop, 2009). Friedrich Schelling was another major source, although his notion of the "dark ground of spirit" seemed to come to Jung mainly through the work of Eduard von Hartmann (McGrath, 2012). Friedrich Hölderlin was a further influence, since he wrote (1801) that the creation of psychological complexes was due to the repression of spirit. Nietzsche was the first to arrive at the view that the collapse of religious mythology "creates" psychology and the sacred needed new cultural containers. These precursors are important to bear in mind, as Jung did not drop from the skies as a lonely genius, but comes from a long line of thinkers, mostly German, who were aware of the cultural significance of modernity's loss of the sacred.

The aftermath of Christian civilisation

In the English-speaking world, Jung seems to have little in common with psychologists or philosophers, but much in common with poets and writers. This is perhaps a reason why Herbert Read, a British literary scholar, became deeply involved in Jung's work and one of the editors of his collected works. As Herbert Read argued, there are parallels between Jung's ideas and the writings of T. S. Eliot, D. H. Lawrence, and W. B. Yeats. All consider that the traditional sources of light have fled from the world and if light is to be found it is to be drawn from "below", the unconscious, body, emotion, and shadow.

In particular W. B. Yeats, and especially his poem "The Second Coming", traces the same developmental shifts in culture that were traced by Jung, using the same mythic language. Both Yeats and Jung see an inevitable enantiodromia taking place as the Christian order collapses to unleash the shadow that had been restrained for ages. For both these figures, the First World War was the first major indication that the beast of scriptural mythology had been unleashed by the laws of reversal that govern the psychological laws of the human soul and its world order.

Jung and Yeats believed that the mythical beast or animal life of the psyche is not going to be content until it is recognised by civilisation as not only real but as ultimately divine in origin. We are talking about the darkness of God, the shadow side of the Christ figure. Hence in Yeats's poem, the "rough beast ... slouches towards Bethlehem to be born" (1919, p. 124), by which he means that the principle of darkness desires to be recognised as archetypal and part of the Godhead. This was also Jung's burden in *Answer to Job*, the 1952 work that shocked his Christian audiences, since he too was arguing for nothing less than the recognition of the collective shadow as an aspect of divinity.

Answer to Job and "The Second Coming" deserve to be read together as masterful testimonies to the dramatic shift or enantiodromia that is one of the most difficult and challenging aspects of our age. Both works call for a radical reconstruction of the image of the sacred; it is as if the shadow of the Judaeo-Christian order is upon us and we are forced to respond in some way. Our civilisation based on the principle of light and good is made to acknowledge that its culture has been one-sided and that darkness has built up in the shadow of Christianity over the course of centuries. Such revelations were difficult for Yeats and Jung to express; indeed, Yeats's poem was a product of an agonising vision that he fought against until it demanded to be expressed, while Jung resisted writing *Answer to Job* for some time until he could no longer delay the writing of a work that he knew would ruin his reputation among Christians.

Today Christian priests are part of this same dramatic exposé or revelation in the way in which the law courts and media mercilessly uncover their sexual abuse and misdemeanours to public gaze. These matters are not local or institutional problems that can be dealt with by awarding large amounts of money to the victims of such crimes. There is an archetypal dimension behind the individual cases, and the beast will not be satiated until it is allowed to be born in Bethlehem.

As a youth growing up in the 1960s, I was aware that I was living in the aftermath of Christian civilisation. While my parents were at church listening to the good news and sermons about loving kindness, I was home listening to the demonic sounds of Led Zeppelin, the Doors, Jimi Hendrix, and Janis Joplin. The tenor of the times was summed up in the Rolling Stones' anthem, "Sympathy for the Devil". The vitality of 1960s and '70s music was based on the eruption of the collective shadow, and the Devil was claiming its due.

This wasn't entirely cause for rejoicing, as the drug culture and upsurge of psychosis and schizophrenia, which impacted my own family, was an indication that the change of orientation would bring pain and suffering. But Jung insisted that any major change in culture rises from below, and is only later registered at the highest levels of society. Popular culture of the 1960s and '70s was the harbinger of changes that would later impact religion, philosophy, and world view. Jung and Yeats got there earlier, but they were prophets of the new dispensation, ahead of their time.

One of the reasons for the splitting of the mind in the 1960s and '70s was that many could not bridge the gap between the dominant cultural discourse of goodness, and the revelation of shadow and darkness in our lived experience. If the dominant discourse pays no attention to the uprising of the shadow, the individual mind has to wrestle with demons that are not purely personal but collective. Under pressure, such minds all too easily split into fragments. That's why it is important that the cultural discourse discontinues the old teaching and attempts to come to grips with the psychic realities of the time. Jung wrote: "One does not become enlightened by imagining figures of light but by making the darkness conscious" (1945a, § 335).

Depth psychology as a mixed blessing

Changes occur from the ground up, and while derelicts and eccentrics are often the first to register them, it seems that popular culture provides the beat and rhythm that makes them audible. Artists and visionaries then supply the forms for what was previously unknown, and the changes are documented by philosophers and sociologists. Only after holding out for a long time do the religions feel the need to respond to the changes. They are fire-walled against change by the adherence to doctrines and time-honoured teachings. As Jung insisted, religions protect the community from an experience of the living God, by delivering an impersonal, abstract teaching about God. That is why Meister Eckhart said, "I pray God to rid me of God." He calls on God to get rid of his preconceptions and destroy the God he has built in his own mind.

In the experience of division between inner and outer worlds, where there is no connecting bridge between soul and ego, the idea of a troublesome unconscious is born. The discovery of the unconscious is the sign that all is not well, that something is wrong with the human situation. Psychology, for Jung, is a product of a sick and ailing world, and herein lies an ambivalence that Jung feels for his own discipline. He probably would rather live in a world where the spiritual impulses are carried by high culture, where art, "*Kunst*", and religion express the soul's life and longings. Jung does not think psychology is adequate for our personal or cultural needs; it serves our temporary needs and is therefore a stopgap. In "The Spiritual Problem of Modern Man" (1931a) he argues that the soul needs a "living religion" in which "all the yearnings and hopes of the soul are adequately expressed".

He did not live to see that living religion, but his psychology provides glimpses of what it might be like. He diagnoses what is missing from traditional religions. For him, technology and the discipline of psychology are mixed blessings or solaces for what might otherwise be a vibrant and rich cultural order. A society that discovers the indwelling psyche is a society that is necessarily poor in spirit. Depth psychology is thus a "consolation prize" in an otherwise gloomy and despairing landscape. Jung is a psychologist by default, and one feels that his conservative nature would prefer to bask in the light of high culture than wander through the gutters and backwaters of the unconscious.

Nietzsche expressed the same sentiment in *The Genealogy of Morals*. Nietzsche said psychology only came into existence due to the inability of the religions to carry the impulses of the spirit.

> All instincts that do not discharge themselves outwardly turn inward—this is what I call the *internalisation* of man: thus it was that man first developed what was later called his soul or psyche. The entire inner world, originally as thin as if it were stretched between two membranes, expanded and extended itself, acquired depth, breadth, and height, in the same measure as outward discharge was inhibited. (1887a, pp. 84–85)

We see here an affinity between Jung and Nietzsche, and in some ways Jung's psychology is an adaptation and development of Nietzsche's philosophy. Presumably the reconstruction of the religions would mean that psychology is no longer necessary, as the sources of our afflictions would find a home in a reconstructed sacred order.

This is the subject of Hölderlin's poetry and Wagner's operas. To make sense of Jung, we have to see him in the context of a tradition of German poetry and music; but to see him as a product of the Freudian school is to make him look a misfit (as argued by Sonu Shamdasani, 2010). The wonder was not that Jung and Freud experienced an acrimonious split, but that Jung ever aligned himself with Freud in the first place. Jung's work, like Nietzsche's, was a response to the religious crisis of his times.

Jung felt that the collapse of our religious cosmos would have cataclysmic consequences for the mental and physical health of individuals and societies. In "Psychotherapists or the Clergy" he wrote:

> It seems to me that, side by side with the decline of religious life, the neuroses grow noticeably more frequent. We are living undeniably in a period of the greatest restlessness, nervous tension, confusion, and disorientation of outlook. (1932, § 514)

The "heap of broken images" of religion, as described by Eliot in "The Waste Land", are not replaced by a vacuum but by psychological illness. The sacred forces which are no longer upheld by culture become expressed in the body-psyche as symptoms, illnesses, and complexes. The "gods" remain but in radically altered form. It then becomes the task of the psychoanalyst to discern which archetype or god is at the core of the patient's neurosis. Hence analysts of the unconscious have to be educated in the history and study of religions, folklore, comparative mythology, and fairytale.

A simple medical training is not enough

A simple medical training is not enough, because the work of analysis is to track the gods that have fallen from the heights into the murk of psychology. Jung believed that a strictly scientific training was insufficient; future analysts ought to study the humanities, literature, and philosophy to prepare themselves for the symbolic languages spoken by the psyche. This is one of the reasons why Jung called his psychology, "complex psychology", not because it is confined to a study of complexes, but because it requires a multidisciplinary approach.

We need a new covenant with sacred forces, but how can we achieve this when the spirit is so activated and disturbed? Jung spoke of the divine as an outraged primal field, with the capacity to obliterate consciousness. In our social order, the psyche might be conceived as a violated feminine figure. It is a Fury capable of tearing us to shreds due to our denial of its reality:

> Seeking revenge for the violence his reason has done to her, outraged Nature only awaits the moment when the partition falls so as to overwhelm the conscious life with destruction. Man has been aware of this danger to the psyche since the earliest times, even in the most primitive stages of culture. It was to arm himself against this threat and to heal the damage done that he developed religious and magical practices. This is why the medicine-man is also the priest; he is the saviour of the soul as well as of the body, and *religions are systems of healing* for psychic illness. This is especially true of the two greatest religions of humanity, Christianity and Buddhism. (Ibid., § 531)

How can we know of this eruption if we think of the sacred only as an illusion of our making? In Greek terms, our failure has been *hubris* or the inflation of the human at the expense of the gods. Greek tragedy expresses the problems of hubris, but due to our lack of mythic imagination we are unable to relate this condition to ourselves and the modern situation. Jung sees the modern psyche as a raging torrent, unruly with anger and wrath:

> The opening up of the unconscious always means the outbreak of intense spiritual suffering: it is as when fertile fields are exposed by the bursting of a dam to a raging torrent. (Ibid.)

The modern encounter with the divine is highly problematical. We do not enter a cosmic sea which is steady, calm, and supportive, as the new age spiritual movement supposes, with its images of tranquillity and peacefulness. We set forth on seas that are stormy and rough, and which are destined to overturn simple vessels unprepared for turbulent conditions.

The churches in all Western nations continue to decline at an extraordinary rate. In my region, there are more churches up for sale than churches used for traditional worship. As they get turned into pizza parlours, apartment buildings, or clothing stores, I reflect on the descent of spirit into commercialism and junk. But the wheels of history are merciless, if the places of worship are no longer connected to the living spirit, but are only engaged in conventional practices. Even as a young boy, Jung had a vision in which God was shitting on his own cathedral, and the boy could have had no idea at this stage what this meant for Christendom as a whole. This was a daytime vision that terminated Jung's relationship with the church, and foreshadowed the rapid decline of the institutions for the next hundred years.

As the moderate churches continue to decline, we see a dramatic rise of hard-line churches, which seem to have some appeal to some people. We are witnessing the return of the religious in various forms, some of them toxic, disruptive, and dangerous. Instead of compassionate and inclusive places of worship, many of these "new" churches are fanatical, right wing, and regressive. These churches are often opposed to modernity and progressive attitudes towards race, class, gender, sexuality, and diversity. They believe they have full possession of what they call "gospel values", but their inability to be inclusive, tolerant, and compassionate suggests otherwise.

On a broader scale, we witness the rise of fundamentalism in all the major religions, especially in the three monotheisms, Christianity, Judaism, and Islam, but also in Hinduism and even formerly peaceable Buddhism. We now live in a world in which religion and violence have been permanently associated, which is a shocking irony given that the scriptures of all religions teach love, peace, and compassion. But once the spirit is defiled, it emerges in distorted forms and nothing other than a change of attitude will alter its destructive course. This wrath is not entirely of human origin, but has its source in an archetypal disposition.

The rise of fanatical religion is a phenomenon that Jung could have foreseen. He would have understood the outbreak of fundamentalism as a reactionary formation to the confusions of the modern era. In "The Spiritual Problem of Modern Man", he said:

> I believe I am not exaggerating when I say that modern man has suffered an almost fatal shock, psychologically speaking, and as a result has fallen into profound uncertainty. (1931a, § 155)

As uncertainty increases, and with it the breakdown of morality and religious values, we discover within ourselves—often against our will—a compensatory desire to assert religious certainty in the face of present doubt and chaos. Jung concedes that this uncertainty will provoke a counter-response:

> Everything has become relative and therefore doubtful. And while man, hesitant and questioning, contemplates a world that is distracted with ... dictatorship, capitalism and Bolshevism, his spirit yearns for an answer that will allay the turmoil of doubt and uncertainty. (Ibid., § 177)

He says the spirit yearns for an answer. It is not only the mind or intellect that wants an answer, but the spirit. The mind can cope with a great deal of uncertainty and survive in the face of it. Many intellectuals thrive on uncertainty and postmodernism turns uncertainty into an art form. But the spirit cares little for this; in a sense it prefers fundamentalism. Spirit is in a rancorous, turbulent mood and moves easily into antisocial expressions. Since the educated have turned against spirit, spirit itself turns against education.

The hard religions that are keen to take over from a failed modernity have not been reconstructed in terms of knowledge or education. Many of these religions are led by the worst, not the best. W. B. Yeats saw this when he wrote, "The best lack all conviction, while the worst/ Are full of passionate intensity" (1919, p. 124). These religions are not post-rational, but pre-rational and hark back to earlier times. They have not benefited from advances in the sciences or theories of knowledge. Rather, they brush this aside and assert a primordial religious impulse. They represent primitive religious instincts seeking to overthrow an advanced but spiritually dysfunctional social order. Commenting on his society, Jung asked, "How are we to explain this zeal, this almost fanatical worship of everything unsavoury?" (1931a, § 177). He answered: "The passionate interest in these movements undoubtedly arises from psychic energy which can no longer be invested in obsolete religious forms" (ibid., § 170).

Our degraded spirit is seething with rage against modernity because it has been locked in a cage by reason. It is keen to topple the cage in whatever way it can. In this climate we see a proliferation of uncompassionate religious leaders, new age frauds, phoneys, charlatans, tricksters, confidence men, militants, and terrorists. These distortions of spirit grow like noxious weeds in the unattended garden of spirituality. The scriptural messages of peace and compassion are ignored, power replaces love, might is right, and the institutions dispense fear rather than transcendence. Jung was under no illusion about the state of the spirit in today's world. He could see it had spent a long time imprisoned in the unconscious, and emerges in a dubious and diseased condition:

> What is now welling up from the unconscious [is] the end-result of the development of Christian consciousness. This end-result is a false spirit of arrogance, hysteria, woolly-mindedness, criminal amorality, and doctrinaire fanaticism, a purveyor of shoddy spiritual goods, spurious art, philosophical stutterings, and Utopian humbug. That is what the post-Christian spirit looks like. (1951, § 67)

Freud said repressed sexuality returns in pathological forms, and we can say the same about spiritual phenomena. The utopian humbug that Jung refers to are the false panaceas and fantasies promulgated by fascism and communism, but today we can add consumer capitalism to the list, since it claims that we can buy our way to a utopian paradise.

The challenge today is not to throw out the situation we have inherited, but to start from where we are, accepting the confusion and turmoil. By bringing care, attention, and insight to bear on our spiritual lives, we might be able to recover a true sense of the sacred. The spirit cannot achieve this endeavour by itself, but needs to be partnered by consciousness, otherwise the results can be devastating. Spirit needs to be educated like any other function of the psyche, and the root for the word *education* means to "lead" or "draw out". "Education is the art of bringing out what is latent" and "a making visible of what is hidden as a seed" (Moore, 1996, p. 3). Jung did not provide us with answers, but he did begin the task of "drawing out" our spiritual impulse, and showing us where it had gone.

Endnote

1. Originally written as "Return of Spirit in the Secular World: Anxiety, Fundamentalism, Spirituality", for Jung Institute, Zurich, summer lectures, June 2009. Revised April 11, 2021, for "Jung and Spirituality", for Moscow Association for Analytical Psychology and Lithuania Association for Analytical Psychology.

CHAPTER 4

The activation of the earth archetype[1]

A concept like physical matter, stripped of its numinous connotation
of the Great Mother, no longer expresses the vast emotional meaning
of Mother Earth. It is a mere intellectual term, dry as dust and entirely
inhuman.

—Jung (1961b, § 584)

Reverberations down below

Contemporary spirituality is influenced by what Jung calls the earth
spirit, or earth archetype. This follows his logic because he says spirit
has fallen from its former height, and has activated earth and the lower
reaches of being. As a result, we experience the sacred today "from
below". It comes from "below" our awareness, and it comes as a surprise, when and where we least expect it, from dimensions that have
not been designated as holy. Indeed, in our time the spirit can rise
from areas of life once designated unholy or profane. Jung is one of the
pioneers of the discovery of what lies below the surface, and in what
follows I explore his ideas relating to the ancestral, the indigenous, the
primordial, and the earthly.

In terms of the unholy or profane aspect of the new spirituality, it is important to realise that Jung referred to the power of earth by using the term "chthonic". It is sometimes believed that "chthonic" refers to the surface of earth, the plants and rocks of nature. However, Jung used the term in the original sense, wherein *chthonos* translates to "under the earth", and in terms of Greek mythology it means "of the underworld". In Jung's understanding, the descent of spirit activates not only the surface of earth, but the underworld forces and deities, personified in Greek mythology as Hades, Persephone, Demeter, Hecate, and the Furies.

The Greeks feared the gods of the underworld because of their associations with the dead and death. So when we look closely at the idea of descent of spirit, in Jung's mind the world of the shades and the dead has been activated, meaning that the situation we find ourselves in today is fraught with danger. As we shall see, there are positive and negative aspects of the activation of the earth archetype.

The earth is personified in Greek and other ancient cultures as Mother Earth, World Mother, or Gaia. In a patriarchal and masculinist civilisation like the West, the earthly aspect of the Mother has been devalued in the same way that women, the body, and the feminine have been devalued. This means that when the Earth Mother awakens, it is often accompanied by storms and chaos, mainly because this archetype, like any neglected figure, has suffered under a repressive regime that has not allowed her to express herself or be revered. As with the gods of old, the archetypes of the present become angered and wrathful when they have not been respected. This leads to instability and suffering on the world stage, in the same way that the feminist movement in society has unleashed large amounts of anger and rage in women, which men find hard to cope with.

Men are intimidated by the rage of women, and seek solace with each other, forming stratagems such as a "men's movement", in which they are able to express their anger and confusion about the loss of masculine prowess and control. It has astounded me that one such manoeuvre, the mythopoetic men's movement, has used Jungian psychology to support the wounded masculine (Bly, 1990). I feel ambivalent about this movement, and have written a book about it (Tacey, 1997), because if anything Jung would be supportive of the liberated feminine, not involved in a rearguard action against it. Just as women have suffered under male domination for centuries, it is time for men to face the wrath of women, accumulated over centuries, and not hide from or guard against it.

Needless to say, spiritual movements based on a repressed archetype or god(dess) will not be always pleasant or nice. They will necessarily make the repressive regime or masculine principle feel unsafe, vulnerable, and uncertain. So in our time, the ecological movement is a major expression of the eruption of this archetype, and many men have tried to deny or ignore the urgent demands of the earth. I have known many men who have been "climate change deniers". It is easy to see that too much is at stake for them, and they run and hide their vulnerability and sense of failure. The climate crisis and ecological catastrophe have arisen because men have failed to treat the Earth Mother with love and respect, but have wrought havoc and destruction in the environmental sphere.

The earth archetype has coloured the experience of spirituality in a different hue. It can no longer be a flight from the earth or the body, but has to involve the whole person, including the bodily and sexual aspects of our existence. It can no longer be an escape from the claims of the body, but must include body, soul, and spirit in a new holistic spiritual expression. I will write on this in Chapter 6, but just want to signal here that a new "embodied" spirituality has been indicated by the changing place and circumstances of spirit in our time. This change is so dramatic that some traditionalists would have a hard time even identifying many of our contemporary experiences as spiritual.

I will also discuss the environmental crisis more fully in the next chapter, but in the present context I want to look at the political, social, and human consequences of the shift in the character of spirituality, especially in postcolonial societies.

The indigenous renaissance

As a way of introducing my discussion on postcolonial societies, I will quote a passage from eco-theologian Thomas Berry:

> Just now one of the significant historical roles of the primal people of the world is not simply to sustain their own traditions, but to call the entire civilized world back to a more authentic mode of being. (1988, p. 4)

I don't agree with his use of the word "civilised", implying that the indigenous people of the world are somehow uncivilised. They simply have a different kind of civilisation to ours, that's all.

In many parts of the world there is growing and widespread support for the recovery of respect for indigenous cultures. We find this in formerly colonial nations, including the United States, Canada, Mexico, New Zealand, Australia, South Africa, many other countries in Africa and South America, and island nations in the Pacific and Atlantic oceans. The colonising nations, the culprits, include Western hegemonic powers, Spain, Portugal, France, Belgium, Germany, Holland, and Britain. Wherever conquering powers imposed themselves upon indigenous peoples in distant lands, we find the same problem: how to acknowledge land rights and award civil rights to the indigenous who have been exploited and denied justice. Many colonial societies are now claiming to be postcolonial, but cannot aspire to this status unless reconciliation has been achieved, or at least started, by demonstrating serious attempts to establish treaties and repair historical wrongs and injustices.

At the heart of such processes of reconciliation are spiritual matters, but these are often ignored or avoided in the political and economic discourses that govern the shift from colonial to postcolonial conditions. As is often the case in the modern world, it is the spiritual dimension of our problems that is neglected in favour of the more tangible economic, political, and legal issues. Yet surely, it is the spiritual dimension that underpins all such negotiations. And as with anything covered up or suppressed, Jung's psychology helps us understand what the spiritual issues are, and gives us the language to begin to reclaim this lost dimension of social experience.

One spiritual aspect of the situation is that transplanted European societies have superimposed themselves on traditionally spiritual cultures. European nations have not been spiritual for many years, in some cases centuries, and yet they find themselves inhabiting geophysical spaces that are intensely spiritual and this has an impact on the invading culture. The colonising power is forced to contend with the possibility that the original and legitimate human condition is innately spiritual, and over time the "modern" societies have lost sight of this ancient perception and have lost their soul. They have literally gained the world and lost their souls, as warned in scripture (Mark 8:36–37; Matthew 16:26; Luke 9:25). The first generations of early colonists may not feel this spiritual problem intensely, but over time, later generations will be plagued by the feeling that they are not legitimate and need to recover their souls. However, as it says in Psalm 49:8, "For the redemption of his soul is costly, and never can payment suffice."

Subsequent generations will suffer greatly for the lack of integrity and self-respect that the absence of soul generates in the human psyche. The irony is that people in the "home" countries might still feel reconciled to not being spiritual, but those who left the security of the home countries to journey abroad have a very different perception of themselves. Those who left "home" feel the spiritual emptiness as debilitating, and the ever-present spiritual lives of those whom they have conquered serve as a constant reminder of their own spiritual emptiness. In this way, as Jung put it: "The foreign land assimilates its conqueror" (1927, § 103).

Thus the failure of the conquering nation to acknowledge or support the spiritual lives of the colonised becomes a mirror image of their neglect and disregard of their own interior lives. In my country, Australia, this has become an acute national problem. As I found as a university teacher, the younger generations are eager to achieve a spiritual integrity and self-respect that the older generations are not concerned about (Tacey, 2003).

But often the colonisers do not want to embark on a spiritual journey. They are too arrogant and have emerged from secularised societies. They view any turn to the spiritual as a weakening of rational authority. They do not wish to engage in any cultural change that appears to be a capitulation to the indigenous people, whom they see as beneath them. There is also much guilt about having dispossessed the indigenous people from their lands and perpetrated extensive violence and numerous wars against them. Moreover, political correctness arises at this time to claim that any cultural exchange with the indigenous is off limits and must be avoided at all costs. These combined barriers and excuses mean that nothing happens and the opportunities of the moment are stymied. There is no leap forward.

This leads to a situation that Jung refers to as the frustration of archetypal intent. Something wants to happen but it is refused. Meanwhile, in such societies, the arts are compelled to express what the society cannot express. Painting, sculpture, architecture, music, dance, poetry, and fiction abound with spiritual themes which express the unlived life of the nation. The arts thrive on what has been repressed and so often these days what nations repress is spiritual in nature. Artists and sensitive people are plagued by a sense of inauthenticity in the new land. This leads to a great division between progressive and conservative people in society. Conservatives refuse to mourn past wrongs and will not accept that they are living on Aboriginal land. The sense that they are illegitimate in the new land is too great a burden to bear. In Australia, successive governments have rejected what they have called the "black armband" view of history, by which they mean the acceptance of the atrocities and massacres of the past. This past is pushed away, hoping it will never resurface. But obviously this achieves nothing; the full acceptance of the atrocities of the past is the only way towards truth and reconciliation.

Aboriginal people correctly claim that their sovereignty has never been ceded: "Always was, always will be, Aboriginal land", is the chant. In the past, colonial societies tried to ignore the problem of legitimacy by pretending to be the rightful owners of lands fought for and won at the time of the invasion. But as time has passed, as the legitimacy of martial takeovers has been rightly questioned, and the glow of colonial conquest has dimmed, transplanted societies have been racked by self-doubt and guilt. This is experienced by sensitive people and the young. They ask: Are we legitimate in this land? Are we intruders in this country, and do we have a right to be here? How can we bond with this place and feel ourselves to be part of it?

Recently, such political questions have acquired a spiritual turn as well as an ecological dimension. Sensitive people cannot help but notice that when it comes to land care and the nurture of earth, indigenous people are way ahead of them in ecological integrity and spiritual belonging. The descendants of colonists and migrants begin to take a new interest in the indigenous people and may even begin to emulate their practices. They become concerned, terrified at the thought that they might be spiritually hollow and unable to attain spiritual belonging or ecological integrity. This demoralising guilt and doubt often trigger a call for action and social change. In this way, spirituality and politics are not opposites but serve each other.

Those who came in conquest are excluded from communion with the spirit of place. It is always the poets who glimpse this sense of exile first, because the average colonist is too busy exploiting the land to notice that they are being shunned by it. The spiritual inadequacy of Australian society is the subject of much of Judith Wright's poetry. She was the first of our poets to articulate the crippling sense of being spurned, never granted admission to a country which had been unjustly seized:

At Cooloolah

The blue crane fishing in Cooloolah's twilight
has fished there longer than our centuries.
He is the certain heir of lake and evening,
and he will wear their colour till he dies;

but I'm a stranger, come of a conquering people.
I cannot share his calm, who watch his lake,
being unloved by all my eyes delight in
and made uneasy, for an old murder's sake.

Those dark-skinned people who once named Cooloolah
knew that no land is lost or won by wars
for earth is spirit; the invader's feet will tangle
in nets there and his blood be thinned by fears. (1955, p. 83)

The seizure of land has a moral dimension and induces a sense of alienation. Conquerors of new lands are eventually conquered by the land, because they are racked by self-doubt and plagued by fears. The natural world seems to turn against them. Their acts of hubris constellate the same consequences that hubris wrought in classic drama: the vengeance of nature and the perishing of the soul. Wright adds a biblical echo to the situation: the "old murder" of Cain against Abel. Conquerors of land can find no solace or satisfaction, if they do not embrace the spirit of place with compassion, allowing them to connect spiritually, organically, to the world around them. We cannot live a real life shut up inside the sterile confines of the ego. Sooner or later, we must break out and risk an encounter with nature. Wright breaks out and finds, to her horror, that nature will not reach out to her.

Land cannot be reduced to a commodity or be expected to embrace the intruders. Belonging to place is a spiritual achievement which gives people a sense of identity and self-worth. Spirituality by definition requires submission to land, nature, and powers greater than ourselves. This is where the colonists are caught in a double bind; the more they strive to subdue the land for material progress, the more the land withholds its gift of belonging. Panic-stricken by the sense of hollow-ness, some descendants of colonists will be tempted to steal the sense of belonging—the cosmology, rituals, or ceremonies—that give the indig-enous their spiritual communion. The new age movement is guilty of such appropriation based on a sense of entitlement; it believes that if it steals the indigenous rites the land will become theirs. It fails to see how this theft merely re-enacts the earlier atrocities of colonisation.

New societies in search of soul

This is where Jung's psychology can help postcolonial societies caught in this cultural dilemma. The task is for the colonising society to dis-cover its soul, its buried indigenous self, and from that depth and being it can begin the important task of re-enchanting its world. But it cannot find its own soul if it does not first do the right thing by the indigenous people. Indeed, the indigenous people are the very embodiment of their souls, given that both have been damaged and bruised. After the glow of colonial conquest has dimmed, what next? Can the colonials send down taproots into the land? The colonisers are too identified with the ego and its point of view; that is why they cannot get beyond the sense that they are hollow and lack the ability to experience the world in a spiritual way. The transformation always arises first of all in the arts: painting, writing, sculpture, dance, music, and architecture of the postcolonial nation begin to imagine the world in a different way.

The more the colonial society can enter a postcolonial space, the less identified it will be with the greedy ego, and the more it will be able to discover soul in its own way. This enables it to relate to the indigenous people in a new way: no longer as threat or danger, but as a guide to soul and enrichment. As the postcolonial society deepens into soul, the more it will appreciate soul in indigenous cultures, and the less tempted it will be to steal or appropriate the spiritual property of the indigenous. That is why reconciliation between the cultures is not only a matter of political negotiation, or an economic or financial exchange, but an artistic and spiritual transformation.

Activation of the primordial mind

According to Jung, the change is essentially archetypal and involves activating what he calls the primordial man or woman within. Jung's premise is that all of us, including urban dwellers, have a deep-seated layer of the psyche at which we remain at one with the natural world. In his essay "Archaic Man", Jung wrote: "Every civilized human being, however high his conscious development, is still an archaic man at the deeper levels of his psyche" (1931c, § 105, pp. 104–147). Jung postulated a phylogenetic component of the psyche based on the theories of evolutionary biology:

> Just as the human body connects us with the mammals and displays numerous vestiges of earlier evolutionary stages going back even to the reptilian age, so the human psyche is a product of an evolution which, when followed back to its origins, shows countless archaic traits. (Ibid., § 105)

He argued that the unconscious stores all the previous forms of psychic functioning that have operated in the course of evolution, which has been attacked by critics as a form of Lamarckism.[2] Nevertheless, Jung believed that although European consciousness has strayed far from its roots and barely recognises its kinship with nature, the earlier forms of consciousness which facilitated human relations with the world for tens of thousands of years have not disappeared but have fallen into the unconscious.

"All those factors … that were essential to our near and remote ancestors will also be essential to us, for they are embedded in the inherited organic system" (Jung, 1928, § 717). Jung refers to this forgotten vestige as the "two million-year-old man that is in all of us" (1936, p. 100). It may not make good science, but it makes good sense, especially at this time when we need to believe that there are resources within the self that can be accessed to revitalise our environmental relations with the world. Jung said:

> In the last analysis, most of our difficulties come from losing contact with our instincts, with the age-old unforgotten wisdom stored up in us. And where do we make contact with this [archaic] man in us? In our dreams. (Ibid.)

He argued that dreams reflect the continued existence of this ancient layer of experience. Whereas our conscious minds speak the language of rationality (mostly), the unconscious still speaks the ancient language of mythos, symbol, and primordial image. This is why we find such difficulty in understanding dreams, because they speak from a layer to which we are no longer related. We not only fail to understand our dreams, we often fear them as well, because they speak from a depth that we are unwilling to explore.

At a deep level, the mind is still at one with nature, because, in Jung's view, the archaic or primordial mind *is* nature and has not yet been disconnected from it. "We have been that [archaic] mind," Jung wrote, "but we have never known it. We got rid of it before understanding it" (1961b, § 591). He believed the primordial mind could be awakened *under certain conditions*, and when it becomes activated we might be amazed at our changed experience of the world, which would be seen as an animated field. Jung's theory of a structural or inbuilt primordial mind influenced a number of the "altered states of mind" investigators of the 1960s, including Charles Tart, Stanislav Grof, and Timothy Leary. That wave of investigation into drugs and mind has come and gone, but other fields have taken up Jung's thinking related to these matters.

Jung's theory of an ever-present but submerged ancestral origin has inspired a lot of research in various fields, including neuroscience, anthropology, psychology, and biology. Harvard neuroscientist Gregg Jacobs has taken up the challenge of a primordial dimension of mind in *The Ancestral Mind* (2003), an important work which concerns itself with ancient levels of the psyche that still connect us to primordial nature. In Jung's time, the social anthropologist Jean Gebser explored the idea of our genetic and ancestral inheritance is his master work, *The Ever-Present Origin* (1949). Psychologist James Hillman (1975) believes this layer of mind is inherently animistic, that is, it experiences the world as an extension of psyche or soul and as animated by personified figures. Hillman's thesis is that the environmental catastrophe is prompting, in fact forcing us to reawaken the perception of the world as a living, animated field. In his writings, Hillman is advocating a postsecular animism (Hillman & Ventura, 1992).

Oxford biologist Anthony Stevens has taken seriously the science underpinning this atavistic theory. In *The Two Million-Year-Old Self*, Stevens claims that the notion of the "two million-year-old man", although a metaphor, is no less scientific than any of the other metaphors of science. He says, "Jung applied it in the same spirit as Neils Bohr, who referred to the atom as a 'miniature solar system': both are valid attempts to create a working image of what cannot otherwise be seen" (1993, p. 3). According to Stevens:

> By personifying this phylogenetic component of the psyche as an archaic being, or "the two million-year-old man that is in us all", Jung lay himself at the mercy of any beady logician wishing to accuse him of falling into a homuncular fallacy—namely, that he believed he had a little old man in there sitting at the controls. (Ibid.)

Stevens claims that Jung's metaphors are too quickly dismissed as implausible, whereas the metaphors of other scientists are taken in the right spirit, as models pointing to what is beyond perception. According to Stevens, the reason Jung's theory was rejected was because it advocated "innate" or intrinsic structures during a time in which cultural relativism reigned supreme. Jung was a structuralist at a time when structures, especially evolutionary ones, were viewed with suspicion.

The indigenous self

Some indigenous writers have taken this view on board. For instance, African writer Malidoma Somé, originally from Burkina Faso, has advanced the notion of an "indigenous archetype":

> There is an indigenous person within each of us. The indigenous archetype within the modern soul is in serious need of acknowledgment. A different set of priorities dwells there, a set of priorities long forgotten in Western society. (1993, p. 34)

I am not sure there is an indigenous archetype as such, but I do believe we all have a primordial self buried in the unconscious. Somé is aware that there can be no predetermined shape to his concept of an indigenous archetype. It can express itself differently in differing contexts, and there can be no "stereotyping" of an archaic vestige in the psyche. Somé is aware that this is at odds with science, but says the "indigenous person" within is a useful metaphor to describe elusive but profound dimensions of experience.

Jung believed Western people living in colonial societies can and do experience an activation of the primordial spirit by virtue of their close proximity to indigenous people. The indigenous community outside activates the primordial spirit inside. Thus, the warlike conqueror of foreign lands, oblivious at first to the spiritual and cultural value of indigenous people, finds himself changed by the indigenous people he has supposedly defeated. I have referred to this in the past (2009) as colonisation in reverse: the coloniser finds himself colonised by those whom he has subjugated. The psyche speaks truth to power. I suppose we might call this karma, or more simply, poetic justice.

What happens in external reality is reversed in the indwelling psyche, and the Aboriginal people of Australia have an explanation for this, which Jung finds intriguing. Basing his observations on the anthropology of Baldwin Spencer and Francis Gillen, and in particular their work, *Native Tribes of Central Australia* (2010), Jung writes:

> Australian Aboriginals assert that one cannot conquer foreign soil, because in it there dwell strange ancestor-spirits who reincarnate themselves in the new-born. There is a great psychological truth in this. The foreign land assimilates its conqueror. (1927, § 103)

Jung never dismisses any archaic idea out of hand; although he may not believe in the notion of ancestor spirits reincarnating in the newborn, he concedes there is "a great psychological truth in this". In other words, he reads such claims psychologically, and that means he reads them symbolically. The psychological truth, he says, is that the foreign land assimilates its conqueror.

This ancient Aboriginal idea, which is still extant in central Australia today, captured Jung's imagination, because he repeats the same observation in his later essay on American psychology:

> Certain very primitive Australian tribes are convinced that it is not possible to usurp foreign territory, because the children born there would inherit the wrong ancestor-spirits who dwell in the trees, the rocks, and the water of that country. There seems to be some subtle truth in this primitive intuition. (1930a, § 969)

Unlike most scientists who would simply smile at this superstition and not give it a second thought, Jung looks for a way of redeeming the archaic idea by giving it a new interpretation. In this case, he amplifies the Aboriginal idea by giving it a colloquial expression: "The foreign country somehow gets under the skin of those born in it" (ibid.). We don't know what getting "under the skin" means any more than we know about the idea of the reincarnation of spirits, nor is it any more scientific as an explanation, but we can feel more at peace with it somehow. In the same essay, Jung says he appreciates the way the original Australians articulate this phenomenon: "I like this picturesque way of putting it," he says. "It is pithy and expresses every conceivable implication" (ibid., § 979). It is a pity that Jung was never able to visit Australia, because there would have been much for him to appreciate in this country.

Jung's reflections on the primordial spirit being awoken by the earth are scattered throughout his collected writings, but are especially located in two essays, "Mind and Earth" (1927) and "The Complications of American Psychology" (1930a). The German title of the first was "Seele und Erde", which might be better translated as "Soul and Earth". Jung's English editors often attempt to bury his spiritual language and disguise it as scientific. This gives a wrong impression of his work to his English-speaking audience. His essays on the impact of earth on the human mind are extraordinary in some ways, because while Jung makes the most mystical of claims about psyche and earth, he does so with the appearance of being cool-headed and empirical.

He speaks of his "findings" on the influence of earth on mind, as if he were delivering a research paper at a scientific conference. He claims he is "not indulging in any psychological mysticism, but am simply trying to grasp scientifically the elementary psychic phenomena which underlie the belief in souls" (1927, § 84). Nevertheless despite these protestations he is indulging the mystical all the time. He was constantly trying to live up to his scientific persona and reputation, which had become a burden by this stage of his life, because his soul was most deeply mystical and spiritual.

What he meant by his claims to being scientific, I assume, is that he wanted to approach the mystical through a scientific method. Some might see this as sleight of hand or deceptive, but a more sympathetic approach might concede that Jung is attempting to bring complicated and "very subtle [matters]" into the realm of thought (ibid., § 54). He is concerned that the relations between mind and earth are often felt, but rarely discussed because we have no language to speak of them. This topic is generally regarded as too difficult to deal with, but Jung wants to bring it into discourse, in the interests of making the unconscious conscious.

Jung wrote "Mind and Earth" after his 1925 visit to East Africa, which had a profound impact on his thinking. In the essay Jung invites his readers to consider what he called the "chthonic portion of the psyche" (ibid., § 53), a portion not easily accessible but expressed indirectly through archetypal configurations. He also expounds on the notion of the *psychoid*, a deep level of mind where matter and psyche meet and interpenetrate. He was always deepening his views with regard to the extent and reach of the psyche, and in the soul and earth essay he postulated that human behaviour was impacted by "the psychic influence of the earth and its laws", and he refers to "the conditioning of the mind by the earth" (ibid., § 52–53). Again, this is the province of poets and writers, who often discuss what they refer to as the "spirit of place" or *genius loci*, as if this is a reality which has so far been unexplained by scientific enquiry.

In speaking of the sway of earth over mind, Jung says he is not talking about the influence of external physical or environmental conditions—not about "the banal facts of sense-perception and conscious adaptation to the environment" (ibid., § 52)—but about things archaic, elemental, chthonic. He sums up the influence of earth over mind by referring to the "night religion" of primitives (his word, not mine) and children:

> What I call "night religion" is the magical form of religion, the meaning and purpose of which is intercourse with the dark powers, devils, witches, magicians, and spirits. Just as the childish fairytale is a phylogenetic repetition of the ancient night religion, so the childish fear [of the dark] is a re-enactment of primitive psychology. (ibid., § 59)

This ancient religion, with its "dark powers, witches, magicians, and spirits", expresses the forces of the earth as they represent themselves to and in the mind. Jung argues that we should not take these figures literally, and we need to separate the "forces themselves" from their "infantile forms" (ibid., § 59). Clearly, Jung treats witches, demons, spirits, etc. as secondary personifications of a more primary, but perhaps no less terrifying, background reality. What this reality is, Jung cannot say, only that it is unknowable. He seems to think that if we grasp this reality psychologically it will be more knowable. As Jung said in another context, in our efforts to "explain" the nature of invisible reality in modern terms, all we can do is offer a "more or less successful translation into another metaphorical language" (1940, § 271).

The primary reality is irrepresentable as such, and can only be known through its symbolic representations. Hence although Jung's scientific persona recoils from the idea of demons and spirits, his second self is forced to embrace them and treat them with more respect than his scientific training would allow. He is forced to have "second thoughts" about symbolic forms that he would normally dismiss as infantile or primitive. That is, he has to take seriously these archaic forms, until new forms come along. Perhaps his poetic vision looks forward to a future time, when a new symbolic order will come into being, and we can move beyond the "infantile forms" that have governed the representation of chthonic forces in the past. Until science comes up with new and compelling metaphors, we are stuck with the old ones.

Experience in the Australian desert

The idea of the influence of the earth on the psyche is important to me personally, because I experienced something similar to this in central Australia. Living alongside indigenous cultures as a young adult, the land and its people had an impact on me that could be described as an activation of the primordial mind. Although as a non-indigenous resident in Alice Springs, recently arrived from the city of Melbourne, I did not understand the Aboriginal Dreaming, but the idea of world-animation seeped into my psyche.

I had intimations, intuitions, and dreams of a living landscape, of ranges and mountains as sentient beings, of plains and gullies as sacred places. None of this tallied with the precise theriomorphic mythology of the indigenous people, and just as well, as then I might have been accused of stealing cultural property. But it was apparent that my imagination had been inspired and activated by their animism. There is a dimension of experience that the policing actions of political correctness cannot control, and that is the spontaneous activity of the psyche.

Some Aboriginal people noticed that my relationship with land had changed, and I experienced it as fluid, living, spirit-filled. They are extremely attentive to the way in which non-indigenous people respond to their land. Some told me in their characteristic half-serious, half-joking fashion that I had begun to "think like a blackfella". The anthropologist Daisy Bates (1938) had claimed to be able to "think black", and this meant, above all, developing an animistic feeling for place, country, objects, and stones. But in the white population in Alice Springs terms such as "thinking black" or "going native" were used in a derogatory sense, referring to drunks, derelicts, and ferals. Rarely were they used in the positive sense of seeing the world as the indigenous see it, as a field which is transparent to sacred energies.

In a way that I have never fully understood, my primordial spirit had come to the fore. By this, I refer to that part of my unconscious that lay ready and latent, awaiting an opportunity to be released by experience. I would suggest that my lifelong interest in Jung and Hillman is almost entirely due to my efforts to understand the impact that the indigenous people had on my psyche. It seemed that no other writers took an interest in this phenomenon, let alone provided an understanding of the process. Something archetypal was being activated by the power of earth, by the geographical and cultural context. This was the Aboriginal gift to me: they invited me to enter the deeper layers of the psyche in which animistic perceptions could still be experienced.

Years later, I was amazed to read the following passage by English-Australian biologist Grant Watson, written after he had immersed himself for years in the cultures of central Australia:

> As I came to fall under the spell of [the indigenous] people, so many thousands of years distinct from our European conventions, so did those same European conventions suffer from an objective devaluation. The process went so far during [my time spent] amongst the Aborigines … that I only just snatched myself back in time to be able to half-believe ever again in the conventions of Europe. I had entered the animism of the savage mind, and found within those mystical, sympathetic identifications the open doorways to the unconscious. It was in a way a unique experience, not so much understood and valued at the time, but valued and partly understood afterwards. It has lifted me, or perhaps sunk me, above or below the orthodox horizon of vision. (1946, p. 108)

I resonate with this confession: such a transformation is "not so much understood at the time, but partly understood afterwards". This was true for me as well; it was after the experience that I reflected on its meaning; it was dimly apprehended at the time.

Grant Watson's testimony is a powerful example of the way in which close proximity to indigenous people awakens the ever-present primordial mind within and draws us into an animistic field. It may seem at first as if he is appropriating cultural property, but when he speaks of discovering "open doorways to the unconscious" we recognise that this is not cultural theft. It is not even an act of will, it happens to him, possibly against his will. We would not speak of a "savage mind" today, but in the 1940s, when this was written, this was an acceptable form of speech. Of great interest is his perception that the consciousness of Europe was in the process of dissolving in the face of this primordial reality; he speaks of "snatching himself" back in time to "half-believe" in the conventions of Europe.

As we might expect, Jung expressed a strong ambivalence about the impact of the ancient earth and the primordial spirit on the European psyche. He saw this process at work in his clinical practice, in modern art, and his travels in Africa and America, but he always cautioned his patients and readers that the tug towards the primal is not only a positive experience of regeneration but is attended by dangers and perils. In his journey to Islamic North Africa in 1920, he could almost feel his European consciousness melt away in a blissful state that was at the same time an indication, he feared, of a pull towards disintegration and inertia (1961a, 268ff.).

Jung admired the revitalisation of the libido through contact with the chthonic earth, and the attendant animism, romanticism, and mysticism that this brought with it, but always feared this activation. His express purpose was to find a balance of the opposites, to hold consciousness and the unconscious in tension, rather than drift into the dream-world of the unconscious. As a depth psychologist, he was always alert to the way in which unconscious dynamics could overturn, subvert, or replace the goals and aspirations of the ego. He never gave unqualified support to the unconscious, but believed that the ego should hold its own in the face of chthonic forces that might attract it downward. In other words, the mysticism was always checked by a critical reserve.

Australian art and literature are full of dramatic examples of what happens when the tug towards the primal is allowed free rein, without the checks and balances that might be offered by the impulse towards consciousness.[3] Australian painting, literature, and cinema provide stark reminders of the dangers, as well as the alluring features, of such a descent into the earth. In Patrick White's novel *Voss*, the German explorer feels the call of the desert, only to allow himself and his explorers to die in utter ruin and desolation in the arms of the primal matrix.

The novel and film *Picnic at Hanging Rock* is a masterpiece which elucidates the grinding tension between the colonial overlay of polite society and the unconscious substratum of ancient and denied realities. In these and other works, the colonising ego seems completely ignorant of the tug of primal forces, until some fall under their spell and find themselves moving irresistibly towards death and ruin. The ego's ignorance of archaic realities leads to tragedy, as the society finds itself at the mercy of the earth, which claims living sacrifices in an attitude of vengeance and retribution.

Jung's warnings and cautions about the primordial mind go unheeded by many of his followers. They tend to see his cautions as outmoded signs of racism, conservatism, or white supremacism. But it is too easy to reduce his warnings to such political issues and ideological battles. Jung spent most of his life trying to strike a yin-yang balance between the opposites, which he believed was the main task of psychology and individuation. He felt many are too willing to give away the gift of consciousness when faced with the lure of returning to the primordial self, nature-worship, and the instinctual life.

He was adopted as a hero of the hippy and back to nature movements of the 1960s and '70s, but these movements had no real inkling of what his real focus was. I explore these misreadings in my book, *Jung and the New Age* (2001). But like the hippies I tend to idealise the unconscious and the state of nature, so that my critique of the hippies is to some extent self-criticism. My idealisation of the Aboriginal people characterised my youth and even in adulthood I tended not to see the shadow or underside of living close to nature. Jung keeps insisting that the perspective of ego-consciousness needs to be maintained at all costs, and if that is unfashionable then he was certainly not fashionable in terms of our resurgent nature romanticism today.

American psyche

We move now to Jung's consideration of the American psyche, where this ambivalence in his thinking is striking. Jung was fascinated by the tension between the ego and the unconscious in all nations, but America in particular. He wrote, "The greatest experiment in the transplantation of a race in modern times was the colonization of the North American continent by a predominantly Germanic population" (1927, § 94). By the term "Germanic", he includes all countries of northern Europe and the British Isles. His experience of the First and Second World Wars made him feel that the Germanic population was more likely to fall under the sway of primitive energies than their counterparts in southern Europe.

Jung was astonished by the way in which North Americans of European descent seemed to demonstrate in their manner, appearance, and gait certain traits of the Native American people. In his study of American psychology he said "the 'Yankee' type is formed", and this is "so similar to the Indian type" that he had occasion to mistake American workers for Indian workers. He then speaks of "the mysterious Indianization of the American people". "The remarkable thing", he went on, "is that [no one seems to] notice the Indian influence." Jung claims he "got to know of this mystery only when I had to treat many American patients analytically" (ibid, § 98, 94). This is a tantalising remark, but Jung typically gives no clinical information, leaving us to guess what he might mean by this statement. Presumably, American Indian culture appeared in significant ways in the inner lives of his American clients, perhaps in a similar way to the role of the Hiawatha motif in the dreams and fantasies of his study of Miss Miller (1912).

Jung was intrigued by the research of the American anthropologist Franz Boas (1858–1942), who sought to prove that anatomical changes begin in the second generation of New York immigrants, "chiefly in the measurements of the skull" (1927, § 94). Jung had already referred to the research of Boas in his earlier essay, "The Role of the Unconscious" (1918). In a work called *The History of the American Race* (1912), Boas claimed that the skull measurements of North Americans of European descent had begun to resemble those of the Native American people. This controversial hypothesis, which anthropologists have alternatively sought to discredit, revalidate, and disprove again, is somewhat shaky in the history of anthropology, but Jung found in it a confirmation of his hunch that mind was impacted by place.

Jung also noted the way in which Americans of African descent, or as he called them, "the Negro", had influenced Americans of European descent, but felt that this influence, while significant, was confined to behaviour, social attitudes, and cultural activities such as music, dancing, talking, partying, and laughter. This influence could be accounted for by theories of the migration and dissemination of cultural styles that did not necessitate a theory of influence through the earth or the "chthonic portion of the psyche". "Only the outward behaviour is influenced by the Negro, but what goes on in the psyche must be the subject of further investigation" (1927, § 98). Jung was convinced that the North Americans were becoming "Indianised" or "going native", and in psychodynamic terms he felt that this was because the unconscious life of the migrants moved "downwards", or sank roots into the native soil of America:

> Thus the American presents a strange picture: a European with Negro behaviour and an Indian soul. Everywhere the virgin earth causes at least the unconscious of the conqueror to sink to the level of its indigenous inhabitants. (Ibid., § 103)

It is a great pity that Jung's metaphor of the psyche sinking its roots "downward" into native soil is fused with the racist idea that indigenous peoples are inferior to, or "below" the level of the European. I like the image of the psyche *sinking* its roots into the earth, as that accords with the process in a culture that has imposed itself from above, but the fact that this is used to support a white supremacist ideology is distinctly unpalatable. Alongside Jung's *spiritual* discourse about the mystery of psychic life is a *moral* discourse about racial inequality and inferiority. He speaks of "the infection of the European by the primitive" (ibid., § 97), of "the heavy downward pull of primitive life", and he asks: "What is more contagious than to live side by side with a rather primitive people?" (1930a, § 962).

Jung delivered a backhanded compliment to indigenous people, by suggesting that newcomers gain vitality, energy, and closeness to nature from their "proximity" to Amerindian people, but at the same time Europeans have to guard against moral collapse and a lowering of ethical standards: "The inferior man has a tremendous pull because he fascinates the inferior layers of our psyche, which has lived through untold ages of similar conditions" (ibid.) Hence the "growing down" into new-old lands activates ancient levels of the psyche, levels that Europeans have presumably dealt with and put to rest in their unconscious. What has been put to sleep in the European comes to new life in the American, and according to Jung this creates internal tension within the New World psyche:

> Thus, in the American, there is a discrepancy between conscious and unconscious that is not found in the European, a tension between

an extremely high conscious level of culture and an unconscious primitivity. This tension forms a psychic potential which endows the American with an indomitable spirit of enterprise and an enviable enthusiasm which we in Europe do not know. (1927, § 103)

The European-descended American tries to resist the process of "going native", and hence in colonial America moral standards were often more rigidly puritanical than back home in Europe. But underneath the pietistic colonial surface, the European in new lands seeks to merge with indigenous nature. The "indomitable spirit of enterprise" is found not only in the rapid emergence of the North East as a centre of culture and industry, but also in the great enthusiasm with which the Americans pursued their westward expansion.

The fabled American West presents us with a complex picture of the American psyche throughout this early period. The conscious aim of the westward project was to expand European civilisation into the remote and wild parts of the continent, but underneath the surface there were other forces at work. These included the notion that the Americans actually sought to return to the earth and become native and indigenous to the place, despite the ambivalent relationship with the tribal peoples, who were the rightful custodians of the land.

In the American mythologisation of the Wild West, in the novels, romances, stories, and movies which were inspired by the westward expansion, we constantly note the tension that Jung described, between "an extremely high conscious level of culture and an unconscious primitivity". In the stories of the West, we often see noble figures, men and women, who do their best for civilised morality and culture, but this stance is always cut across by the defector, the outlaws or bad cowboys, who allow their instincts to run amok in these wild places. Or sometimes the deputy sheriff himself hands in his badge and joins the bad boys of the town.

According to Jung, American women often carried "the more conservative element" (1930a, § 970), while men often yielded to moral laxity and the call of the wild. We see this pattern in Western movies, where the woman on the vast ranch or in the remote village battles to maintain the civilised codes of conduct, while the men in her life abandon all decorum and fall foul of the law. Hence "nature versus culture" was often enacted as a battle of the sexes in colonial America.

However, it must be said that returning to the wild is by no means synonymous with breaking the law or being immoral. Sometimes it means that American characters of unusual calibre discover a new integrity in their relationship with the land and primitive conditions, as in, for instance, the memorable *Dances with Wolves*. Such characters are not only highly sensitive to the American land but deeply respectful of Indian cultures and values. In this new, chthonic kind of moral balance, there is often a note of cosmic spirituality, since becoming at one with the land means becoming at one with the forces that govern the cosmos and the deep unconscious.

Germanic people and the barbarian within

Jung maintains that what he calls the "Germanic population"—and he includes all of Northern Europe and the British Isles in this category—is more likely to fall under the sway of primitive energies than their counterparts in Southern Europe. In 1918 he said: "This chthonic quality is found in dangerous concentration in the Germanic peoples" (1918, § 18). His argument is that the Germanic northern peoples have come more "recently" to civilisation and to Christianity than have their counterparts in the south, and thus are closer to the pagan and pre-Christian barbarian. In his view, the "uncivilized" parts of the northern psyche are more easily activated when the social controls of the conscious life are weakened:

> The primitive man ... reminds us of our prehistory, which would take us back not more than about twelve hundred years so far as the Germanic races are concerned. The barbarian in us is still wonderfully strong and he yields easily to the lure of his youthful memories. Therefore he needs very definite defenses. The Latin peoples being older don't need to be so much on their guard, hence their approach to the colored man is different. (1930a, § 962)

It is difficult to find evidence for Jung's intuitions, but they are suggestive of differences between national psychologies. I have noticed in my experience that "Latin peoples" relate differently to the indigenous people of Australia than those from northern European or Anglo-Saxon origin. Somehow, relations with the indigenous people are easier, more relaxed, and less defended than the Anglo-Saxons. I had never seen this difference pointed out until I read Jung's essays on America.

But Jung's intuitions about national differences were highly pro-phetic, given the fact that he was making these observations in the 1920s and early '30s. He warned that the Germanic type had a dan-gerously close relation to the barbarian within, and less than a decade after his pronouncements the world witnessed the spectacle of the "barbarian" let loose in the German people, personified by the "blond beast" of National Socialism. In 1918 Jung had given a description of the Germanic psyche which was a snapshot of the Nazi character which emerged in the late 1930s:

> Christianity split the Germanic barbarian into an upper and a lower half, and enabled him, by repressing the dark side, to domesticate the brighter half and fit it for civilization. But the lower, darker half still awaits redemption and a second spell of domestication. Until then, it will remain associated with the vestiges of the prehistoric age, with the collective unconscious, which is subject to a peculiar and ever-increasing activation.
>
> As the Christian view of the world loses its authority, the more menacingly will the "blond beast" be heard prowling about in its underground prison, ready at any moment to burst out with devas-tating consequences. When this happens in the individual it brings about a psychological revolution, but it can also take a social form. (1918, § 17)

Jung's prescience seems uncanny, suggesting he had some kind of fore-knowledge of the devastation about to happen in Europe. He says that the activation of the lower layers of the psyche is "ever-increasing", due to the collapse of the Christian view of the world, and to the collapse of the inhibitions and restraints that had formerly been placed on the psyche by the superego, which had been formed by Judaeo-Christianity.

Many feel relieved and liberated by the collapse of the Christian superego and its restraint on the instincts, and are happy to give an extra shove to the superego as it falls over the precipice. Most of the progressive revolutions of the last hundred years, including the sex-ual and love revolutions, have targeted Christian restraint and piety as a source of oppression. We are happy to "shed the inhibitions" of the past, but as Jung says, this is often done without any awareness of the consequences that follow, and what might be unleashed by such moral freedoms. The fact is that, as he puts it, "the lower, darker half [of the psyche] still awaits redemption and a second spell of domestication". Although we are keen to shed our inhibitions, we don't seem to have many ideas about how we might tame the beast that has been let loose by liberations.

Jung thinks that the breaking of rigid Christian ethics was inevitable, but that as we move to a less inhibited form of culture—which had been indicated by Freudian psychoanalysis from the beginning—we need to become more aware of and responsible for the evil within the psyche which is let loose as our sexual and instinctual libido is unleashed. I have long felt this to be a particular burden of our time—we sing the praises of our new-found liberation, failing to take into account the moral shadow and evil that trails behind the freedom that the modern condition allows. A permissive attitude towards instinctual life comes at a considerable price, and not least is the challenge to civilised conduct and ethics that is part of the general relaxation of moral control.

One is not sure whether Jung admires or abhors the American psyche by the time we finish his analysis of its psychology. There is considerable ambivalence in his depiction of the opposition in Americans between what he calls "an extremely high level of culture" and "an unconscious primitivity". The positive element of this clash is that enormous energy is created in the American psyche, and Jung concedes that "there are many Europeans who are infected by feelings of inferiority when they contact America".

But the main sense emerging in Jung's analysis is that America represents an experiment that could go horribly wrong, for the clash of opposites may not be transformed or its energies contained, and this could lead to pathologies on a huge scale. America's desire to control the world, and act as an unchecked and unregulated superpower could be seen as a symptomatic expression of its desire to gain control over itself, to submit its own unbounded energy to some countervailing force. Jung does not spell out his particular unease over America, but comments ominously: "A nation in the making is naturally a big risk, to itself as well as others" (1930a, § 980).

We must not forget that Jung's essay on America was first published in *Forum* magazine in New York under the controversial title, "Your Negroid and Indian Behaviour". Jung did not want to be too critical of Americans, because wealthy Americans were his major patrons and supporters. He did not want to be written off as a fool. He found himself in a double bind: he wanted to tell Americans that they had a great asset in the activation of primordial forces, but in explaining this process he had to resort to ideas that seemed oddly unconvincing and unscientific. Hence the desire to distance himself from the primordial mode he was trying to uncover.

Endnotes

1. This chapter is based on talks delivered to the Moscow Association for Analytical Psychology, November and December 2021. Chair: Alexander Pilipyuk; translator: Natela Hanelia.
2. This evolutionary biological view of the psyche is expounded by Anthony Stevens in his work *Archetypes: A Natural History of the Self* (1982).
3. My *Edge of the Sacred* (1995) provides examples of this process.

CHAPTER 5

The spirituality of nature

Nature seemed to me full of wonders, and I wanted to steep myself in them. Every stone, every plant, every single thing seemed alive and indescribably marvellous. I immersed myself in nature, crawled, as it were, into the very essence of nature and away from the whole human world.

—Jung (1961a, p. 32)

Childhood and nature

In the first chapter we looked at the nature of spirituality and in this chapter I want to explore the spirituality of nature. What Jung describes in the above quotation represents our primal urge, which I think is to immerse ourselves in nature, and seek it as refuge, protector, and true abode. What he describes as his childhood experience is close to my own, where I found nature a great consolation and companion in my early life, and still today, as far as possible. Such proximity to nature is the primal urge, because it is where we were all immersed in long ages past, and I think this urge is still evident in the unconscious lives of modern people. Today we might have replaced natural immersion with entanglements with relationships, family, sports clubs, and nationalism.

We have removed ourselves from nature and now find our primary bonding in the human, social, and national spheres. But some of us, like Jung, have maintained the primal connection with nature, and I find this especially in artists, writers, and sensitive souls.

When I was a child, some people around me found my desire to be close to nature as eccentric or weird, but I could not explain it in terms that adults would have understood. It was a desire to be close to what is greater than society, with its filth and corruption and false promises. I distrusted society but found nature comforting and secure. That is why when I eventually moved to the desert country of central Australia, I found the lifestyle and spirituality of the indigenous people much to my satisfaction and enjoyment. It was also my spirituality long before I had even heard of the word "spirituality". To some extent, we only use the word spirituality when we no longer have it. It represents something we desire in our lives, something we can only aspire to. My spirit and soul felt content and satisfied when I was ensconced in nature, and my whole being felt healthy in an inexplicable way. I was pleased to read that Jung had said, "Enchantment is the oldest form of medicine" (1977, p. 419), and wondered to what extent our ailments and diseases are in part a result of being alienated from the primal source.

As a mature adult, Jung spent much of his time building what he would call his tower, a rough-hewn stone cottage beside the lake in Zurich. The purpose of this tower, in one sense, was to recapitulate the harmony with nature that he experienced as a boy heading off into the forests in rural Switzerland, near Basel. The tower would be the place where he felt truly alone, not in the sense of being lonely, but in the sense of a solitude in which his being rediscovered a sense of communion with nature:

> At times I feel as though I am spread out over the landscape and inside things, and am myself living inside every tree, in the splashing of the waves, in the clouds and animals that come and go, in the procession of the seasons. There is nothing with which I am not linked. (1961a, p. 225)

To some, this retreat into the oneness of all beings might be seen as regressive, or as autistic to some extent, a union with the life force at a non- or pre-human level. Perhaps it might be called extreme introversion, but at the same time it is an attempt to reconnect with the source of life which gives our human lives new energy and vitality to face the demands and exigencies of the world. It is close to the true meaning of ecstasy, which literally means to "stand outside" ourselves and lose the egocentric self in moments of bliss and harmony. Again, to what extent is the desire to lose our identity in drugs, alcoholism, consumerism, or any other form of harmful escape from reality a kind of pathological replacement for the natural ecstasy that Jung describes finding in his connection with nature?

The ecological emergency

When alienation becomes the norm, it takes a great deal to convince people that we need to reconsider our relationship with nature. But the ecological emergency serves as a harsh wake-up call about the dangers of our alienation. When we stray far from nature, there is what popular culture calls a "disturbance in the force", and a breakdown of the order of things becomes a possibility. We have become all too familiar with the components of this breakdown: pollution, depletion of the ozone layer, loss of biodiversity, climate change, and a rapid increase in extreme weather events. Weather events that have been described as "once in a hundred years" episodes, now seem to happen every few years. Things are not right, and many of us feel threatened and in danger.

Even people without romantic attachment to nature are saying: "Gaia is angry." James Lovelock's (1979) hypothesis, that earth is a unified biophysical system and we have disturbed its self-regulation, seems to have hit a nerve in popular consciousness. There are things going on in the natural world that are unprecedented, and part of our response to the disorder is to think of nature as a unified whole, and resort to phrases like the "anger of Gaia" to account for it. This strikes me as one good thing that arises from the crisis: we are forced to think in holistic terms about nature and this means the crisis is reawakening the ancient mythological bond with the world. This bond had been lost for ages, and although it is too early to talk about a spiritual reconnection with nature, the ecological emergency will likely jolt us in this direction.

In ancient times there was world-animation, and every indigenous culture that has survived the onslaught of colonisation bears testimony to some kind of enchantment. Then, with modernisation and secularisation, we entered a world where there was no animation of the world, and now we are entering a post-rational phase where the possibility of the invisible is returning. But how are we to imagine this return? How are we to conceptualise world-animation in the future? Clearly, in order to move forward we have to go back, to recover lost visions that can inspire our future. Meanwhile, as Annie Dillard puts it:

> It is difficult to undo our own damage, and to recall to our presence that which we have asked to leave. It is hard to desecrate a sacred grove and change your mind .... We doused the burning bush and cannot rekindle it; we are lighting matches in vain under every green tree. Did the wind once cry, and the hills shout forth praise? Now speech has perished from among the lifeless things of earth, and living things say very little to very few. (1984, p. 70)

It is easier to lose world-animation than to win it back. Destroying visions of a unified world was quickly achieved by science, but now we have to go back to the past and find out what those ancient visions were pointing to. Once we refused their assertions and scorned their claims, but now we must adopt a more respectful attitude and use our best resources to "recall to our presence that which we have asked to leave".

If we go back in time, we find religions, myths, and cosmologies that claim that the world hangs by a gossamer thread, and if the thread is broken, disaster strikes. The thread has different names in different cultures: spirit or soul in the West, the Tao and the One in China, Indra's net in India, and in Aboriginal cultures, the Dreaming. The diverse names and cultures ought not to blind us to the similarities. If the thread is not attended to and nourished by cultural practices, sacrifices, rituals, and prayers the world falls apart. The idea that runs through much of the world's visionary literature is that there is a subtle reality, call it a "dream thread", that maintains the integrity of the universe and the unity of creation. Our responsibility as human beings is to recognise this subtle reality, or invisible order, identify it, serve it and by doing so the whole of creation is sustained.

Cosmology and ecology

In ancient Chinese culture, we see that the thread that holds the world is called the One, or the Tao. The *Tao Te Ching* advises that humans ought to respect the Tao, and not think of themselves as too haughty or proud, too full of their own knowledge, to ignore the One and concern themselves only with human tasks. They have a cosmic responsibility which is readily forgotten or overlooked. When the One is honoured it is said that "earth is settled" and the "gods have their potencies". "The valley is full, the myriad creatures are alive, and lords and princes become leaders in the empire: It is the One that makes these what they are." However, "when humanity forgets the oneness of infinity" then:

> The sky, lacking clarity, would break apart;
> The earth, lacking tranquillity, would erupt;
> The gods, lacking divinity, would vanish;
> The valley, lacking abundance, would wither;
> Myriad things, lacking life, would be extinct.

This sounds alarmingly like the ecological emergency that is unfolding today. The *Tao Te Ching* urges that the only way to restore order is for humans to recover their sense of the sacramental life, to return to reverence and humility:

> Therefore, the superior must have the inferior as root;
> The high must have the low as base.
> Therefore, the highest renown is without renown,
> Do not wish to be shiny like jade,
> Nor aloof like stone.

The emphasis in this text is to avoid the arrogance of pride and the folly of hubris, because when we succumb to such errors, we lose our respect for the One from which all things flow. The Way of the Tao is the way of healing, and one heals oneself and the world by remaining mindful of the unseen hand behind creation, the spirit of the world.

The American poet Walt Whitman wrote that the soul is an unseen force that binds the world. He said it is like a "noiseless patient spider" which "launches filament, filament, filament out of itself". It throws out its web into "measureless oceans of space", "seeking the spheres to connect them". Its one hope is that its "gossamer thread" will "catch somewhere" and its threads "hold", forming a "bridge" across the spheres. When I first read Whitman's poem, "A Noiseless, Patient Spider" (1868, p. 1085), I was reminded of the Aboriginal Dreaming, which throws out a web of mystical threads into geographical and cosmic space, binding humanity to nature and nature to humanity.[1] Then I thought about

Wordsworth, Coleridge, and the Romantic poets, and how they were creating not only a new poetry but a new mythology about our bond with nature. Art seems to have taken over the spiritual responsibility that was previously the arena of religious cosmologies. In our society, art is one of the remaining carriers of the sacred, and that is why art is more important today than ever before, because it carries the spiritual vision in a disbelieving age.

The subtle threads that bind us to nature have always interested me, not only now, as we struggle to find ways to reconnect with nature in an ecological crisis. Even as a boy I sensed that the depth connection to nature is a religious or spiritual problem, not something that governments could fix by moral decrees or environmental laws. While the laws and decrees are necessary in a reckless age, there is something more fundamental that is rarely talked about. The environmental crisis is the result of our inability to love fully and without reservation. It is our failure to love the world as part of our selves and as God's creation. Once we recover our ability to love fully and unconditionally there is no longer any need to be told by authorities to care more about the environment. Such external voices are no longer necessary because there is no longer any impulse to mistreat the world or behave thoughtlessly towards it. This might seem simple, but it has always been my basic thought about the environmental problem. Ultimately we have misnamed it as an environmental crisis, because it is rather a crisis of human consciousness; it is our fault, not the fault of the environment.

Something like love or fellow-feeling is absent from our relations with the world. We have confined our love to human persons dear to us, family, friends, partners, and children. Or we confine love to our ideas, religions, ideologies, and systems of meaning. Our love seems to dwindle and finally stop or disappear when we reach beyond the human to the world. Intellectuals refer to this as "anthropocentricism", that is, being bound to or caught up in the human. Depth psychologists might refer to it, critically, as egotism or narcissism, that is, a failure to live beyond the ego, and beyond that which the ego sees as related to its own interests or edification. But the world can't be bracketed out in this way. The cut between self and world is entirely illusory.

If we humans care only about ourselves, then the notion of what constitutes *self* has to be broadened to take in the world. If our love can be expanded to include the cosmos, there can be real change. We draw the circles of our belonging too narrowly, and live in tight and ever-narrowing circles of compassion. We have to learn to fall in love with the world. We have to care for the world as if it were ourselves. Alice Walker put it well: *Anything We Love, Can Be Saved*. This is a source of hope amid the gloom about the state of the world. If our love can be expanded, the rest looks after itself.

Indigenous spirituality and nature

Indigenous societies taught members that they belonged to the universe and not only to a family group or tribe. What facilitated this broader sense of belonging was spirituality, namely, the experience of the world as an intelligent, living, and spiritually significant field, charged with forces and energies that have a direct bearing on human beings. These forces were often personified, or if you like, mythologised, as a cosmic mother or father, as ancestral spirits, or as gods and goddesses who embodied the powers of nature and the powers in human nature. In other words, there was no exact division or cut between outside and inside; both were felt to relate to the other, to interpenetrate and move across boundaries that we experience as solid. Boundaries were fluid and pervious that have now become impervious. What facilitated this fluidity was the sense that the human being is more than human, in our understanding of the term. The person is not merely flesh and blood, not mere personal ego, but a complex web of archetypal forces that animate the human self and the more-than-human world.

These transpersonal and yet personal forces are not revealed to the ordinary mind or normal sight but are only revealed to the trained mind and insight. They form the basis of sacred knowledge, and are kept out of profane life and announced only in the context of ceremony and ritual. Indigenous people are aware that the so-called "natural" man or woman would be unable to experience these forces, and would most likely regard them as unreal, fantastic, or illusory. Hence the initiation ceremony was introduced as a vital aspect of all indigenous cultures. One has to be initiated into an understanding of these forces, and the purpose of the initiation ceremony is to terminate the natural, ego-bound state and put it to death.

During the initiation ceremony, the novice is introduced to the cultural, that is to say, spiritual point of view. He or she is made to see that the personal ego is a working illusion or enabling fiction. The real person is actually a spiritual essence, with a connection that goes right back into the past and extends into the future as well. The present, literal, empirical person is an "incarnation" of a spiritual life which far transcends the individual being, but which has chosen to incarnate in him or her. This is the spiritual knowledge that underpins the ecological vision that is found in all ancient cultures, but which is absent in ours. It is the sense of oneself as a spiritual reality that provides the fluidity that links one to the past and future, to inside and outside, and to physical and environmental domains.

The secret of indigenous spirituality is a different way of knowing, which I would describe as non-dualism. There is no separation between spirit and matter, because spirit is felt to imbue the whole of reality. This vision of one world, or *unus mundus*, is imparted to young adults at the time of their initiation. In the ceremony they are taught that the spirit that animates their lives is the same spirit that animates the world. Unlike Westerners, they do not live in a dualistic world, where spirit is found in some things but not others, making the world appear purely physical and objectified as a realm that can be exploited by humans. As we make our way to a new sense of the sacred, we need to observe with care the non-dualistic vision that can usher in a profoundly ecological consciousness. We, however, seem to believe that an ecological layer of awareness can be "added" to our existing consciousness, which divides the world into sacred and profane. But unless we aspire to a non-dual awareness there can be no ecological revolution.

While growing up in central Australia, I was moved by the cosmology of the Aboriginal people. These people have used myths of ancestor spirits to facilitate the animation of place, transforming the world from a collection of objects, as it appears to dualistic perception, into a communion of subjects, as it appears to indigenous perception.[2] Rocks, trees, mountain ranges, gullies, gorges are not just material objects in space, but sacred traces of the movements of ancestral beings. The natural world is embraced as a geography of the sacred. Nature is personified as mother, or Kunapipi, and experienced as an elaborate and complex family network, a field of transpersonal forces that defines the lives of individuals and the tribe.

Their world is alive and speaks to them because the spirit which animates their lives animates the world. Moreover, elders attend sacred sites to "sing up" the spirits of place through ritual, song, and ceremony. These performances keep the spirits of place alive, and in turn they enliven and keep sustainable the lives of the tribes.

Aboriginal author Vicki Grieves has made freely available her comprehensive and insightful account of Aboriginal spirituality (2009). She quotes Aboriginal elder Silas Roberts saying: "Our connection to all things natural is spiritual."

The efficacy of this ecology of soul can hardly be underestimated seeing that it has sustained these cultures in harsh landscapes for millennia. Political commentators often pay lip service to the "special relationship" between Aboriginal people and land, and praise them for their ecologically sustainable cultures, but without grasping the vision that supports and enables it. It is their cosmology that is responsible for their ecological intelligence, and we will not achieve full ecological integrity unless we re-sacralise our relationship with earth.[3] In his "Apology to Indigenous Peoples" (2008), Prime Minister Kevin Rudd said that Aboriginal peoples are "the oldest continuing cultures in human history". He did not, however, point out that their survival and longevity is due almost entirely to their spiritual pact with the world. This is too difficult for white people to understand, and, as well, many non-indigenous find it embarrassing to even discuss this subject.

The Aboriginal Dreaming encompasses the visible and invisible in a unity which cannot be appreciated by a dualistic consciousness. This primal bond with nature is not to be dismissed by rational minds as a remnant of a useless or unscientific way of viewing the world. Their vision is to be respected as a psychological and cultural achievement with real survival value. It is the *survival value* of their vision that needs to be emphasised, whereas the scientific world view, which encourages the despiritualisation of nature, has a questionable record.

The things that are regarded by modernity as irrelevant, such as spirituality and cosmology, prove to be the vital elements for wellbeing, longevity, and ecology. I do not want to sentimentalise indigenous people or suggest they did not harm the land or have an impact on it. Anthropological studies have shown this is not the case (Flannery, 2002). Their impact was considerable but they were aware of the ecology of the whole, the rhythms of nature, and the earth's need to recover from human impact. Their awareness was not just the result of natural science or farming technique but based on a vision of the interconnectedness of things. We need to reanimate the world by rediscovering its sacredness. Once we manage to do this, we will act differently towards it. Spirituality in this sense is political and has real impact.

The earth has a soul

Our attempts to become ecologically sensitive are modest and largely ineffective because they are based on a defective consciousness. The point is that it is not only our conscience that has to be activated; only a change of consciousness can usher in the ecological awareness that the world requires. I am in favour of green politics and environmental laws, and support these wherever I can. But they do not go far enough, and many in the environmental movement are aware of this. In her analysis of the green movement, *Groundswell*, Amanda Lohrey (2002) suggests there is a spiritual underpinning to much of this environmentalism, but it is nascent and often unexpressed. We need something more solid upon which to base our vision of the environment. This is why some environmental groups and researchers are looking for something more than politics. As Fritjof Capra (2005) put it in his cover endorsement of Warwick Fox, "Ecology and spirituality are fundamentally connected, because deep ecological awareness, ultimately, is spiritual awareness." Capra is a physicist making this claim, not a sentimental onlooker.

When Jung announced that "the earth has a soul" (1958, p. 432), he set in motion a spiritual interest in the natural world that eventually led to the development of eco-psychology (Roszak, Gomes, & Kanner, 1995). Today, ecological philosophers and eco-theologians have become aware that the model they are searching for is already demonstrated in the ancient cosmologies of indigenous peoples. Thomas Berry, a student of Teilhard de Chardin, wrote:

> Just now one of the significant historical roles of the primal people of the world is not simply to sustain their own traditions, but to call the entire civilized world back to a more authentic mode of being. (1988, p. 4)

I don't like the word "civilised" in this sentence, suggesting indigenous people are uncivilised. I experienced them as having more wisdom than my own culture, in that they recognise the unity of humanity and nature, a unity that gave them an innate, not a forced or guilt-driven awareness of ecological realities.

In the process of development and modernisation we have narrowed our focus to the ego and cut ourselves off from the subtle forces that have been acknowledged and respected in all traditional cultures. As James

Hillman would put it, we have confined the psyche to a narrow space inside the human skull, and have failed to realise that the psyche is not inside us, but rather we are inside the psyche. Psyche or soul is greater than ourselves, and only our myopia or rationalism could imagine that it can be limited to the human. In late medieval times, the psyche or soul was referred to as *anima mundi*, the soul of the world, and that is the dimension of soul that seems to have been fully realised in early or archaic cultures. We have to get that dimension of psychic reality back somehow.

A half century before Hillman explored the ecological dimensions of the psyche, Jung was arguing that "the psyche is ... a world of cosmic proportions". He said, "The loss of this great relationship is the prime evil of neurosis" (1934b, § 367). When we lose our connection with the largeness of soul and the totality of its nature, we become separated from the foundations of our lives and succumb to neurosis. But Jung was writing before the impact of this dissociation was expressing itself as a global ecological emergency. What he saw as a cause of personal sickness is now revealed as a cause of sickness in the world. Our lack of psychic connection to the world is responsible for our mistreatment of the world and lack of emotional affect as we respond to its enormous suffering.

In my view, the environmental movement has done a great deal of good for the imperilled earth, and has brought the critical nature of the problem to international attention. But green politics and social awareness are not enough. These discourses have focused mainly on externals, and we now need to introduce a spiritual or depth psychological dimension. The fact is that the consciousness that brought the environmental emergency into existence is not the same one that can heal it. As Einstein put it, no problem can be solved by the same consciousness that created it. Our consciousness has said there is no spiritual life in nature; the only subjectivity is inside ourselves. We have denied spirit in the world, seeing it as a static background to human endeavours.

We have to deepen the debate from appeals to our conscience to changes in our consciousness. Everywhere today we find environmental appeals to our conscience, but guilt about our environmental damage can only get us so far. Punishing ourselves for what we have done is not enough. We need less of the stick and more of the carrot. What is the carrot apart from the invitation to inhabit a new mind, a new kind of awareness? Metanoia is what the Greeks called it. A turnabout, a change of orientation to reality. We need an alternative vision about to how to live, and an environmental spirituality, or what literary culture might call a return of Romanticism. It is true that guilt about environmental damage must be acknowledged and can spur us on to reparation. Guilt can be useful if it is shifted towards a cultural grief that brings action. But guilt can also paralyse us and make us unable to do anything. So can the fashionable pessimism that we have gone too far in our environmental damage, and reparation is no longer possible.

The greatest resource for change is not our guilty conscience but our potential for *the recovery of a unitary consciousness*. We had that unitary consciousness once, but lost it. Jung put it well when he said:

> We *have been* that [primordial] mind, but we have never *known* it.
> We got rid of it before understanding it. (Ibid., § 591)

This realisation is what holds the key to the much-needed revolution. We had this non-duality once, but didn't know what great prize we had until we lost it and were inducted into the alienation of modernity. The Vatican speaks of our need for an ecological "conversion", and I agree, as nothing short of a conversion experience will save us. Common sense and social action alone will not bring about the desired change.

We need to work from the inside, and not only on the outside. I found this idea well expressed in a work about a group of young Australians who trekked from the mouth to the source of the Yarra River. In *The Comfort of Water* Maya Ward describes a pilgrimage to the source as an induction or initiation into a new mode of consciousness. "There is a web, around us, unravelling" (2011, p. 22), she writes, and describes a journey into a new kind of consciousness in which we are no longer strangers in the world but grounded in it. Ward describes her motivations for this journey: she felt "a sense of displacement [with] my surroundings" and at the same time "an ache to belong" (ibid., p. 25).

We feel this separation everywhere where modernity has driven a wedge between humanity and nature, but in new world countries like Australia, the sense of alienation is particularly acute. We live on the land, but do not feel grounded in it, and this sense of being a rootless intruder is the spiritual legacy of our colonial origins. The history books tell us that we "conquered" the land, but land is not just an object to be conquered; it has a more subtle dimension captured by the phrase "spirit of place". The spirit of place does not easily invite a conquering people into its embrace, and it may turn hostile and repel the intruder.

Hence the chronic sense of homelessness often experienced by non-indigenous Australians.

To achieve a sense of belonging, sacrifices will need to be performed, or rituals of atonement undergone, not only for the land but also for the indigenous people of the land. That is how I see Maya Ward's pilgrimage, as a ritual of atonement, in which she sacrifices her time, effort, and security to risk a deeper connection to place. If we perform these rituals, the place might, just might, open up to us. As she puts it, "I was searching for a way to sink deeper into my home place" (ibid., p. 25). In this sense, the book presents us not only with a journal of an expedition, but a rite of passage into a deeper belonging. This rite is a form of sacred geography, and its meaning is not only personal, for Ward and her team, but collective, insofar as it represents an attempt to atone for colonial mistakes and insensitivities. The book shows us how to be postcolonial, and the spiritual sensitivity that the new state entails. Underlying the whole book is the question of the ecological crisis. How are we to respond to this crisis? Ward feels that we are not doing enough. She writes:

> There has finally arrived a sense that we must stop affecting the earth in the way that we do, and do it urgently. The calls to change how we source our material needs are growing ever louder. Yet while society is slowly acknowledging the truth of this, there also seems to be a corresponding simplification and smoothing over of the depths contained in these challenges. It is as if change were an external thing, with all the holes in the web of the world fixed with a few new laws and a switch to "green" buying. As if nothing needed to change on the inside. I feel the problems are far deeper than our culture seems ready to admit. (Ibid., pp. 26–27)

The ecological crisis will not be solved by Band-Aid solutions, by switching to green buying or establishing an emissions trading scheme. These are external approaches, and while useful in a practical sense, they do not get to the heart of the problem.

Ecology and religion

The spiritual elements of the environmental crisis lead into religious questions. If the central issues are love, compassion, respect for nature as a sacred force, we find ourselves in religious territory. Jung repeatedly argued that the human alienation from nature is at bottom a religious problem. He lived before we had become fully aware of an ecological crisis, but it was clear to him that our separation from nature was a deep-seated problem of our religious life. One of his close associates, Joseph Henderson, put Jung's view in these terms:

> Nature has lost her divinity, hence any cure for our alienation from nature would have to awaken spirit to new life. The relevance of this theme for us today may be that it is a problem we are still trying to solve on too personal, psychological a level, or on a purely cultural level without fully realizing it is at bottom a religious problem and not psychological or social at all. (1990, p. 279)

These reflections concur with the ideas of the pioneering ecological thinker Lynn White, professor of history at Stanford, who said in 1967:

> More science and technology are not going to get us out of the present ecological crisis until we find a new religion, or rethink our old one. Since the roots of our trouble are so largely religious, the remedy must also be essentially religious, whether we call it that or not. (p. 1206)

These lines are from his article "The Historical Roots of Our Ecological Crisis", which has been called the foundational document of environmental history. White, who was a practising Christian, was the first to attribute the crisis to the problems inherent in the Christian religion, with its destructive views of nature as a fallen world in need of redemption. He believes that the impact of Christianity on the natural world is a major contributor to its demise, and I will return to this in a moment.

Religion and sacred stories have traditionally regulated our relationship with what lies beyond the self. The very word "religion", from the Latin *religio*, means to "rebind", or "reconnect". Religion binds us to that which is other than ourselves and enables us to make meaningful connections with the other. Religion teaches us to love the other as we love ourselves, and to do unto others as we would have them do unto us (Luke 6:31). Religion and spirituality represent powerful sources for right action and morality, and as secular society cuts loose from religion, one wonders where the resources for civilised morality are going to come from. In my view, to sacralise the other is to guarantee a moral relationship with it. Only if we understand that the world is sacred, and the earth is not just a material resource but a work of divine creation, can we act responsibly towards it.

If nothing is sacred nothing matters, and this is why a fully secularised society is heading for disaster, because there are no resources for morality and ethics, apart from expediency and self-interest. In this way, all indigenous cultures are wiser and more enlightened than modern society. They understand that to sacralise the other and the world is the only guarantee of responsible living. We set out on this course of secularisation not knowing where it would lead. To some extent, the experiment has been successful insofar as it has led to relatively stable politics, economics, education, and social situations. Except where extremist ideologies have held sway, such as fascism and communism, most secular societies have led to rational social structures and fair-minded codes of conduct. Secularism has in some ways proved to be more humane than the theocracies it replaced. Secularism has understood the importance of tolerance, diversity, and plurality, whereas religions tend towards absolutism, rigidity, and oppression. There have been advantages to secular living which ought not to be treated lightly.

We have prospered materially under secular governance, but spiritually we have become impoverished. The secular West has won the world but lost the soul, fulfilling the warnings of scripture. The question now is, where to from here? The Western world faces a dilemma: it needs religion but does not want it. We cannot live purely secular lives, because much of our existence is spiritual and not purely material. Our spirits have to be nourished, but we remain unsure how this will happen. I am hoping that the green movement will move in this direction, and appreciate that the relationship with the world cannot be understood solely in material terms. We have to open to the horizons of spirit, which alone gives us the ability to love the world as it should be loved.

Western religious traditions have been caught unawares, as they only know how to think of spirit in traditional forms, but that is not what is required. If the traditions have a future, they will have to figure out how to communicate spirit to secular people who are, if anything, becoming more secular as time passes. Religious traditions are stunned by the present situation, and have been unable to act effectively. They have been astonished by the triumph of secularism and unable to present a convincing counter-position. This has rendered traditions silent on a number of cultural issues, including, until recently, the ecological emergency. Pope Francis's encyclical on the environment, *Laudato Si*, is important and encouraging but somewhat belated.

Scientists and philosophers like James Lovelock and David Suzuki have been speaking of the need to resacralise the earth, and revision the planet as a spiritual creation, for the last sixty years. Indeed, as the Gaia hypothesis suggests, nature scientists have been harking back to prehistoric conceptions of the earth as an animated field. Contemporary science is finding that the ancient religious conceptions of the world, previously dismissed as delusional, are correct on a number of points. Humanity is not a passive onlooker in nature, but an active participant who can work good or evil in the order of things. Humanity has agency, and while we are aware of our detrimental impact, this can be experienced in reverse: we can become agents for good if we understand the ecological principles and abide by them.

Christian domination over nature

Christianity has a chequered history when it comes to respect for nature. Although Christians all over the world are scrambling to make of this tradition an ecological faith, there remain real historical and scriptural obstacles to the greening of Christianity, which cannot be willed away merely because our time is in need of an ecological religion. Ecological critics point out that Genesis institutes the anthropocentric attitude that they hold responsible for the despoliation of the world:

> And God blessed them, and God said unto them, Be fruitful, and multiply, and replenish the earth, and subdue it: and have dominion over the fish of the sea, and over the fowl of the air, and over every living thing that moves upon the earth. (Genesis 1:26–28)

In his landmark essay Lynn White argues that "Christianity is the most anthropocentric religion the world has ever seen" (1967, p. 1205). Having desacralised and instrumentalised nature to human ends, it bears a substantial "burden of guilt" for the environmental crisis (ibid., p. 1206). He argues that this anthropocentric vision enabled Christianity to give its unqualified blessing to industrial uses and abuses of natural resources, and by extension, to the capitalist, consumerist society in which such industries existed. Some ecologists argue that Christianity not only established a dualism of man and nature but insisted that it is God's will that man exploit nature for his proper end (Williams, Roberts, & McIntosh, 2012).

It seems ironic that two recent popes, John Paul II and Francis, have implored the world to undergo an ecological conversion, because Christianity is itself in need of such a conversion. What Francis's encyclical *Laudato Si* does not do, and this omission is inexcusable, is grapple with the difficult issues involved in resacralising nature, after Christianity has spent centuries trying to desacralise it.[4] In a memorable passage, Lynn White challenges Christianity's recent attempt to represent itself as a force for the greening of the earth:

> In antiquity every tree, every spring, every stream, every hill had its own *genius loci*, its guardian spirit. These spirits were accessible to men, but were very unlike men; centaurs, fauns, and mermaids show their ambivalence. Before one cut a tree, mined a mountain, or dammed a brook, it was important to placate the spirit in charge of that particular situation, and to keep it placated. By destroying pagan animism, Christianity made it possible to exploit nature in a mood of indifference to the feelings of natural objects. The spirits in natural objects, which formerly had protected nature from man, evaporated. Man's effective monopoly on spirit in this world was confirmed, and the old inhibitions to the exploitation of nature crumbled. (1969, p. 1205)

The history of Christianity, apart from the startling exceptions of St Francis of Assisi and Teilhard de Chardin, is not green but various shades of grey. Obviously we cannot go back to archaic animism, with individual spirits in every tree, but we might move forward to a new animism in which "the spirit that rolls through all things", as Wordsworth put it, is felt to infuse the world.

A Christian can grow up believing that humans have no essential relationship with the natural world, no responsibilities to nature, and no sense of identity with the world. In Christianity earth and nature are slightly unreal, not important: humanity lives on earth, but, in St. Paul's phrase, "Our citizenship is in heaven, and we eagerly await a Saviour from there" (Philippians 3:20). Norman Habel writes: "Numerous scholars in recent writings have sought to demonstrate the green credentials of God as Creator. Few, however, have sought to face the fact that the portraits of God, especially in the Old Testament, are often grey rather than green" (2009, p. xxi). Across the Christian world theologians are trying to bring God back to earth through eco-theology, eco-spirituality, and reinterpretation of scripture. I wish them well in this endeavour, but it is not going to be easy.

Christian apologists disagree, but they admit there are problems. They insist that we can reinterpret the Bible and search for its affirmations of the created world. Since God made nature, nature must somehow reveal the divine mentality. These affirmations are, however, always in tension with the negative references to fallen nature and the degraded natural state. Thomas Berry, a Catholic theologian, argues that Christians have had a "spiritual aversion" to the natural world (1988, p. 3). He traces this aversion back to Genesis 3, where God cursed the earth and subjected it to futility.[5] Norman Habel, a Lutheran, traces the problem to what he aptly calls "heavenism" (2002, pp. 3–4). Christians who see salvation as an otherworldly reality more important than life on earth are not easily challenged in their faith by the destruction of the earth.

St Francis of Assisi

One person who rebelled against the dogma of man's transcendence of, and mastery over, nature was St Francis of Assisi. He tried to substitute the idea of the equality of all creatures, including man, for the orthodox idea of man's limitless rule of the world and its life forms. Francis saw that everything, dogs, cats, birds, flowers, sun, rivers, mountains, is a creation of God. But Francis is not quite the simple-minded ecological hero that popular imagination wants him to be. Francis is a Christian, meaning he can never be content with the natural order as it is. The natural order may be created by God, but it is fallen, along with humanity, and its godliness has to be redeemed. The divine element in creation and humanity has become obscured and the *imago dei* in both has to be recovered. Christianity is and always has been a religion that emphasises the potential of redemption. If Francis saw nature as an expression of the divine, this was a potential, not an actual redemption. He saw through the fallenness to the divine possibility. If nature was already perfect, there would be no need of redemption and hence no need of Jesus.

Indeed, if Francis were what popular culture wants him to be, he would be a pantheist or heretic. He would have been despised as a nature worshipper, not canonised as a saint. If things are perfect as they are, the Christian drama becomes irrelevant and Jesus becomes irrelevant. When Francis celebrated nature he celebrated the potential of the natural order to overcome itself and reach towards God. Like Paul, he saw creation "groaning" to be brought into perfection.[6] In *The Travail of Nature: The Ambiguous Ecological Promise of Christian Theology*, Paul Santmire (1985) points out that Francis's radical aspect was not in denying the need for redemption, but in downplaying the supremacy of humanity in the natural order. Francis wanted to institute a radical democracy of all God's creatures. Bonaventure thought he was moving dangerously close to paganism and tried to suppress the early accounts of Franciscanism. The Franciscan doctrine of the animal soul, for instance, was quickly stamped out by orthodoxy (White, 1967, p. 1207).

According to Lynn White, "The prime miracle of St Francis is the fact that he did not end at the stake, as many of his left-wing followers did" (ibid.). The biography of St Francis by Bonaventure documents the demise of some of his followers, who were put to the stake by the church. What brought Francis back from the edge of heresy was his repeated insistence that Jesus emphasised humility, and he, Francis, was advocating the humility of humanity within the ecological matrix of creation. He was trying to dismantle the old hierarchy that saw humanity as the apex of creation and institute a species-wide humility.

In returning to the radical vision of St Francis, Pope Francis is bound to face criticism from his conservative colleagues. They claim he should not be supporting climate science when this is not within the purview or scope of theology. The Catholic Right do not like his downplaying of the uniqueness of the human species in creation, or of the right of humanity to have dominion over and subdue the natural world. This, critics say, is basic to scripture and creed, and he is flying against them. While all Catholics would agree, technically, in the importance of humility, the specifically ecological humility shown by Assisi and amplified by the pope remains in question and controversially at odds with convention. Francis of Assisi failed in his endeavour to generate an ecological vision, if success might be judged in terms of convincing the church and Christendom of the sanctity of creation. Similarly, it remains to be seen whether Pope Francis will succeed in following in his footsteps.

Panentheism

The eternal fear of Christian leaders is that the sacralisation of nature will result in pantheism, the denial of the transcendence of God. In recent times, a theoretical resolution has been suggested, which might at least call a truce between the warring parties of the proponents of nature and heaven. In contrast to pantheism and its apparent evils, theologians and philosophers have proposed the idea of *pan-en-theism* as the way forward for Christianity, to get it out of this tight corner.

Panentheism means "all in God", in the sense that all creation resides within a transcendent divinity. The German philosopher Karl Krause who invented this term in 1828 had St Paul in mind: "For in Him we live and move and have our being" (Acts 17:28). Pantheism, on the other hand, means God in all things, as if God were no greater than things. Pantheism does not allow room for God's transcendence, but sees God as present in the things of the world, hence from the Judaeo-Christian point of view, pantheism is idolatry. Panentheism, by contrast, upholds the transcendence of God at the same time as recognising God's immanence in the natural world. In the best definition of panentheism, God transcends yet also includes all beings as their true identity, their true selves, the only one who can say "I am that I am". Thus, in pure panentheism, God is beyond all beings and persons as their source, and within all as their essential substance.

My sense is that many notable figures of the past, including nature poet William Wordsworth and Jewish philosopher of nature Baruch Spinoza, were wrongly charged with pantheism by religions, whereas they can be more sensibly aligned with panentheism. In the seventeenth century, Spinoza, possibly the greatest ecological philosopher, identified God with the most universal and active causal principles of nature, and not with any modes of substance. And yet he was charged with pantheistic crimes against the transcendence of God, even though he insisted that the reality of God exists not only in nature but in an infinity of other dimensions beyond our power to conceive. When Spinoza wrote *Deus sive Natura* (God or Nature) he did not mean to say that God and nature are interchangeable, but that God's transcendence is attested by its infinitely many attributes. Due to the absence of the idea of panentheism at the time, and the logic that attends this idea, he was viewed and condemned in an inappropriate way. Spinoza, however, has come into his own in our time, where his influence on the thinking of deep ecologists is profound (Lloyd, 1996).

Panentheism declares God's simultaneous transcendence and immanence, the divine beyond all yet within all. It is a wonderful solution to the age-old conflict between paganism and Judaeo-Christianity, and while many remain suspicious of it, seeing it as paganism through the back door, I think of it as a wonderful release from the destructive dualism that has kept spirit and matter, masculine and feminine, heaven and earth, apart for centuries of religious thought. In the solution of panentheism, the gender war is potentially resolved between God and Mother, as between men and women, and between heaven and earth.

Endnotes

1. The best indigenous exploration of the Aboriginal Dreaming is Vicki Grieves, *Aboriginal Spirituality: Aboriginal Philosophy: The Basis of Aboriginal Social and Emotional Wellbeing.* (2009). This work by an Aboriginal writer can be downloaded at: http://crcah.org.au/publications/downloads/DP9-Aboriginal-Spirituality.pdf

2. This is a paraphrase of Thomas Berry's statement in Berry and Swimme, *The Universe Story* (1992, p. 243).

3. This is the argument put by David Suzuki and Amanda McConnell in *The Sacred Balance: Rediscovering Our Place in Nature* (1997).

4. By desacralising nature I mean rendering it a utilitarian resource. In the United States, for instance, the exploitation of natural resources and the rise of unecological industries was completely supported by the churches. As far as I can tell, the churches have always given their blessing to the ideal of progress without limitations.

5. Genesis 3:17: God says to Adam: 'Cursed is the ground because of you'.

6. Romans 8:22: 'We know that the whole creation has been groaning as in the pains of childbirth right up to the present time'.

CHAPTER 6

Individuation as a spiritual journey[1]

I want to explore the notion that what we call "spirituality" is close to what Jung meant by "individuation". This is debatable, of course, but I believe such an investigation is worthwhile. Clinicians would likely question whether spirituality and individuation have much in common. They would probably say individuation is a much wider and broader concept. They would emphasise the psychological work of individuation and point out that spirituality can be an escape from the psychological domain. This was perhaps true in the past, but I believe spirituality has changed its character, and is no longer what many imagine.

In this context, it is worth considering the work of American psychotherapist John Welwood. One of his important contributions was to introduce the term "spiritual bypassing" into the language of psychotherapy. This term was coined by him in his book, *Toward a Psychology of Awakening* (1984). Welwood, a Buddhist teacher as well as a psychotherapist, was not against spirituality; he encouraged it in his Buddhist teaching. But as a therapist he became aware of the way it was being used to escape the developmental tasks which were the domain of psychotherapeutic work. He argued that spirituality can be used to avoid, suppress, or bypass the less savoury elements of our lives, such as emotional wounds, neuroses, complexes, and developmental blocks. He thought a number of people were attracted to spirituality for the wrong reasons, and this could stall their emotional and psychological lives. There is ample evidence that such avoidance is more, rather than less, evident today. Welwood's warnings are to be heeded. I am sure Jung would have agreed with him, almost absolutely.

But meanwhile, over time, spirituality has changed its tune. It is not what it used to be. In the late medieval age and up until modern times, it was often a disembodied, transcendental flight towards rarefied experiences. It was about leaving behind what psychology is concerned with. Spirituality was once a flight from suffering and an escape from psychology, but it has changed its character. Many might be surprised by what I am about to argue. I want to focus on the content of individuation and the substance and pursuit of spirituality, and draw out similarities.

Jung's term "individuation" did not become popular in his time, nor has it gained currency in ours. The term did not catch on in the wider community, and is used mainly in clinical contexts. But the word "spirituality" has widespread currency. It is found globally today, and is by no means confined to Western Europe or North America. Jung did not use the word "spirituality" very much, but he talked about "spirit" and the "spiritual problem" of modern man. In referring to the experience of his clients, he preferred the term "religious attitude" to refer to the state of mind that was necessary for us to approach the unconscious and understand its symbolic language. Jung's term "religious attitude" is another term that did not become popular. And as "religion" acquires increasingly negative connotations in the world, it is even less likely that his "religious attitude" will gain traction.

Spirituality and wholeness

If you look up the meaning of spirituality in dictionaries, they will indicate that during the nineteenth and twentieth centuries, the word was defined as something in opposition to the body and physical life. It is used in the Pauline biblical sense, where spirit is opposed to body, and leads to a rarefied existence, aiming for perfection and at-one-ment with the divine. In the past, a spiritual person was often reclusive, in a monastery or cloister, apart from the world, who viewed the body as evil and tried their best to transcend it through spiritual exercises and ascetic practices. But today, spirituality has taken on a new meaning.

Today it has nothing to do with overcoming the body, but with living more fully and completely in the body. The body-hating emphasis, that was still evident when Jung was writing, has almost disappeared. Spirituality today means the search for wholeness, not the search for perfection. Hardly anyone using the term today is using it in the old negative sense, as that which is antithetical to the body and the physical. So a shift has taken place, which means the term is closer to what Jung meant by individuation, which he often defined as the path to the integration of personality. In *The Integration of the Personality*, he wrote:

> I will try to explain the term "individuation" as simply as possible.
> By it I mean the psychological process that makes of a human being
> an individual, a unique indivisible unit, or "whole" man. (1939c,
> p. 490)

I find it interesting that many in America use the term "embodied spirituality", as a way of ensuring that they are not misunderstood as referring to spirituality in the body-negating sense.

Today the imperative of our time is for a spirituality that is *incarnational*, that is, to incarnate in creation, to take on flesh. The spirit of our time is not in favour of the medieval desire to overcome the body in a bid to achieve a state of pure spirit. The imperative for us is for an embodied or incarnational spirituality, a quest in which body, soul, and spirit are brought into balanced relationship. There has been a shift in the direction of spirit, and this is linked to the ecological sensibility of our time.

In the same way that we are becoming more aware of the ecology of the natural world and our human impact on it, so we are becoming aware of an internal ecology, in which body, soul, spirit are viewed in a new light, not as competing but as complementary. I am not suggesting that the spirit's redirection is influenced by our new ideologies. I am suggesting that there is something profound going on in spiritual life itself, that it is essentially different to what it was in the past.

Has spirit changed, or are we perceiving it in a different way? Arguably, the desire of spirit has always been incarnational; after all, the meaning of Christianity, long lost to conventional belief, is that spirit incarnates in the person of Jesus. Jung says: But why only Jesus? Spirit incarnates in all of us, and does not stop at Jesus. Spirit is the power of eternity, longing to take on flesh and enter time. Why has Christianity not perceived this from the beginning, but instead developed a religion based on heavenism or transcendentalism? The desire of spirit has perhaps never been understood by religion, as it involves a paradoxical awareness that the transcendental can be found in the immanental. The transcendent has been interpreted literally, as that which is above creation, rather than that which is sublime within creation.

In an essay entitled, "Spirituality: The Emergence of a New Cultural Category", Jewish scholar Boaz Huss announced: "The contemporary definitions and applications of spirituality are significantly different from its pre-modern uses." He continues:

> In the second half of the twentieth century, the term spirituality underwent a major shift. The opposition of the spiritual on the one hand and the fleshly and material on the other, which was central to the earlier perception of spirituality, became blurred; instead, a new defining dichotomy emerged, juxtaposing spirituality with the category it was previously closely related to, namely the religious. (2014, p. 47)

This shows that the shift is not limited to Christianity, but found in Judaism and other religions as well. My sense is that spirit, an intelligent force, realises that human life, and indeed all life, is imperilled because humanity has not loved the physical enough. Is this one reason why Jung's God let fly a great turd that demolished the Basel Cathedral? (1961a, pp. 52–53). It was a vision that the boy Jung was unable to accept, because he was at that stage part of the church community.

But the vision was forced on him by the spirit. Later he saw it as a sign that the spirit is not impressed with what we have made of the religious expression of the spirit. We have built binary, dualistic structures that have prevented, rather than facilitated, its entry into time, space, and body. We have looked down on the physical, the bodily, and the sexual and seen these as devoid of spirit. Since the greatest longing of spirit is to bring the eternal into time and space, spirit knows that a misinterpretation of its meaning is jeopardising life on earth.

Our spirituality has to follow a new direction and, in this endeavour, indigenous spiritualities from around the world, and Aboriginal spirituality here in Australia, point the way to the future. Spirituality of the land, creation, body, and flesh is what indigenous spiritualities know about. Those of us who come from Europe have little knowledge of this incarnational spirituality, and have to listen carefully to what indigenous people say about spirituality. I am hoping it is becoming clearer how spirituality and individuation are moving closer, and how they are beginning to mirror each other.

Spirituality and individuation

So we must look at some of the clearly spiritual features of Jung's theory of individuation. Jung began with a basically Freudian view of the psyche, but rapidly outgrew and transcended it, as his reflections deepened and broadened. Whereas Freud seemed to emphasise the importance of the ego, and the need to strengthen and develop the ego in the course of experience, Jung tended to emphasise the unconscious, and our need to befriend and understand its mystery. For Freud, the ego seemed to *create* the unconscious, by virtue of the suppression of once-conscious contents. The unconscious seemed to Freud like a rubbish dump, a place where unacceptable contents and desires were placed and forgotten. For Freud, the aim of therapy was to empty the unconscious and integrate as much of it as possible into consciousness. "Where there was id, there shall ego be" was his motto.

Jung's research seemed to reverse the Freudian schema. It was the *unconscious that created the ego*, not the other way around. The unconscious for Jung was vast, mysterious, and timeless. The deeper we move into it, the more vast and mysterious it becomes. Jung personified the integrative function of the unconscious as the Self, and claimed the Self is present before the ego; it is primary and the ego develops from it. In the Freudian system, the self (differently conceived) is described as a by-product of ego development. In every way, Jung and Freud have opposite stories of origination, different creation stories. What is difficult to conceive is not that they parted acrimoniously, but that they ever shared common ground.

In *Memories, Dreams, Reflections,* Jung refers to the inner world as "truly infinite, in no way poorer than the outer world" (1961a, p. 345). It is from this unfathomable mystery that life emerges, the ego is formed, and consciousness arises. Jung believed the unconscious was not personal but contained a collective dimension, and in it there were archetypes, primordial elements of psyche which are expressed in frequently occurring symbols. Many exponents of Jungian thought today seem to overlook the fact that this view of the unconscious is highly spiritual. That is, it is cosmic in outlook and based on vision rather than empiricism.

To pretend that Jung's archetypal theory is mainly clinical, based on scientific observations in the clinical setting, is unrealistic and improbable. His theory is closer to poetry and philosophy than it is to science. Jung's concept of psyche can be characterised as a mixture of Platonism and Romanticism, while Freud's concept is Aristotelian and rational. One is working with a model of reality that opens up to cosmic mystery, the other with a closed model that distrusts mystery and is concerned with the management of daily life and building muscle. Freud's psychology is worldly, while Jung's is concerned with the intersection of the world with cosmic forces that move beyond and through it.

For Jung, the ego is like a tiny island that is thrust up from the ocean, which is his favourite metaphor for the collective unconscious. The point of the ego is to provide dry land or stability upon which the various aspects of the unconscious can *become conscious* of themselves. In Jung's view, there is intentionality and direction in the unconscious—hence the "unconscious" turns out to be a problematical term, since whatever it is that we call "the unconscious" appears to have a consciousness in itself. Indeed, it has a consciousness far greater than ours. Here are some of the echoes of Eastern philosophy in Jung's psychological system.

This entity or field is only "unconscious" to and for the ego, but in itself, it appears to have intentionality, goals, and direction. In Eastern philosophies we do not hear about an "unconscious" but about Supreme Consciousness. We in the West identify consciousness with ego, and therefore we can only arrive at the idea of an *a priori* universal or cosmic wisdom through the idea of an unconscious. Ironically, in the Eastern system it is the ego that is the primary site of unconsciousness, and the first stage of enlightenment requires that the ego must recognise the depth and extent of its ignorance. The idea that consciousness arises in the wider universe, in matter, and outside the range of the human ego is anathema in the West. In this sense, Eastern cosmology is the opposite of Western psychology.

The ever-present origin

In addition to his psychological discourse, Jung provides us, especially in his late work and memoirs, with a theological language. When he operates theologically, Jung seems to revert to the Eastern approach, finding the ego to be the seat of unconsciousness, and locating conscious intention in forces outside the ego. But for Jung, God is not all-knowing, omnipotent, and wise. Rather, Jung adopts the expressly heretical view that God's knowing is incomplete and partial. God's wisdom is only a potentiality within the infinite realm of "his" or "its" being. God longs to become conscious of itself, and thus has a need for creation, and in particular a need for human consciousness, which is like a mirror in which "he" beholds his own unknown face. This is a radical departure from Christian orthodoxy and Western religion, where God is imagined as perfect, needing nothing from our world, other than our obedience and devotion.

Western religion emphasises God's omnipotence and self-sufficiency and the insufficiency of the human. But Jung emphasises God's dependence on humanity, since humanity is God's best chance of becoming conscious of itself. In Jung's psychology, the ego's task is to become conscious of as much psychic reality as possible, but this reality is not merely personal, but reaches into the cosmos. The psyche might appear narrow as we first encounter it, but as we move further in, it seems to open out like a funnel until it becomes identical with the universe. The ego is not only faced with the task of knowing its own personal history, recovering its memories, or facing its traumatic past. The ego is engaged in a larger cosmological project, which is to become aware of transpersonal reality, the archetypes, and the collective unconscious.

The task of the ego is to "remember" more than its personal background; it has to remember the lost wisdom or legacy of the human experience. In Platonic style, the ego's role is to reach into the mind of God, remembering the ideas or forms of its unconscious beginnings. This idea finds powerful expression in Wordsworth's "Ode: Intimations of Immortality":

> Our birth is but a sleep and a forgetting:
> The Soul that rises with us, our life's Star,
>   Hath elsewhere its setting,
>   And comes from afar:
>   Not in entire forgetfulness,
>   And not in utter nakedness,
> But trailing clouds of glory do we come
>   From God, who is our home. (1807, lines 58–65)

These ideas can be traced to Plato, who believed that at birth the human soul detaches from the pleroma and traverses the plains of forgetfulness, losing much of the cosmic glory from wherever it came. It enters the world of time and space and experiences a certain amnesia regarding its sublime origins. However, the forgetting of our origins is not complete, as we come "trailing clouds of glory", or as Jung would put it, the ego becomes aware of a cosmic background to its separate and timebound reality. In popular spirituality today, this experience of a cosmic background is often understood in terms of an increasing awareness of past lives in previous incarnations.

It is the vague awareness that "something is missing" that sets us off on our spiritual journeys. The recent book by sociologist Jürgen Habermas, *An Awareness of What is Missing* (2010), outlines the importance of this sentiment in initiating spiritual and religious experiences. Our painful alienation from our cosmic origins is archetypal and this is what initiates the spiritual quest. Freud looked upon this as fantasy, an escape from the rigours and difficulties of adapting to the harsh realities of lived experience.

Wordsworth, Plato, and Jung believed that we do not enter the world as a *tabula rasa* or empty slate, but traces of our ever-present origin are imprinted on the indwelling soul. There is a template at the core of our lives which constitutes our archetypal background. As the ego matures and deepens, the numinosity of its original ground becomes clearer and more evident, or we might say that the cosmic source rises above the threshold of awareness, and beckons to us as a treasure chest of riches and wisdom from the depths of the unconscious. If the ego is sensitive to this background, which it can access through intuition and introverted feeling, it may be able to bring up the lost glory into consciousness and thus transform itself and enter a translucent world. It does this best through art, love, relationships, and intimacy with the natural world. This is the Romantic and Platonic version of paradise regained, of returning to the past of the human species and recovering a link with a lost reality. Hence nostalgia, sentiment, romance, and longing are all major drivers of the spiritual quest.

For Freud the goal of psychotherapy, as he once famously said, is to transform neurotic suffering or misery into common unhappiness. For Jung, a Platonic thinker, the goal of therapy is to draw closer to the archetypal background and ask the decisive question: "Are we related to something infinite or not?" (1961a, p. 357). His answer is yes.

But how we might imagine or conceptualise this cosmic Other depends on our upbringing and culture. Precisely because it is infinite, it has no form, shape, or being. It is the groundless ground upon which existence rests and from which all life springs. It can appear in a myriad of different forms, and none of these is absolute, but all are ways of imagining that which is beyond form.

The fact that there are so many truths does not mean that all are false, as cynics and nihilists like to say. It only means that all are relatively true. The absolute can only express itself in and through the relative. René Girard put it this way: "We must admit that truth can coexist with the arbitrary and perhaps even derive from it" (2005, p. 329). And in William Blake's language: "Eternity is in love with the productions of time" (1793, p. 151). It is important that we recognise the relativity of truth, lest we fall into the error of fundamentalism of the philosophical or religious kind. When we accept the relativity of truth, there can be peaceful coexistence among religions, races, nations, and ideologies. The nature of any fixed ideology is to assert its dominance over other models of reality. This is why all ideologies are warlike and dangerous. The key to peace on earth is the recognition that what lies beyond remains beyond.

Once the ego becomes aware of this background, it recognises that the unconscious is more than just the "unconscious", but represents a link or bridge to the World Soul or *anima mundi*. At the same time, the ego recognises that the psyche is not only "psychological", but profoundly spiritual. At this moment, the psyche returns to its origins, and is renamed the soul, the ancient term that modernity hardly uses without a blush of embarrassment. As the cosmic dimension rises like a star above the horizon of consciousness, the humanist conception of the psyche dissolves and gives rise to a more mystical apprehension.

This is what Jung explored, especially in his *Modern Man in Search of a Soul* (1933). Soul, for Jung, is the vessel or container of spirit; it is in the soul that the universal mind becomes conscious of itself. That, for Jung, is the meaning of life—we are instruments through which the cosmic forces (Plato's ideas or Jung's archetypes) become conscious. Our lives are not "about" us; we are servants of archetypes, or in the old language, instruments of the gods. These are immortal and we are mortal, and just as the ego emerges like an island from the sea, so it is taken back into the sea at the end of our lives. We "pass away", as we say, but the archetypes or gods live on, because they have never fully crossed the threshold into time/space, but remain anchored in eternity. It is our task to serve this larger design as best we can.

According to Jung, we gain the most satisfaction from life if we do not live for ourselves alone. If we live for the archetypes or "gods" (cosmic forces), there is enormous satisfaction awarded to the personality, and the individual feels a sense of accomplishment. However, if we live only for the ego, we feel life to be empty, shallow, and essentially worthless. This is ironic because many of us assume that the way to live a fulfilling life is to indulge our personal ego, to be selfish and wallow in our narcissism.

But Jung, following the wisdom of religious traditions, believes that to live an ego-bound life is not rewarding, and modern society cannot teach us how to fulfil ourselves, because it only teaches us how to live in and through the ego. It teaches us the egoic art of "getting on", not the spiritual art of linking (*religio*) to the source. Therefore, he concludes, we feel unhappy much of the time, because the larger life that we might live but are not living is not expressed in daily reality. Consumerism and materialism arise as symptoms of the unfulfilled life.

We long to have *more*, but the "more" we want cannot be supplied by society and its commercial industries. This unabated longing is apparent to the industries and producers, who exploit it in their advertising campaigns to enhance their products. Hence banks refer to themselves as "more than money", sports industries refer to themselves as "more than a game", and car manufacturers refer to their products as "more than a car". Always the presence of *more* ghosts our lives and never lets us rest. Behind every advertising campaign is a gesture towards the archetypal background and source from which we have been sundered. Consumerism depends on the expectation that our hopes can never be fulfilled, thereby leading us to repeat experiences.

Confrontation with the opposites

In the course of becoming conscious, we are forced to wrestle with a series of opposites, such as good and evil, light and darkness, spirit and body, heaven and earth. For Jung the aim of individuation is to bring these opposites into a creative relationship. The journey of individuation is a journey into wholeness, and the ego needs to become familiar with both sides of every psychic content or archetype. He felt that the ego was prone to identifying with one aspect of the archetype, usually the good or light side, and suppressing or repressing the dark. But individuation urges us beyond one-sidedness into a broader frame of reference in which we learn to understand good and bad, the spiritual and the instinctual, the masculine and the feminine, the intellectual and the physical.

Jung claimed that our dreams encourage us to move away from one-sidedness towards a holistic understanding of the psyche. A major function of dreams is to act in a compensatory way to the one-sided attitude of the ego. The dream is thus for Jung a source of great wisdom—it provides the messages that enable the ego to find its way between the opposites, and negotiate its course through inner and outer worlds.

In the Bible, especially the Old Testament, dreams are featured as prophetic, visionary, and full of symbolic advice about how to live the good life. It is therefore ironic, if not tragic, that Judaeo-Christian culture has chosen to forget about the spiritual dimension of dreams, and view with suspicion the products of the unconscious. But in the ancient past, there was no unconscious as such, only God or gods. So dreams were regarded as the language of God, and unattended dreams were seen as unopened letters from God. It is imperative that psychotherapy today rediscovers the sacred dimension of dreams.

The Self that is not the self

As indicated, Jung conceptualised the integrative function of the unconscious as the Self, and claimed the Self exists prior to the ego; it is primary and the ego develops from it. The archetype of the Self, he believed, together with the "transcendent function", helps to facilitate the individuation process and the coming-to-wholeness of the personality. The word "Self" is perhaps an odd choice of term for something that is essentially *other* than the ego, given the fact that the ego is universally and colloquially referred to as the "self". In the secondary Jungian literature, therefore, the Self is usually capitalised to distinguish it from the everyday usage of "self", and to avoid confusion with the ego. Jung's Self is not the self. Or to put it in other terms: the Self is in the psyche, but transcends ego and the conscious arena.

The theological equivalent of Jung's Self is *panentheism*, a term invented to describe the relation between God and world. The term is derived from the Greek *pan-en-theos*, and means all things in God. It contends that the presence of God is within the world and yet the world is within God. The term is understood as a third option over against the alternatives of pantheism (God in all things) and classical theism (God as separate from world). Over against these alternatives, panentheism emphasises the closeness between God and world (God's immanence), as well as positing that God is more than world (God's transcendence). The term was coined in 1828 by the German philosopher Karl Krause. Interestingly, Krause came up with the idea after reviewing Hindu scriptures. This is relevant to Jung's work, because he came up with the idea of the immanence and transcendence of the Self after studying Hindu scriptures. The Self and panentheism are coterminous with each other. As far as I know there has yet to be a comparative study of these two terms.

Dangers abound for new or inexperienced readers of Jung. In Jung's writings, the Self is unfortunately not capitalised, and the chances of confusing ego and Self are high. They are vastly different, if related, concepts. The Self is a highly technical and specific term in Jung's psychology. It has no equivalent in the Freudian system, and there is almost nothing comparable in the whole of Western philosophy or psychology. Its closest counterpart appears to be the god within in the world's mystical traditions and the *Atman*, Purusha, or divine Person that dwells within in Hinduism. Related to the personal self, but not the personal self, it is the sacred principle that sustains and guides life.

In Hindu cosmology the Atman is a silent spectator of our lives and only comes into our awareness through self-realisation. This is similar to Jung's Self which watches, waits, and provides commentary on our lives through dreams, hunches, intuitions, and synchronicities. If we do not engage in considerable introspection, we will never notice it. But if forced to intrude into our lives due to our ignorance or mistaken pathways, the Self has no option other than to make its presence felt in either positive or negative ways.

Some of Jung's followers became too unrealistic about the Self, assuming it would always be present and extricate us from trouble in times of crisis. But given the prevalence of mental illness, and the propensity of the psyche to lose balance and become disturbed, the holistic function of the Self is not something that can be taken for granted. The Self is not to be reified as a "thing"; it is more like a process or direction of the psyche. It is an intuitive idea or hypothesis—critics refer to it as wishful thinking on Jung's part. The danger of this idea is that it can make us unduly confident about our experience of the psyche, giving us a sense of security in a territory that is fraught with perils. We need to be aware that the goal of coming-to-wholeness is a tendency only, and certainly not guaranteed.

Jung admits that his idea of the Self is provisional, and he calls it a "borderline concept". Although he writes about it at length, and arguably it is the central focus of his work, there is always in Jung the suggestion that we must not suppose that the Self will arrange life for us, and we should understand that the ego has to do the primary work in the task of individuation. For Jung, the ego is the centre of consciousness, the locus of our personal identity, whereas the Self is the centre of the entire psyche, conscious and unconscious, and thus the locus or seat of our transpersonal identity.

In Jung's theological reflections, it is clear that he sees God on a par with the collective unconscious; both are vast, oceanic, infinite, and extensive. Jung's Self, however, appears to represent a differentiation or concentration of the collective unconscious, an intensity which changes in some way the nature of God. His Self appears to correspond with the figure of Christ in the West, and with Buddha in the East. The Self is an archetypal figure that connects the human and the divine, a bridge or link to ultimate reality.

The Self is a transcendental concept, and as such it is larger than life. It cannot be known directly by the ego, but only indirectly through symbol, dream, and myth. In the idea of the Self, it is as if Jung is reinventing the concept of a redeemer for a psychological age. He sees our scientific age as having largely rejected religion, but Jung seems to want to reinvent religion in psychological terms, replacing the Christ figure of his Christian background with the archetype of the Self, replacing God with the collective unconscious, and replacing the Holy Spirit with the mysterious healing process that Jung calls the "transcendent function"—the function that helps us heal the tension between the opposites.

While religious people might wonder why Jung feels the need to reinvent the religious wheel, and protest at his arrogance in attempting to do so, in his defence Jung would say that religious terms and concepts have lost their meaning for modern men and women. He feels the need to provide a new terminology for the eternal ideas that have been found in religious and cosmological systems. Moreover, Jung does not seek to replace religion with his psychological terms, rather, he sees his analytical psychology as a kind of adjunct to the life of the spirit, which might be helpful even to those who already have a faith and live and work within a religious setting. But the majority of people in the West, he argued, are entirely secular, do not have the benefit of religion, and thus are in need of a new science of the life of the spirit. Jung seems to look forward to a future time in which the insights of depth psychology and the wisdom of religion can come together and work towards the benefit of humanity.

The Self is for Jung the master archetype, and has power which can override all other psychic contents and complexes in its bid to inaugurate a reign of wholeness. The Self has the power to override the ego and its wishes, and to ignore the promptings of the Self is to court disaster. The Self is a kind of benevolent ruler who must be obeyed, but rarely does the ego realise that the Self is calling for its transformation. The Self can therefore be the architect of change and growth, or the instigator of ruin, depending on the ego's attitude. If the ego recognises there is a greater force that must be obeyed, the Self is mostly a benign force. Although it is hard to predict how the Self will behave, because it is a paradoxical archetype which cannot be assumed to be ego-syntonic. All we can say is that it is less likely to be hostile if the ego forges a respectful relationship with it.

Again, we can hear a spiritual parallel behind Jung's theories of ego and Self. He is giving a new, modern language to the ancient relationship between man and God, or humanity and the divine. Jung was aware of this, but as a scientist he did not wish to use an explicitly religious language. In his memoirs, he reveals his ambivalent attitude towards religious language, and admits that, although it is outmoded and archaic, it nevertheless continues to have evocative power, which he finds attractive. Religious terms like "mana", "daimon", or "god" have "the great merit of including and evoking the emotional quality of numinosity". It is the numinous that humanity sorely needs, and yet as a scientist he is impelled to use the term "unconscious", which he admits is "banal and closer to reality" (1961a, p. 369).

But even though he preferred psychological terms in his scientific writings, he "knew [he] might equally well speak of God or daimon if [he] wished to express [himself] in mythic language" (ibid.). He paints a picture of himself as a somewhat divided figure and a reluctant scientist, aware that "the unconscious is too neutral and rational a term to give most impetus to the imagination". He says his intellect preferred science but his imagination preferred myth and religion. So it is with this in mind that we must understand that Jung was ambivalent about his own psychological terms, and we should not attach ourselves to them too strongly, because he was aware of their limitations. He was aware that just as religious fundamentalism is a problem, so a Jungian fundamentalism can be a similar problem.

So his term "Self" must be accepted with all these caveats, as a provisional construct designed for a non-religious world, and not as an article of faith for a new religious orthodoxy. The archetype of the Self, together with the transcendent function, helps to facilitate the individuation process and the coming-to-wholeness of the personality. I was struck by the similarities between Jung's Self and the Holy Spirit as this term is used by St Augustine. Augustine says the Holy Spirit stands behind and within our lives as a supreme authority, and urges us to the unification of personality and an in-gathering of human attributes around the authority of God. The Holy Spirit warns us of danger and shows us the way forward in dreams and visions. This is close to Jung's Self, and one can see that Jung's psychology is an attempt to rescue the spiritual world view for an increasingly secular world.

* * *

The stages of life

All of this spiritual foundation and infrastructure impacts on Jung's theory of the stages of life. The main source for his thinking on the developmental stages is found in "The Stages of Life" (1931d, § 749–795). It is from this essay that his well-known theory of the life cycle and the so-called "midlife crisis" arises.

Jung's theory of the archetypal life cycle appropriates the biblical mythology of a threefold human experience: Innocence, Experience, Innocence Regained. Or to use other terms: Garden of Eden, Paradise Lost, and New Jerusalem. Jung deliberately bases his psychological theory on the theological mythology of the Jewish and Christian Testaments. He makes no apology for appropriating this mythology and reshaping it in his own psychospiritual terms.

In early life, in a state of relative innocence we are embraced and contained by a mystery that some call God. This experience is mythologised in the Bible as life lived in innocence, under God's care in the Garden of Eden. Adam is said to walk with God in the cool of the evening.

It is a wonderful story, but if taken as fact, as tradition once believed, it is disastrous. In the first few years, as long as the social and familial context is congenial and not traumatic, we live in blissful ignorance of the problems of the social fabric and familial environment. We have no awareness of the impending disaster that is about to befall us. We do not know that the ego is soon to be expelled from the paradisal state, and sent out into the world to fend for itself.

The second stage begins as consciousness emerges from the sea of unconscious life and instinct. The ego forms like a tiny island in this sea, and Jung believes the larger, cosmic purpose of the ego is to allow the Self, or Atman, to become conscious of itself. This is the age-old belief of gnostic traditions, found also in alchemical and mystical traditions. The individual becomes aware that he or she cannot remain in the Garden, and that "God" will kick them out of Eden as soon as the person becomes conscious of him- or herself as a separate being, apart from the parents. In mythological terms, eating the fruit of the Tree of the Knowledge of Good and Evil is the act which initiates awareness. The knowledge of good and evil, quite obviously, represents the emergence of the clash of opposites and the dualities we will have to reconcile in life. To eat of this fruit terminates the bliss that is known only as oneness and the oceanic unity of all things.

As soon as this awareness arises, the age of paradise is terminated. Jung says it is ironic that in the biblical story God appears to be enraged by the act of eating the forbidden fruit, because this hides or disguises the fact that God has willed this disobedience from the beginning. God wants us out of the Garden, so God can increase his, her, or its self-awareness through the agency of created beings. God orchestrates the whole process, but archaic society must have been unable to understand this, and hence produces a mythic story in which God is displeased of the coming to consciousness and characterises it as an evil to be rectified at a later time. Christians believe that the Fall from Grace is only rectified through Christ.

The idea of original sin, occurring at the time of sexual awakening, is an archaic depiction of the shame and guilt felt by early humanity as it faces the painful consequences of moving from bliss into the emergence of consciousness. People were not ashamed of their sexuality, on the contrary, sexuality is one of the many instincts that accompanies the unconscious state. Jung cautions that the intensity of the original sin concept reflects the fear that the journey into consciousness may not be successful, but might lead humanity astray and into disaster and ruin. As he puts it: "We are beset by an all-too-human fear that consciousness—our Promethean conquest—may in the end not be able to serve us as well as nature" (1931d, § 750). This is what the world is currently experiencing in view of the ecological emergency, brought about because we have turned away from nature.

We are on a journey of continuing and increasing consciousness, whether we like it or not. A child at the brink of puberty is full of fear of the future, and an excitement about what lies ahead. Jung argues that the "undisturbed sway of instinct" is challenged by a spirit of progress, which makes humanity nervous, and this challenge is accompanied by fear and shame. Christians, but not Jews, interpret this shame as the awareness of sexuality. Christianity mistakenly, in my view, blames the body, sex, and the feminine as personified by Eve, as the sources of defilement. In reality the loss of innocence and expulsion from Eden is programmed into the human psyche, and coincides with, but is not caused by, sexual awakening.

We feel disturbed by the rise of consciousness, and the awareness that what happens is our responsibility, no longer in the hands of fate, parents, or God. Jung argues that the idea that this shame is due to sexual awakening is a moralistic cover for the dread that we carry as an existential burden. In the course of life, the shame of consciousness arises at the same time as the awakening of sexuality, because at that moment we are most certainly no longer under parental guidance and care. A *daimon* has got into us, which can be tamed but not controlled by parents and society. We are alone in our selves for the first time. Our burden is not sexuality as such but a fear that consciousness might move in a direction contrary to the universe, and against Mother Nature. Jung points out that the drive towards consciousness has always been constructed as an *opus contra naturam*, a work against nature.

As ego consciousness develops it is torn away from the primal source and struggles to make its way in the world. It doesn't know who or what it is, but it is always looking for signs of what it must do, signs of a calling or vocation that might bring some contentment and happiness. The bliss of the past can never be recaptured, but the contentment of hard work and dedication is within its reach. With his belief in hard work and concentrated effort, Jung reflects the Protestant work ethic of his upbringing, now converted into psychological proficiency.

According to Jung, the ego is not meant to return to the state of bliss, for its task is to bring wholeness into the world, not regress to the first paradise and lose the ground it has gained. Jung often says that one of the great tragedies of life is that we do not know the extent to which our lonely journey into consciousness is inspired and supported by God. We feel we are alone, and technically we are, but spiritually we are in league with God and the Holy Spirit, if not with Mother Nature and her beckoning back to paradisal sleep in her womb. That which inspires us onward Jung saw as mythologically masculine, and that which lures us to paradise he saw as feminine. Masculine and feminine principles are not to be confused with male and female, or father and mother. Jung felt that the importance of religion is that it has acted as a guarantor of the human journey, in that it gives the individual a sense that something transcendent is supporting them through the journey. But in secular modern times, this support is sorely lacking.

Jung finds in the refusal to let go of the primal situation of dependence and innocence the archetypal background to many psychic afflictions, neuroses, and addictions. We refuse to grow up, as we see this is going to bring suffering and discomfort. But clinging to the source ultimately brings a suffering of its own, because the expulsion from Eden is a necessity, a spiritual demand placed on us by the Creator. Jung argues that the modern epidemic of people who refuse to grow up, the *puer* problem (in the male) and the *puella* problem (female), is a reflection of the power of the source and the inability of people to break from it to build their lives. The pathological person has a "fatal" tie to the source, and won't let go. But he or she must let go, so that some version of the original condition can be realised "later", in a conscious state, which Jung saw as the third stage.

In her classic work on this topic, *The Problem of the Puer Aeternus* (2000), Marie-Louise von Franz argues that the high incidence of puer and puella pathology in our time is an indication that the breakdown of traditional structures of meaning and purpose has made it harder for people to individuate. The archetypal source exerts a higher than usual allure, when we no longer know how to make the passage into manhood or womanhood due to the collapse of the rites of passage into maturity and adulthood. If a bridge into maturity is not found, or cannot be believed, the source exerts a gravitational pull which can hardly be resisted by the ego which has not the confidence to live its own life and discover its own truth.

The ego requires what Jung calls a "faithless eros" to break away from the parental bonds and the security of hearth and home. But now, with young adults clinging to their parents for financial and emotional security, the developmental impulse has atrophied and the challenge of individuation is easily betrayed. All of this is done, of course, in the name of high-minded ideals such as frugality, thrift, familial bonds, and anti-consumerism. Idealistic youth argue that staying at home is better for the environment: save the world by staying at home. Perhaps this saves resources, but one's development is betrayed. The ego has to feel the fear, and do it anyway.

What the ego does not realise is that while the break from the source may be painful, there is support waiting for it after its separation. The archetypal source the ego longs for is found not in moving back but going forward. This is the paradox of individuation. The Self represents the origin of the ego, and at the same time it is the goal towards which the ego strives. The Self is alpha and omega, beginning and end. But the ego cannot fast forward to the end, but has to go through the lonely road of psychological development, involving adjustment to society and the creation of a personal identity. So the ego must toil in the fields of social reality, and develop in strength, courage, and stamina, only to endure the deconstruction of its identity at around the time of midlife. Another paradox: the ego must build itself up in order to be reduced and sacrificed.

The traditionalism of Jung's concept of individuation is evident in his emphasis on the theme of sacrifice. Sacrifice is the key element in any religious cosmology, and Jung's spiritual psychology is no exception. The Self is the spiritual guarantor of the ego and supports it in its journey of individuation, but the ego, or conscious person, must sacrifice certain aspects of itself for the sake of the Self. Jung defines the individuation process by using terms that remind us of the Christian spiritual path, which is referred to as the Way of the Cross, involving suffering, loss, sacrifice. Jung writes:

> Human nature has an invincible dread of becoming more conscious of itself. What drives us to greater consciousness is the self, which demands sacrifice by sacrificing itself to us. (1942b, § 400)

Individuation involves two-way sacrifice. The Self sacrifices itself to us, by incarnating in the limited human being, and losing its infinity and grandeur. In Christian theology this is called *kenosis*, which means "to empty". The divine empties itself, divests itself of its *plerosis* or fullness, to become something which is part human and part divine.[2] This is the archetypal idea embodied in the figure of Jesus. For Jung, this process of kenosis is not confined to Jesus, but something that each one of us must endure and witness. Jung has been influenced by St Paul, who argues that God's humility in the incarnation is a call to Christians to be similarly selfless and subservient to others. One can see how Jung has adapted this theology to his psychological system, which could be called a kind of mixture of Christianity and Gnosticism, or a Christian gnosis.

The midlife transition

In Jung's theory, the foundations of the renunciation of ego are laid at the time of the midlife transition. His vision is that in the "first half" of life the ego grows strong, becomes grounded in reality, and secures itself a footing in social life. I don't think this happens anymore, if it ever did, but it is part of his theory. I'm sceptical of the simplistic, formulaic nature of his theory. He believes the ego is displaced at about midlife, to allow the Self to emerge. He employs the metaphor of the rise and descent of the sun to describe our journey:

> At the stroke of noon the descent begins. And the descent means the reversal of all the ideals and values that were cherished in the morning. The sun falls into contradiction with itself. It is as though it should draw in its rays instead of emitting them. (1931d, § 778)

The ego must rise, so the incarnation of the Self can begin, but the ego must fall so the Self can replace it when the ego becomes full of itself. In this way the cosmic Self plays hide and seek with its own creation: it emerges from the pleroma to incarnate in time, and having experienced temporal consciousness, it enfolds that back into itself. In Hindu terms, God the Creator, Brahma, is replaced by God the Destroyer, Shiva. We belong to a universal rhythm that is not about us. We serve an extraordinary and unfathomable mystery; it does not serve us.

Human existence is predicated on this tragicomic impulse: the fall of the ego that has struggled to get itself established in the world and solidified around a point of conscious stability. The theory of the stages of life may need a few modifications, to make room for postmodern complexity, individual differences, and the ever-present threat of psychic disruption, which by no means happens at the stroke of noon.

The theory has dated and reflects a time in which society seemed more stable than it is today. The ego nowadays is not given the luxury of developing for a thirty-five-year period, unimpeded by disruptions or trauma. From decades of teaching university students, it is evident to me that early childhood trauma is common in youth today.

The young adults who enrolled in their hundreds in my spirituality course had been impacted by trauma either at an early age, or during the period of adolescence. That was why they were attracted to the study and practice of spirituality, because it gave them a sense of psychological stability in a world in which many things appear to be swirling at a great rate of change. A revised Jungian psychology will need to consider the possibility that these two processes, grounding the ego in the world and ungrounding the ego from its static position, may need to be thought of as parallel movements, or simultaneous developments in which now one and now the other predominates. Jung's theory of a linear movement from stability to instability seems to us today to be quaintly old-fashioned and fanciful.

With the collapse of many social traditions, customs, and forms of containment, the modern ego is unable to feel secure in society for half a lifetime. We often find that people have to go in search of meaning at an early age, since meaning is not provided by secular society. This is especially the case for young people who suffer trauma, disruption, mental illness, or family breakdown. They may be forced to go in search of meaning as it were ahead of the Jungian schedule (Tacey, 2003). In that case, the midlife crisis might become a quarter-life crisis, or a problem suffered in the teenage years or early adulthood. An ego which is not yet established may need to look for secure spiritual ground upon which to base its existence, in which case we might say that such young adults are "wise before their time". Second half issues have intruded into the morning of life.

Although Jung's theory asserts that a displacement of ego occurs at midlife, this is not always the case—as he himself makes clear. By the time of midlife, the ego often becomes full of itself, blown up with self-importance and status, with defences erected to protect its fortress. The ego takes the illusion of power seriously, and strives to protect itself against attack from the forces of the Self. The ego forgets—or never knew—that its role is secondary. Under secular conditions, belief that the ego is "number one" is reinforced by social attitudes, commercialism, and consumerism.

> The nearer we approach to the middle of life, and the better we
> have succeeded in entrenching ourselves in our personal attitudes
> and social positions, the more it appears as if we had discovered
> the right course and the right ideals and principles of behaviour.
> For this reason we suppose them to be eternally valid, and make a
> virtue of unchangeably clinging to them. (1931d, § 772)

We grow used to being egos, entities with free will and volition. As
human subjects who stray from the divine presence, we move so far
from it we wonder if there is any divine presence. Was it merely a dream
of the ancient past, a *poetic* idea enshrined in literature and sacred tradition? The divine becomes a rumour, and the ego cannot be bothered
with it, but attempts to "get on" without it.

Thus the ego grows strong and more secure, keen to connect with the
world and fit in with the social structures that surround it. The ego is
programmed to keep on keeping on, to be part of the larger scheme of
things, to wear a social persona and work towards achievement, goals,
and belonging.

Ironically, we only recover our true nature when we go through a second exile or alienation. This second exile is our eventual estrangement
from our familiar ego-selves, from the ego-bound world we have constructed, and in which we feel familiar and at home. It was the poet Rilke
who said *we long to become strangers to ourselves*, for deep down we realise
we are not who we say we are or appear to be. Awakening inside us, at a
deeper level, and often barely discernible at first, is the ancient memory
of our true belonging, our true home in God, the universe, or the cosmos.
Being an ego is a kind of game we play with ourselves, and although it is
an important game, we know it is not essentially who we are.

The recalcitrant ego is not keen to volunteer for individuation, or put
itself through the daunting encounter with the unconscious. It wants to
remain connected to the world and fit in with social structures. In Jung's
memoirs he is candid about this:

> As a rule many people end by surrendering their individual goal
> to their craving for collective conformity—a procedure which all
> the opinions, beliefs, and ideals of their environment encourage.
> (1961a, pp. 376–377)

The ego that has not glimpsed a deeper meaning wants more power,
because its emptiness is cloaked by greed and disguised by riches.

It wants to conquer greater heights and achieve greater goals. So at midlife, in affluent societies, instead of individuation, we often find individuation in reverse, which leads to a hubristic ego that can never allow itself to serve a greater mystery. It wants to keep winning, and cannot bear to lose. As poet Emily Dickinson put it, we lose, because we win.

It has become a joke these days to refer to some people going through a "midlife crisis" by clinging to their youth by seeking excitement and diversions in an attempt to avoid the introversion that the midlife transition demands. They don't want to look at themselves but become obsessed with diversions and amusements. The showy cars, ostentatious houses, exotic travels become attractive, but there is something forced, they are compensating for a lack, an absence. Inner substance is being replaced by outer extravagance. They know their time is up as pure egos, but cannot face it. This can end up being ugly, as the egoic charade refuses to sacrifice itself for a greater reality. Such people are identified too strongly with the goals of society, and not critical enough of those goals. It is not their fault that they continue this charade without seeing through it. Increasingly, society lives in denial of the nonegoic, and goes out of its way to berate or condemn the nonego.

Jung once said that the defeat of the ego is a victory for the Self, and this idea runs through all religious thinking, all cosmologies, mythologies, and theological systems. Naturally, the ego tries to shirk this dreadful experience, because it has become too familiar with the world as it is revealed to its common senses. It therefore requires a real shock, a nudge, a violent disruption, to push it out of its comfort zone and into a larger encounter with the whole of reality, visible and invisible. In this crisis of development, the integrity of the ego has to be maintained, because the ego has important work to do, and must not be crushed or destroyed by the disruptions that life is bound to deliver. In this individuation crisis, the ego is made to realise that its role is not to lead or control, but to serve a greater mystery that remains unknowable.

The importance of art, literature, religion, mythology, music, theatre, poetry, dance, ritual, ceremony, and the symbolic realm of expression, is to help the ego negotiate its way to the larger Self that remains outside its comprehension. Without the assistance of art and the productions of *mythos*, the ego remains trapped in logical thinking and critical thought that adjusts it to visible reality, and which alienates it from the unseen world which requires acknowledgement. The importance of art and music is, as Shakespeare said in *The Tempest*, to give form to things unknown. We would not need to make this adjustment to invisible reality, if we were merely material beings with a purely political, social, or economic meaning. But since the imprint of the cosmic Creator is upon our soul, there is no way we can escape making an adjustment to the spiritual. The impulse to seek our true home is archetypal, and no amount of common sense can squash this or suggest otherwise.

Jung accepted the importance of secularism in modernity, yet bemoaned the fact that it has left human beings without a road map to transformation. He said the exhortation of Christian culture to "put off the old Adam", and the aim of "the rebirth rituals of primitive races" was to "transform the human being into the new, future man, and to allow the old to die away" (1931d, § 766). We have no replacements for these ancient rituals and sacred languages. Therefore, almost by definition, individuation cannot take place and the Self cannot be born in the soul. The secular condition of the ego means it is unable to respect historical symbols, nor is it equipped to imagine new symbols, since it receives no support for this endeavour from society. The stages of life cannot be completed and this is why modernity is obsessed with youth and seeks to prolong the state of youth. We no longer value the wisdom that comes with age; we have old people today but rarely are they respected as elders.

The Self has always been symbolised and upheld by cultures and religions, so that the individual is able to sense the full reality of the Self and to understand its gravity. Buddha, Christ, Mohammed, Confucius, Lao Tzu, and others have served as powerful symbols of the Self, namely, that aspect of humanity that reaches into the divine and has a relationship with ultimate reality. The purpose of culture is to give form to a dimension of human being that might otherwise not be grasped, given its elusiveness and subtlety. The individual must not be led to believe that the Self is a work of fantasy, that it is a phantom or illusion. It has to be *real* and felt to be real, and cultures have expended a great deal of energy on building up images of the Self, and extolling their virtues to the people.

If the ego hands over authority to another source, it has to give over to something which has value and can be trusted. This is what Jung believes is one of the most difficult aspects of modernity. We have to surrender to something, but what is it to be, if religious language has become ineffective in conveying these terms? More often than not, the nation state asks us to sacrifice ourselves to it, or to one of the political ideologies that organise the state and define its meaning.

As everyone knows, Jung was hostile to the idea that the nation can replace and stand in for the Self, as the nation is invariably corrupt and its appropriation of religious status is bogus. Naturally it is easy to assert in the abstract that the ego must give over to a greater life, but if there is a crisis in culture there is a crisis in the ego as well. This means there is a lack of imagination in the ego as to what it must do, and to whom or what it must surrender.

It is here that Jung becomes a critic of modernity. He cannot accept the banality and stupidity of modern life, yet he is modern himself and has to accept his own position in it. He warns that we may not survive a direct encounter with the unconscious without religion:

> Modern thought has unfortunately overlooked the fact that man has never yet been able single-handed to hold his own against the powers of darkness, that is, of the unconscious. Man has always stood in need of the spiritual help which his particular religion held out to him. (1932, § 531)

In this mood, Jung fears for modern man in his aloneness and uprootedness. We are at the brink of a new spiritual dispensation, but without the guiding images, symbols, words, rituals, and myths that might direct us at this time. The individual in a process of transformation needs resources, historical parallels, shared languages, and community support—in a word, tradition. But by definition the modern individual is outside tradition, and cannot be rescued by it. However, Jung believed there were positive forces at work in the psyche, which could be called upon to guide us through the most difficult crises.

The third stage of life, which in mythology is called Paradise Regained or the New Jerusalem, is the most difficult of all to achieve. In the work of Erich Neumann, Jung's closest associate, it is called the re-establishment of the ego/Self axis, a connection severed when the ego was banished from Eden. It involves subordinating the ego to the greater power and guidance of the Self. The ego must surrender, but cannot entirely capitulate to the Self, otherwise it could become psychotic or dismembered. The individuated ego must not destroy itself in the arms of the Self, even if at times it wants to. It has to hold to its ground, as that is the ground upon which the Self must realise itself. The point of the ego in the first place is not to serve humanity but serve the Self in its passion to become conscious. It must walk with God, not be overwhelmed by God, otherwise the incarnation cannot take place. As Jung puts it:

> Individuation is an heroic and often tragic task, the most difficult of all, it involves suffering, a passion of the ego: the ordinary empirical man we once were is burdened with the fate of losing himself in a greater dimension and being robbed of his fancied freedom of will. He suffers, so to speak, from the violence done to him by the self. (1942a, § 233)

The third stage of ego/Self reconnection cannot be attained by an ego which is stuck in the phase of alienation. The disconnection has to be overcome by faith in the existence of a higher authority, a power greater than human. Naturally this is where instinct and intuition of the individual become supremely important, if society cannot offer images of that to which the ego must surrender. In Jung's view, unless modern individuals are prepared to risk the encounter with the unconscious, we cannot succeed in completing the life cycle by moving towards the source from where we came.

Endnotes

1. This text is adapted from my lecture course, "Jung and Spirituality" delivered to the Jung Society of Melbourne, November 23, 2021; and before that, to the Moscow Association for Analytical Psychology, October 17, 2021.
2. The kenotic ethic is an interpretation of Philippians 2:7. For further on kenosis see Thomas Jay Oord, "Essential Kenosis", in *The Nature of Love: A Theology* (2010, pp. 149–155).

CHAPTER 7

Dreams: The hidden doorway to the soul

The dream is a little hidden door in the innermost and most secret recesses of the soul, opening into that cosmic night which was psyche long before there was any ego-consciousness, and which will remain psyche no matter how far our ego-consciousness extends.

—Jung (1934c, § 304)

I was struck by the above quote for personal reasons. When I was a boy in primary school, I became obsessed with the image of a secret doorway, leading into a mysterious place. The door was obscured by creepers, ivy, and trees. In reality, there was indeed a partially hidden doorway to the basement below the school building. I often wondered where it led, but never found out. I would paint or draw the doorway in art class, and take it home to think about at night. My teachers asked where my doorway was leading, but I could not answer. It never occurred to me, at that young age, that this was the doorway to the soul, and I was not looking for a real doorway but a symbolic opening that was more important than a real door.

Some readers might recall Jung's early childhood dream of a secret doorway leading to an underground chamber, with a ritual phallus installed on a throne. This is discussed at length in his *Memories,*

Dreams, Reflections (1961a). He was only four years old at the time, but that dream stayed with him for a lifetime.

Dreams as products of the unconscious

Theories of the unconscious and knowledge of dreams may give us the sense that we know what dreams are about. Jung said such assumptions are wrong. He said, the peculiar fact about the unconscious is that it *is* unconscious; therefore, dreams, as messages from the unconscious, cannot by definition be known in advance. To avoid the pitfalls of such assumptions, Jung developed the habit of saying, before interpreting a dream: "I do not know what this dream is about." He would utter this quietly in his mind, and proceed from there. This habit seems important; the ego needs to divest itself of any illusions of having superior knowledge, and the act of surrender can put us in the position of being more able to understand the dream, because we have respected the otherness or mystery of the dream.

Some people are better with dreams than others, and have a natural affinity for dream language. But such people can make exaggerated claims if they believe they understand every dream of their patients, friends, or family. Often untrained people have a special affinity for dreams, especially women. In Australia I found a woman in Adelaide, Molly Scrymgour, who had the knack for dreams, and interpreted mine for several years without charging a fee. She was not a therapist but a typist at the university. The staff at the university had no understanding of her intuitive knowledge, and she was treated badly. She was what Toni Wolff would call a *medial* or mediumistic type of woman,[1] who had hunches about people, and often could tell what they were like even before she spoke to them.

In her 1934 paper on the four structural types of women, Toni Wolff said: "The medial woman is immersed in the psychic atmosphere of her environment and the spirit of her period, but above all in the collective unconscious". That kind of ability can be scary, but also wonderful if you can be open to this style. Molly started me on my dream journey, by saying some things that totally startled me. Molly died early, totally unrecognised, and her gifts were only acknowledged by me and a couple of others.

Eventually I began to consult professional therapists, not because I was mentally ill, but because I was so intrigued by dreams and wanted to learn more. I was often amazed at the capacity of Jungian therapists to interpret dreams. Such people had a personal gift, but had complemented it by undergoing a training. I worked with Janice Daw in Sydney and James Hillman in Dallas, both trained in Zurich. Any doubts I might have had that dreams were not worth considering were quickly dispelled by the work I did with them. And yet, there is a persistent view in the general public, and in the medical and health professions, that dreams are nonsensical and merely the chatter of the brain while we are asleep. Even sleep specialists, and REM experts, can have strong prejudices against dreams. They often imagine they are random, chaotic, and meaningless. Why? Because they cannot understand them. They have not bothered to learn the language. Any language can seem meaningless if we do not understand it.

I have heard some people say that the notion that dreams have meaning is a superstition. In other words, it is a falsehood to believe that they have anything to say. Contrast this with Robert Johnson's view, expressed in his popular book *Inner Work* (1986), that dreams are the most direct contact that anyone is likely to have with his or her spiritual life. There is no exact key to dreams. There is no single or right interpretation of a dream. But dreams are sources of revelation. A book by Edward C. Whitmont and Sylvia Perera is called, *Dreams: A Portal to the Source* (1989). In other words, they subscribe to the secret doorway approach. I feel hurt and offended when I hear people say that the notion that dreams have meaning is a superstition. It seems a gross undervaluation of the inner Self and its ability to provide guidance and direction.

Dreams are indispensable and give us an up to the minute guide of our inner experience. Marie-Louise von Franz puts it this way, in contrasting dreams with other forms of intuitive or prophetic knowledge:

> Some intuitive arts, such as horoscopy, graphology, chiromancy, phrenology, and the like, can indeed also often provide surprising bits of self-knowledge, but dreams have a great advantage over these techniques in that they give us a dynamic, continuous self-diagnosis and also clarify smaller fluctuations and momentary erroneous attitudes or specific modes of reaction.
>
> For instance, a person can, in principle, be modest, never overvaluing himself, but can become momentarily inflated as the result of some success. A dream will correct this immediately and in

doing so will inform the dreamer not only that he or she may, as a general rule, be such-and-such, but that "yesterday in connection with that matter, you were on the wrong track in such-and-such a way". (2014)

She is right in that no other form of knowledge is able to respond so immediately to changes or imbalances in the psychological economy. Dreams will rarely flatter us, but like a good and devoted friend, will always tell us if something is wrong or if our lives have gone awry without our being aware of it.

Dreams speak another language

The dream will never tell us something that is superfluous, it will never tell us something we already know. It won't waste our time, or its time. So I'm inclined to the view that to engage in dream work is to build holy ground. I can't explain why dreams are so knowledgeable or wise, except to say this appears to be so. Most scientists cannot affirm the meaningfulness of dreams, because this idea postulates that there is something within us that is watching us through our days, and is in possession of a higher wisdom. There is some kind of hidden eye that observes our actions and behaviour during the day and responds to us at night. To put forward this view is too spiritual for most scientists to be able to deal with. As soon as such ideas are put forward, science gets twitchy.

To understand dreams is to learn another language. It requires an initiation into a foreign tongue and only those who are willing to risk the work come back with a modicum of knowledge. I have been watching my dreams for fifty years, but instead of knowing the language, I still find it mysterious and difficult, and often need help in interpreting them. I dare say it would be easier for an English speaker to learn to read Russian or Chinese than to learn the language of dreams. This is because Russian and Chinese are fixed language systems, but dreams are different.

There is no fixed language, no simple code, and every book that claims to be a guidebook to the art of interpretation is usually rubbish. Every dream presents us with a new challenge, and we have to learn to read this language when we are presented with a new dream. I sometimes have no idea what has been expressed in my dream of the previous night, and anyway, it is advised by the great interpreters not to assume that we can interpret every dream that comes our way. Even Freud, Jung, and Hillman were often stumped by their dreams, and sought advice from others.

The dream speaks the language of myth, metaphor, and symbol. To understand this discourse is to enter foreign territory. It's an ancient language but new to us moderns. The mystery is that it operates subliminally and impresses itself on us from below. It does not arise from conscious thought but operates autonomously. It speaks from psychic depths that we do not understand and can only guess at.

It is little wonder that, before the discovery of the unconscious in the nineteenth century, this language was believed to come from the "gods" or "spirit beings" of the nether world. Dreams have been referred to as God's Forgotten Language (Sanford, 1989). Although the Bible contains many examples of the divine origin and purpose of dreams, Christians today, through fear and the constraints of dogma, have come to reject the visions through which God speaks to humanity. There's an old saying from the Jewish *Talmud*, "A dream unexamined is like a letter unopened."

An intelligence in the unconscious speaks to us, even today, in myth and symbol and we can only marvel at this phenomenon. We encounter this language as something belonging to early childhood, or found in the disturbed world of schizophrenics, or in prehistoric humanity with its rites and ceremonies. Dream language is distant from, and yet close to, us. If we use the language of neuroscience, we could say that we need to connect with the right hemisphere of our brain to understand the symbolic code of dreams. Everything is a representation of something else that is not easily expressed, except via the symbolic image or metaphor.

It is as if we have an ancestral part of the mind, which is present but not the product of conscious intention. Modern people claim to have outgrown the world of myth, since we see ourselves as civilised and rational. But just as an "inner child" continues to haunt the psyche of the adult, so an ancient dimension of life continues to dwell in the modern person.

Is it that the psyche contains traces of earlier evolutionary stages, going back to the dawn of time and the origin of the species? Jung said in "Archaic Man": "Every civilized human being, however high his conscious development, is still an archaic man at the deeper levels of his psyche" (1931c, § 105). This archaic man or woman speaks to us every night in our dreams. It may be the original symbolic language long before modern language systems were invented. In *The Interpretation of Dreams*, Freud noted the prevalence of mythical thinking in dreams, and commented:

> What once dominated waking life, while the mind was still young and incompetent, seems now to have been banished into the night. (1900a, p. 567)

"Young" and "incompetent" expresses Freud's prejudice about this kind of thinking. Psychoanalyst Karl Abraham similarly found archaic thinking in the modern psyche, and wrote that "The myth is a fragment of a superseded infantile psychic life of the race" (1909, p. 36). Again the Freudian prejudice is found, that dream language is infantile and incompetent. Even Jung's supervisor, Eugen Bleuler, dismissed mythical thinking as "autoerotic" and "autistic" (1910, p. 6). To counter these negative assertions, Jung wrote:

> The unconscious bases of dreams and fantasies are only apparently infantile reminiscences. In reality we are concerned with primitive or archaic thought-forms, based on instinct, which naturally emerge more clearly in childhood than they do later. But they are not in themselves infantile, much less pathological. (1912b, § 38)

We may not use the language of myth today, but the psyche does. The psyche is not *us*; but it is *within* us. It is not our conscious selves. What the ancient Greeks called *mythos* or sacred story is its native tongue. We need no elaborate scientific experiments to establish this fact. All we need is to recall last night's dream, and the dreams we have every night, which sometimes bear a striking resemblance to the productions of myth, fairy tale, folklore, and religion. This language goes on all the time, in the hinterland of our consciousness. It goes on even while we are awake, but is drowned out by the light and noise of conscious thought.

Here there is an analogy with the day and night time cycles. When the sun is out in the day, all the stars disappear from above, but that does not mean they are not there. The same thing happens with the psyche, when the light of consciousness is shining, it blocks out the other figures and presences in the psyche, which are still present but not noticed. Daydreams or reveries reflect what the psyche is doing while we are awake, when the threshold of awareness is lowered. Our dreams are never complete or whole myths, but contain fragments or echoes of myth, as if emanating from the same source as myths and religions.

If we reflect on this, it is enough to make even the most sceptical person develop a sense of awe and wonder. Evidence of a spiritual heritage is apparent every day and before our eyes. All we have to do is tune in to the psyche and listen to its frequency. It's like trying to dial into a new radio station on our radios. The impulses that drive mythic formations are found in every culture of the world, and especially in those we call tribal or indigenous. But the mythic life is preserved in modern day religions: Jung writes that "Religious thought keeps alive the archaic state of mind even today, in a time bereft of gods" (ibid., § 138).

Is "the unconscious" a good enough term?

The habit in depth psychology of saying that the wisdom of dreams comes "from the unconscious" is strangely inept. As I think more about it, calling this locus of wisdom the "unconscious" is disrespectful. To call it the unconscious is to say nothing about its nature or origin; it is only that we don't know anything about it. It seems that, given the unbelievable knowledge displayed in dreams, we cannot speak of the "unconscious" with a clear conscience any more. It is apparent that what we call the unconscious is infinitely more aware and conscious than we are. Why would we denigrate this source by applying the term "unconscious"? The answer is: out of habit, and for lack of a better term for describing the source from which this knowledge comes. The "unconscious" is only a provisional term, until we come up with a more specific term.

Aware of this anomaly, Marie-Louise von Franz says that dreams are not produced by the unconscious but by the "dream spirit". In her book on dreams she writes:

> The dream spirit that creates the dreams appears to us at times rather like a conscious being full of intentions and at other times rather like an impersonal mirror. (2014, p. 36)

I don't know if the term "dream spirit" solves the problem. What is clear is that we have a crisis in our psychological language, and the term "the unconscious" is a confession of ignorance about the sources of life that nourish, guide, direct, and sustain us. I think the term "God within" is probably better than "dream spirit", but each of us has to arrive at a term that suits us and meets our psychological and intellectual needs.

Psychology tries to secularise all these terms and processes, but clearly we are walking on sacred ground, even if we do not wish to use religious language. Even if we are non-religious or anti-religious we are nevertheless obliged to acknowledge sacredness when we see it. Jungian psychology expects us to adopt a religious attitude without religious language. It's a difficult act to perform, and possibly one reason why Jungian psychology itself won't last very long, because it is incomplete. Is Jungian psychology, as Jung himself believed, a temporary stand-in until we arrive at a new religion that is more complete and comprehensive? Jung saw his psychology as a temporary system of thought and belief which would prepare us for what is to come, which will need to be a religious orientation which is profoundly psychological and aware of the God within.

Freud called the dream the *via regia* ("the royal road") to the unconscious and used the dreams of his patients to help them become conscious of their repressed sexual and instinctual urges, the repression of which, according to Freud, determined the nature of all neurotic disturbances. Dreams, in his view, contain, in concealed form, allusions to instinctual or sexual desires which might have been conscious once but have fallen into the unconscious because the mind was not able to handle them at the conscious level. This was the background for his idea of a "dream censor".

Freud believed that dream images were residues or reflections of the persons or events of our day world. He interpreted dreams and fantasies largely at the objective level, as referring to external things or processes. Jung saw this as a Western cultural prejudice, and argued that we automatically (and wrongly) respond to dreams as reflections of external phenomena. To understand dreams, he argued, we need to postulate an interior reality, inhabited by internal persons and archetypes.

Jung was wary of the Freudian method, in which the patient "free associates" on the images and actions of the dream. To Jung, this was mistaken because it takes us away from the actual content of the dream. "Stick to the image!" he used to exclaim to readers and students (1931e, § 320). The dream is a self-revelation of the psyche, and its meaning cannot be ascertained by activating the resources of personal memory or childhood history. It almost requires what for Plato was called the memory of the human race, *memoria*, to encompass the extent and reach of the dream. It is a "transpersonal" message from the depths, and we should adopt a position of humility towards it. Jung believed the dream had to be approached with surprise and wonder, and we should be prepared for insights, unpleasant and pleasant, that would be made known to us.

Jung's method of interpretation involves not free association but *amplification*. This is a skill developed by the analyst in his or her clinical training. The object is to amplify the dream images by relating them to the myths and legends of religions, fairy tales, literature, and cosmologies. Instead of reducing the dream to the biography of the patient, Jung relates the dream to the history of humanity, to the symbolic systems that have enshrined wisdom in every age.

Jung argues that personal dreams are more important today than ever before. In the past, Western man and woman had primary access to the universal level through myths and religions. We entered into the core of reality through ritual, ceremony, narratives, and story. But in our time, these reservoirs of meaning have dried up, as we have become more rational and cerebral. The increase of interest in the phenomenon of dreams is an indication that, since secular society has no "dreaming" or mythos of its own, the individual is forced to carry the burden of the myth-making process, and this is done by concentrating on, interpreting, and analysing one's dreams.

The compensatory and complementary function of dreams

Jung felt that dreams have a *compensatory or complementary function*. This means that the dream almost never represents something already conscious, but brings contents which balance a one-sided attitude of consciousness (in which case they are compensatory) or completes what is lacking in consciousness (in which case they are complementary). Compensation means that the psyche is trying to put us back on the right course, address a problem, or adjust our consciousness so that we allow more into our frame of reference than is currently allowed. The law of compensation explains many of our dreams, perhaps most of them.

This function of the psyche begs many questions: Who or What is trying to adjust our lives so that we get the best chance to live according to the way we are meant to live? Is there some kind of blueprint for our lives that we are unaware of? How can we fathom or understand this process without positing some kind of God or guiding force in the psyche that tries to put us on the optimal course for us? What or where is the user's manual that might allow us to be better informed about the choices and decisions we make?

If I am too high and mighty, dreams bring me down to earth. If, on the other hand, my self-esteem is low or I am depressed, dreams will attempt to fill me with inspiration and lift me up. If I consider myself too pious or proper, dreams will show me the side of myself that I don't want to see: the shadow or darker side of my thoughts and desires. If I am too spiritual, dreams will remind me that I have instincts and sexual desires. If, on the other hand, I live only on the material or instinctual level, dreams will remind me that I have spiritual obligations and religious needs.

If I am indulging certain aspects of my life at the expense of others, dreams will urge me to live a more balanced life, and be more critical of my desires and longings. It is as if dreams know who and what I should be more than I myself know who and what I should be. There is a constant moral, guiding, and directing discourse emerging from dreams, of which I may be completely unconscious.

By "moral" I do not, of course, mean dreams are "moralistic". On the contrary, the dreams may have the reverse effect of moralism: if I consider myself above certain instinctual activities, dreams will reveal that I have secret longings that my self-image will not allow. If I am homophobic in life, dreams will throw up images of homosexual encounter and longing. If I am exclusively homosexual in life, dreams will show that I have secret longings for the opposite sex, and so on. If I think of myself as completely masculine, dreams will indicate that I have aspects of myself that are feminine, and vice versa.

Contrasexuality and transsexuality

This line of thought leads us to the contemporary interest in transsexuality, which is an area that Jungian psychology could shine a light on, if it were given a chance to do so. As early as 1909 Jung was saying that there is an anima in the man and an animus in the woman, which is often referred to as his theory of contrasexuality; also referred to as the *syzygy*, a Greek word meaning "yoked together".[2] For Jung the term means the archetypal pairing of contrasexual opposites, and the communication and coming together of the conscious and unconscious minds. No human is exclusively male or female, but he or she contains the counterpart of their biological sexuality in the form of contrasexual archetypes, which Jung thought are becoming more pronounced in modern times due to the fact that the archetype of wholeness, the Self, is pushing for greater expression. He spoke of the goal of individuation as the conjunction of two archetypal figures without the loss of identity.

This was a highly controversial thesis in Jung's time, and it greatly unsettled conventional understandings that men are decidedly masculine, and women firmly feminine. He wrote entire volumes, such as *Mysterium Coniunctionis* (1955–56), on the topic of the separation and synthesis of opposites in alchemy. The problem with this and other works like it is that it is too complicated for most people to digest and understand. One has to have much time and patience to work through Jung's writings on alchemy, in which he argues that the rise of the androgyne or hermaphrodite is a central motif of the achievement of individuation.

He saw the rise of such imagery in the dreams and fantasies of patients, and realised that an alchemical process was underway in the modern psyche which could be likened to the laboratory experiments of the ancient alchemists and metaphysicians. But his work is mostly too esoteric and complicated for medical professionals and students to take seriously, and that is why in the current rise of interest in contrasexuality Jung's theories have been almost entirely ignored.

In Jung's theory, the process of individuation begins when the person realises that he or she is not a single self, but composed of several selves or personalities. People become fearful of this, thinking Jung is leading them into madness or multiple personality disorder. He is saying that the plurality of the personality is a fact, and needs to be experienced before individuation can begin. Jung predicted that the human experience of identity would become more fluid and relative as time goes by, because the other voices, other selves, would be clamouring for attention and breaking open the hegemony of the ego, which considers itself to be the master of the house. In our time, the ruling ego is being overturned and we can see this in a number of ways, including the new interest in contrasexuality.

Upon reading some of the published case studies on contrasexuality, one can see that a psychological understanding of this phenomenon is lacking. People sense there is another sexual identity within their

being, and often begin the process of transitioning into the other identity. This can happen to very young adolescents, whose identity has yet
to be established. When they glimpse the other gender in their personalities, they are inclined to think that there is a hidden man or woman
inside them.

In one case I read, a man has a vivid dream in which he looks into a
full-length mirror, and staring back at him is a tall red-haired woman.
He wakes up and thinks to himself, I am really that red-haired woman
in the mirror, not the man I think I am. If he discusses this with therapists or doctors who have no knowledge of the unconscious—which
includes virtually the entire medical and therapeutic establishment—
the person will often be encouraged to begin the process of transitioning to the opposite gender glimpsed at the core of their identities.

There is an increasing tendency towards gender dysphoria today,
which is a sense that one's gender identity conflicts with one's biological sex. Such people experience a strong desire to hide or be rid of physical signs of their biological sex, such as breasts or facial hair. This might
lead to the desire to transition to the other gender, and permanently
transition to the gender with which they identify, often seeking medical assistance to help them align their body with their identified gender. Jung would intervene in this process and say: Not so fast with the
surgery. There is a need to become psychologically aware that we are
composed of several personalities. The man who dreams that a tall red-
haired woman is looking at him is seeing his anima looking back at him.

The dream was saying: Look, you are also this woman. The dream
was not saying, this woman is the real you and you should make haste
to become this woman. Jung would view the surgical option as a sign
of lack of imagination, a sign that we are unable to hold the tension
between the opposites and accept the possibly terrifying prospect that
the biological sex does not define the whole person. It is hard for us to
accept multiplicity if the consciousness of the time does not allow for
a fluid nature of identity. So this is an important way in which Jungian
dream work can contribute to a contemporary phenomenon, that some
Jungian analysts have defined as a psychic epidemic (Marchiano, 2017,
pp. 345–366).

The popular commentator Jordan Peterson has been outspoken
on this matter. Peterson, with a following of millions, calls himself
a Jungian but he is a dubious asset to the Jungian movement. He is

highly opinionated and the opposite of tactful. He often makes valid arguments, but they are spoilt by his crude manner of expression. In one of his videos he declares that the doctors who perform transsexual operations ought to be arrested and jailed because of their lack of psychological insight. He decries the medical and psychotherapeutic practices that fail to deal with the psychological dimension of trans gender and gender nonconforming patients. He says that there are industries that exploit this situation, offering "trans affirmative care" and resources. Peterson argues that the situation has got out of hand and appears to him as a form of indoctrination, so young people who are uncertain about their identity are preyed upon by therapists and exploited by medical and therapeutic interests.

If one googles, Jordan Peterson's "Arrest Them" on YouTube, one will find his outburst on this situation. Acting as provocateur he blames extremists and ideologues for promulgating this crisis in the modern world, but loses his temper and starts shouting and wailing. I often get the sense that Peterson is at the edge of a nervous breakdown, because he is too easily excited and loses professional control. I would point out that, despite Peterson's politicisation of this process, the problem is one of medical literalism and unimaginativeness versus depth psychological and symbolic literacy.

But one wonders that, if there were more psychological literacy in the world, and more understanding of Jungian thought, the fraught situation facing vulnerable adolescents might be less critical. Jungians have been slow in coming forward with their approach to this matter, although it is crying out for greater understanding at an archetypal level. Perhaps Jungians are afraid of entering the fray, and people don't want to be branded as reactionary or contrary to contemporary culture. Peterson comes out punching and fighting, which is his style. I feel sorry for Jordan Peterson: he has glimpsed something, but he can't seem to contain himself to present a sound and coherent argument, without hitting out at people and turning it all into a political bun fight and heated rant.

I will add here an astute comment from Jungian analyst Lisa Marchiano, based in Pittsburgh, Pennsylvania. Marchiano has braved the storm of protest, by describing gender dysphoria as a psychic epidemic of our time. It is an epidemic, she claims, which is not resolved by surgeons and therapists, but which is made worse by them, particularly in the way in which teenagers are encouraged to have transsexual operations in an attempt to resolve the dysphoria. She writes:

> Having lived through both World Wars, Jung was aware of the dangers of what he termed "psychic epidemics". He discussed the spontaneous manifestation of an archetype within collective life as indicative of a critical time during which there is a serious risk of a destructive psychic epidemic.
>
> Currently, we appear to be experiencing a significant psychic epidemic that is manifesting as children and young people coming to believe that they are the opposite sex, and in some cases taking drastic measures to change their bodies. Of particular concern to the author is the number of teens and tweens suddenly coming out as transgender without a prior history of discomfort with their sex. (2021, p. 813)

Her work is worth reading, especially because she argues that a Jungian approach to gender and contrasexuality, as a psychological experience of the opposites, might help our time to extricate itself from this crisis and lead to a more complex understanding of the human psyche.

What is the point of dream work?

Dreams rarely support our pet interests or personal preferences. Instead, they critique and undermine the things we have become attached to. They cut through much that has become precious to us to reveal the other side of the argument. They cut through all of this and simply tell us what we are neglecting or have left out of the equation.

Years ago, when I tried to live a strict vegetarian lifestyle, I had dreams about eating hot meat pies with tomato sauce. When I tried to live a strictly religious life, dreams showed that I might prefer watching sport to attending church. When I stopped attending church, my dreams indicated that my life lacked something sacred and holy. When I tried to be sensitive, aesthetic, and artistic, my dreams showed that I needed to play rugged team sport, get into football, and enjoy all-male company.

Our ideologies and fashions are always one-sided and hence not condoned by our dreams. Dreams are constantly trying to deconstruct any fixed moral code we have adopted. If I am strictly Jungian, the psyche will give me Freudian dreams. If I am Freudian, I will have Jungian dreams about unmet spiritual desires. Dreams always hound and annoy us, because we always prefer a particular kind of one-sidedness and the psyche demands wholeness. That's why it is never satisfied with how we live. It always keeps us on our toes; no wonder many have great resistance to recording and exploring their dreams, because of the constant moral commentary on the lives we lead.

In his essay on dreams in *Modern Man in Search of a Soul*, Jung summarises this adversarial and contrarian aspect this way:

> The psyche is a self-regulating system that maintains its equilibrium just as the body does. Every process that goes too far immediately and inevitably calls forth compensations, and without these there would be neither a normal metabolism nor a normal psyche. In this sense we can take the theory of compensation as a basic law of psychic behaviour. Too little on one side results in too much on the other. Similarly, the relation between conscious and unconscious is compensatory. This is one of the best-proven rules of dream interpretation. When we set out to interpret a dream, it is always helpful to ask: What conscious attitude does it compensate? (1931e, § 330)

Jung's theory of the purposeful nature of dreams begs questions of a metaphysical order. Is there a God Within that is beyond our knowing or comprehension? How and why is this wisdom within us, and if so, why isn't this wisdom better known and more respected? What are we to do about it? How can we live in alignment with this other will? We can see why a former age believed that God or the gods had eyes that watched our movements; something cares about us even more than we care about ourselves.

Jung believes it is a grave error if people are tempted to identify with the unconscious compensation which is indicated in dreams. For instance, a celibate priest might be tempted to live a promiscuous sexual life because his dreams ask him to become aware of sexuality. But ever-watchful of our tendency to literalise and act out even the contrarian aspect of our behaviour, Jung warns:

> If it should occur to anyone to replace the conscious content by an unconscious one he would only succeed in repressing it, and it would then reappear as an unconscious compensation. The unconscious would thus have changed its face completely: it would now

be timidly reasonable, in striking contrast to its former tone. It is
not generally believed that the unconscious operates in this way,
yet such reversals constantly take place and constitute its proper
function. That is why every dream is an organ of information and
control, and why dreams are our most effective aid in building up
the personality. (Ibid., § 332)

He says the goal of dream work is not to become the images that have
arisen to compensate our practices, but to integrate the images of the
soul, and not to be assimilated by them. If we become the image of
the soul, he calls this possession, which generates an imbalance or one-
sidedness in the opposite direction. Then the ego becomes swamped
and will need to be returned to the person as an unconscious compensation. But if the ego is tempted to act out the shadow, rather than take
it into the personality as an integral part, the unconscious will change
its attitude completely. It will become timidly reasonable, he says, in
striking contrast to its former tone. Thus the unconscious is constantly
monitoring the tone, direction, and character of the conscious, and if
that attitude changes, so will the unconscious change its approach.

In the conclusion of this essay, Jung refers to the end to which all
dream work points:

The way of successive assimilations [of the messages in dreams]
goes far beyond the curative results that specifically concern the
doctor. It leads in the end to that distant goal which may perhaps
have been the first urge to life: the complete actualization of the
whole human being, that is, individuation. We physicians may well
be the first conscious observers of this dark process of nature. As a
rule we see only the pathological phase of development, and we
lose sight of the patient as soon as he is cured. (Ibid., § 352)

So the "distant goal" of all dream work is individuation, that is, the
actualisation of the whole human being. The dreams help tirelessly,
and at every point, to actualise our best approximation of a life well
lived. The depth psychologist, he says, may well be the first conscious
observers of this process, because since they work with the dreams of
the client, they are front line workers in the art of tending to and nurtur-
ing the wholeness of personality. But he laments that patients naturally
leave analysis when the personality is on the way to a relative degree

of health, in which case they only observe the "pathological phase" of human development.

In similar vein, Marie-Louise von Franz describes the end point or goal of dream work as follows:

> Through constantly taking dreams into consideration something is produced which resembles a continuous dialogue of the conscious ego with the irrational background of the personality, a dialogue by means of which the ego is constantly revealed from the other side, as if there were a mirror, as it were, in which the dreamer can examine his own nature. (2014, p. 24)

So in answer to the question, often asked by people who can't be bothered to record and reflect on their dreams: what is the point of taking notice of our dreams?, von Franz answers: increased self-knowledge is the point. If one takes them seriously as subjective dramas, dreams constantly provide us with new insights about ourselves. If we take them seriously, dreams can be immensely practical, in that they can help us avoid making huge mistakes and errors in our life-direction. But more importantly, they help show the way forward towards the life we are meant to be living, according to the fates of our nature. They are promptings that show us how to live the life that we are meant to be living.

Endnotes

1. The term medial relates to a medium or to mediumship, as in medial faculties or mediumistic phenomena.
2. Syzygy can be traced to the Greek *syzygos*, a combination of *syn* (together with) and *zygon* (yoke).

CHAPTER 8

The individuation of God[1]

If the Creator were conscious of Himself, He would not need conscious creatures

—Jung (1961a, p. 371)

The not-yet God

Some readers dislike Jung's writings on God for different reasons. Atheists and humanists don't like them because they believe there is no God, and Jung's reflections are pointless. On the other hand, religious believers often dislike Jung's approach to God because they view it as heretical and cavalier. He refers to God in ways that believers find problematic and even indecent. Some Jungians do not like Jung on God, and refuse to take his reflections seriously. For instance, James Hillman suggested we should take note of his psychology, but ignore his theology (1975, p. xviii).

This is easy to say, but I don't think we can leave such a significant part of Jung's work out of the picture. Jung's late writings and memoirs are preoccupied with the issue of God, as he wrote to a clergyman: "I find that all my thoughts circle around God like the planets around the sun, and are as irresistibly attracted by Him. I would feel it to be the grossest sin if I were to oppose any resistance to this force" (1961a, p. 13). However, Jung was reluctant to declare his belief in God in his major works because he spent much time and energy trying to be a scientist, and in his day, being a scientist and a believer in God were not compatible. However, today it is far more common to see scientists espouse a belief in God, and the two views are no longer seen as incompatible.

An argument could be made that if you can't cope with Jung on God, you can't cope with Jung, whether as a psychologist or theologian. It also needs to be said that Jung does not believe in some kind of supernatural figure in the sky; although he does persist in the convention of referring to God as He, which can be annoying. But let us say that "God" for Jung is actually a proper noun for eternity. He is fully aware that there is no man in heaven, and as such he has much in common with atheists who similarly refuse to believe in such an anthropomorphic fiction. God is a hypothesis for Jung, and one in which he firmly believed, but he rarely said as much in his scientific papers. Nor did he say what God is in itself, but we can infer from his reflections that God for Jung is the primal energy of life, the process that directs and regulates the course towards consciousness, and as such, the guarantor of the individuation process.

But God is "not yet" God, because it is in the process of making itself. As in the process theology of A. N. Whitehead and others, Jung sees God as a cosmic life which is being shaped and completed by the process of coming-to-consciousness taking place in humanity. Our coming to consciousness is not just about us, nor is it solely about our personal individuation, but it is about the individuation of God. The two processes are inextricably linked, and this is why Jung's reflections on God cannot be seen as extrinsic to his work on the individuation process, because both processes involve each other and thus individuation has a theological dimension.

Secret knowledge

Among the works that directly concern the problem of God are Jung's late works *Aion* and *Answer to Job*. These works are probably among the most difficult in his long career, but they were written at a time when he was tired of making his ideas understandable to non-specialists. After a serious illness in 1944, during which he experienced a psychological rebirth, Jung decided to write the way he wanted to, with not too many concessions to his readers. They would have to meet him where he was, rather than him going to lengths to meet them, wherever they might be. This puts an extra burden on the readers of the late works. Jung said about *Aion*:

> Before my illness [in 1944] I had often asked myself if I were permitted to publish or even speak of my secret knowledge. I later set it all down in *Aion*. I realized it was my duty to communicate these thoughts, yet I doubted whether I was allowed to give expression to them. During my illness I received confirmation [from the psyche] and I now knew that everything had meaning and that everything was perfect.[2]

He meant conditions were perfect for him to abandon his hesitations and divulge his so-called "secret knowledge". He did not want to worry too much about his audience, as he had done for the past forty years. If people did not like it, they could set it aside, which many did. He was a wise but cantankerous old man, who felt an urgency to say things he had gleaned over his long career. *Aion* was the place where he told his secret knowledge, the knowledge he had developed over a lifetime but felt he was not "permitted" to speak. It is not certain who exactly was refusing him permission, but my guess is that it was his own conscience as a scientist.

The basic message of *Aion* is simple, if shocking to those who subscribe to conventional religious ideas. Jung argues that the God who had died in our civilisation is not dead, but in the process of incarnating in the modern individual. The God who was above, in a metaphysical heaven, had been a projection of the human imagination, and in modern times this projection has collapsed. But God was not dead, only the image had died. Jung believes it died for a purpose, which is to reveal the secret that lies buried in the human soul. All of this had been pre-dicted by arcane sciences and mystical traditions of the East and West. Esoteric Christianity has many hints and suggestions that indicate that we might have expected this transformation.

From a Christian view, the first stage of God's incarnation is found in the myth of Christ as the Son of God. But now this myth is collaps-ing, to make way for a more radical myth about God incarnating in every individual. Jung calls it, following his spiritual mentor Meister Eckhart, the ongoing incarnation of God:

> The future indwelling of the Holy Ghost in man amounts to a continuing incarnation of God. Christ, as the begotten son of God and pre-existing mediator, is a first-born and a divine paradigm which will be followed by further incarnations of the Holy Ghost in the empirical man. (1952a, § 693)

By "myth" I don't mean it isn't true; it is a truth of the spirit, and like all truths of the spirit it is revealed in story or narrative form. Myth and story are the best, indeed the only ways to speak of such transformations in history and culture.

For Jung the decline of Christianity in recent times is not an indication of the collapse of religion *per se,* but an indication that the previous dispensation, based on the projection of God upon Christ, needed to collapse so we can experience the ongoing incarnation of God into humanity. This had been happening all along, but in modern times we are becoming more aware of this radical transformation. In this new myth, the human is perceived as a necessary partner of God.

Jung admits that he is writing not for those who already have religious faith. He is writing for the "mythless ones" who might encounter this new myth and become gripped by its numinosity. They might, he says, become drafted into its service, and contribute to the ongoing incarnation. Such people will not only have discovered the meaning of their lives, but the meaning of all lives. Jung wrote:

> We live in the age of the decline of Christianity, when metaphysical premises of morality are collapsing. That causes reactions in the unconscious, restlessness and longing for the fulfilment of the times. This is called chiliasm.[3] When the confusion is at its height a new revelation comes. This follows psychological rules.[4]

For those who can endure the chaos and uncertainty of the present, there is a new dispensation that arises as it were to compensate for the confusion of the times. If we can be alert to the new, rising archetypal configuration, we can overcome much personal and collective suffering to discern the deeper truths which are emerging at this time.

The "secret knowledge" is that consciousness is the meaning of creation, and the individual is given the responsibility of supporting God by helping it become conscious of itself. I try to avoid referring to God as He, wherever possible, since it seems to me that this anthropomorphic construction is part of the reason why the idea of God has been lost in our time. The sexism of this is too excruciating for many to bear, and so the whole idea of God goes out of the window. However, because the Bible speaks of God as He, and the churches have for 2,000 years continued this convention, and Jung also speaks in these terms, it is often impossible to avoid the use of masculine pronouns when referring to the Western deity.

To refer to God as "he" aids in the decline of God because it makes him seem like an improbable and ridiculous proposition. I think Paul Tillich rescued the idea of God for me when he said that God is not a being, but Being itself. That makes more sense than the silly notion of an old man in the sky. God is not a supernatural being, but a philosophical concept or reality, rather like the Chinese Tao. In this regard, theology has helped to kill off God with its familiar personifications of what should remain mysterious, vague, and abstract. As Jung put it: "The finite will never be able to grasp the infinite" (1931b, § 283). But a critic of Jung might add: well, if that's so, why does he often speak of God in definitive terms, as if God were familiar and known? The answer is: he is speaking into the Western theological discourse, which speaks in these terms.

According to Jung, the human eye that beholds our experience is the eye of God looking upon creation to know itself. The individual is an instrument of the divine to permit the divine to apprehend itself. This is Jung's secret knowledge, or what seems to be his new religious myth for modernity. However, despite what it may seem, this myth is by no means new. Jung is giving expression to an ancient idea found in mystical philosophy and esoteric thought. For those who know the work of Meister Eckhart, Jung's secret knowledge is instantly recognisable as a central platform of Eckhart's mystical thinking. Eckhart wrote: "The eye wherein I see God is the same eye wherein God sees me: my eye and God's eye are one eye, one vision, one knowing, one love" (1956, p. 240).

Eckhart was deemed heretical for his ideas, which revolved around the theme that God wants to give birth to itself in the human soul. God is not satisfied with incarnating in Jesus of Nazareth, but wants to move into a process that Eckhart calls continuing or ongoing incarnation.

For this radical idea, Eckhart was harshly judged and punished. He was summoned from Paris to Rome to explain himself to the Vatican, but historians believe it is likely that on his way to Rome he was murdered by the Vatican army before any inquisition could take place. So this mystical idea of ongoing incarnation comes with a weight of condemnation, and Jung inherits the condemnation that was placed on Eckhart.[5]

So if we look at Jung's secret knowledge from the point of view of conventional religion, it will seem scandalous. The idea that God needs humanity to become conscious of itself is a heresy if we recall that in orthodox theology God is said to be omnipotent, omniscient, and omnipresent. These attributes of deity are often referred to as the three Omni's of God. If God is omniscient and all-knowing, there would be no need for humanity as such, except to know and praise God in worship and service. But central to Jung's thesis is that God is dependent on human consciousness to allow God to know itself. What we do impacts on God. As Jung put it: "Whoever knows God has an effect on him" (1952a, § 617).

Without the consciousness that is developed in the course of evolution, God remains in the pleroma and undifferentiated. In *Aion*, Jung quotes many sources from Gnosticism and alchemy that indicate that "the Godhead is essentially unconscious". He also quotes from the *Rig Veda* of Hindu scriptures saying that God is not conscious but could be dreaming. In this case, we may be the dreams that God is dreaming in his unconscious state, an idea that comes up in the writings of Edgar Allan Poe: "All that we see or seem is but a dream within a dream" (1849). Edinger reflects: "Ordinarily we think that suprapersonal powers and images are projections of our own mind, but if reciprocity exists, we equally may be projections of the transpersonal other" (1984, p. 55). In this sense, our lives gain dignity and value if seen as the dreams of some incomprehensible deity. In *Aion* Jung summarises his conclusions:

> The unconscious God-image can alter the state of consciousness, just as the latter can modify the God-image once it has become conscious ....
>
> Psychologically, however, the idea of God's *agnosia* (ignorance) or of the *anennoetos theos* (unconscious God) is of the utmost importance, because it identifies the Deity with the numinosity of the unconscious. The *atman/purusha* philosophy of the East and, as

we have seen, Meister Eckhart in the West both bear witness to this.
(1951, § 303)

But the bulk of *Aion* consists of hundreds of examples of quotes and postulates arguing that God is unconscious and requires humanity to enable it to become conscious of itself. Eckhart actually refers to God as the "not yet God", as God is involved in the ongoing process of becoming. This is a phrase that has been used as the title of a recent book on Jung and Teilhard de Chardin by American theologian Ilia Delio (2023). Jung quotes Eckhart as saying in one of his sermons: "Love God as he is: a not-God, a not-spirit, a not-person, a not-image; as a sheer pure, clear one, which he is … and in this One let us sink eternally from nothing to nothing" (1951, § 301).

The two sides of God

Jung argues that the two hands of God, the right and left, the good and evil, are undifferentiated and not gathered into a workable or conscious unity. Neither hand knows what the other is doing. This is not a paradox, but a contradictory situation. In *Aion* and *Answer to Job* Jung refers to Yahweh as irascible and unreliable. God is a jealous god, testy, petulant, cantankerous, and unpredictable. On the other hand, Yahweh is capable of showing tenderness, mercy, and compassion. Jung refers to the nature of Yahweh as a condition of complex opposites, or *complexio oppositorum*, using the terminology of medieval alchemy. Such a condition reflects a nature which is not integrated; it is conflicted and chaotic. Jung sees this conflict at the heart of the God-image that is being worked through in the Book of Job.

Jung gives as an example of this conflicted situation the dynamics at play in the Garden of Eden. In Jung's view, Yahweh and the serpent are personifications of the right and left hands of God. Yahweh is rigidly conservative and expects humanity to follow his rules and commandments. The wily serpent, who is said to be "more clever than any of the wild animals the Lord God had made" (Genesis 3:1), tempts Eve to contradict Yahweh's commands and eat of the forbidden fruit of the tree of the knowledge of good and evil.

The tree of good and evil is naturally a symbol of the world of opposites which greets the young adult as he or she leaves childhood innocence and enters the conflicted world of experience. Good and evil,

Jung argues, are the primary pair of opposites that characterises the conscious realm of choice and decision making. The adolescent who emerges from childhood is faced with a bewildering world where choices have to be made at every turn; whereas in the infantile condition no choices are made, but instinct chooses on our behalf.

The Lord God is imagined as a patriarchal king who has zero tolerance of free will or independence and insists that humanity obeys rules designed to keep it in a state of innocence. One thinks in this regard of the many brutish dictators in the world of politics who claim to be religious and yet show no mercy or grant no freedom to their people. They are acting in the image of the brutish, unconscious God. This prevents humanity from moving into consciousness and freedom, so it remains held in the bosom of the Lord God. As Jung puts it in *Answer to Job*:

> The Creator needs conscious man even though, from sheer uncon-
> sciousness, he would like to prevent him from becoming conscious.
> And that is also why Yahweh needs the acclamation of a small group
> of people. One can imagine what would happen if this assembly
> suddenly decided to stop the applause: there would be a state of high
> excitation, with outbursts of blind destructive rage, then a withdrawal
> into hellish loneliness and the torture of non-existence, followed by a
> gradual reawakening of an unutterable longing for something which
> would make him conscious of himself. (1952a, § 575)

The blind rage of Yahweh is characteristic of a narcissistic, unconscious being who cannot bear to witness the coming to awareness of his creatures. This would make his creatures morally superior to him, which is a theme hinted at in a number of places in the Book of Job. Jung is arguing that the good side of Yahweh and his evil side are not related, but are in fact split off elements personified as God and Satan.

Jung argues that one aspect of God wants to prevent Adam and Eve from becoming conscious, and another undermines this view and encourages Eve, and then Adam, to eat the forbidden fruit. But why is the primal impulse towards consciousness represented as an evil transgression? The answer is that this impulse introduces humanity into a world of turmoil and travail, as indicated in Genesis 3: 14–24. "See, the man has become like one of us, knowing good and evil … therefore the Lord God sent him forth from the garden of Eden."

We might ask, to whom does the plural "us" refer? Is this Yahweh and Satan, or perhaps Yahweh and the feminine Lilith or Sophia? Whomever it refers to, it seems that the idea of monotheism was invented by theologians, as it does not tally with scripture. But consciousness drives the first humans out of paradise and introduces them to a world of suffering that cannot be avoided if we are to take on the burden of consciousness.

Jung's assessment is that the God of the Old Testament is split into two antithetical parts, just as, in the Christian story, Jesus and the devil are eternally warring antagonists. This is shocking for the Judaeo-Christian narrative, which insists that God and devil are two agencies who have nothing to do with each other. However, this is contradicted in the Book of Job, where Yahweh and Satan get together to make a wager as to whether Job can be corrupted or not. In this context they are seen as co-conspirators, not enemies. Jung argues that the Bible is full of hints that there is only one figure, split into different parts, which is why, until he becomes conscious, we find that "The 'just' God can go on committing injustices, and the 'Omniscient' can behave like a clueless and thoughtless human being" (ibid., § 617).

This is where the human burden comes in: God cannot heal his own split character but the hope of the ages is that humanity might reconcile the opposites within its own nature. That is why the process of individuation is always characterised as a painful and difficult wrestling match with the opposites within our nature, ego and shadow, ego and anima or animus, with the hope of achieving a reconciliation when the Self is constellated as an archetype capable of putting a stop to the war between opposites. For this to happen, the so-called transcendent function needs to be constellated, so that the war of opposites achieves a yin/yang balance, in which case the stress and tension is toned down: war and conflict resolves into a dance of binary polarities. Jung always points to the East as having the philosophical and moral capabilities of transforming war into interplay. This is why he says we must defer to the East, for its greater moral and philosophical sophistication.

The more Christianity accentuates the light, the darker the shadow becomes, by way of compensation. It is because we make no room for evil that it attempts to destroy us. If we could adopt a yin/yang Chinese Taoist understanding of good and evil, we would be in much better shape. Instead, we don't see how darkness and light are complementary, but make them diabolical opponents. Hence Jung says: Christianity has "enthroned an eternal dark antagonist alongside the omnipotent God" (1961a, p. 370). He says the West needs to learn lessons from the East, especially Chinese Taoism:

> We must beware of thinking of good and evil as absolute opposites. The criterion of ethical action can no longer consist in the simple view that good has the force of a categorical imperative, while so-called evil can resolutely be shunned. Recognition of the reality of evil necessarily relativizes the good, and the evil likewise, converting both into halves of a paradoxical whole. (Ibid., p. 361)

If we followed Taoism and created a paradoxical image of the Creator God we would not be bedevilled by such catastrophic outbreaks of evil. "We have no imagination for evil, but evil has us in its grip" (ibid., p. 363).

Imagining the future

At this point, Jung's religious critics protest that Jung is not talking about the Judaeo-Christian God, but something else, some other arche-typal figure such as Hermes, Dionysus, or Abraxas, or the Chinese Tao, all of which are paradoxical and morally ambivalent. Some say Jung wants us to abandon the West and follow the East. They say Jung is not talking about a recognisable Western God, but some other archetypal agency that he has concocted from his imagination. They say Jung is inventing a God-image of his own, and his thinking does not belong to the West. We in the West find it almost impossible to think of a God through this paradoxical lens, although the evidence is there in the Bible pointing in just this direction.

Jung draws on astrological configurations, arguing that the Piscean fish swimming in opposite directions is the synchronistic counterpart to the Christ and Anti-Christ binary. The symbolism of the Aquarian age represents a shift of perspective from the struggle of opposites to the new symbol of the Water Bearer, as a symbol of the Self. Jung believed that each of the great shifts in history is represented by a new astrological aeon reflected in the imagery of the presiding zodiacal constellation and its planetary ruler.

As Liz Greene puts it in "'The Way of What Is to Come': Jung's Vision of the Aquarian Age":

> Jung believed wholeheartedly that a new epoch reflecting the symbolism of the constellation of Aquarius was about to dawn and that his psychology might make a significant contribution to the conflicts arising from such a profound shift in the collective psyche. (2017, p. 156)

Jung is aware that what he is advocating is preposterous from a Judaeo-Christian view. But he is doing some hard thinking that is unfamiliar to Western theology. He does not regard his reflections as alien to the West, but as drawing attention to a hidden or unconscious undercurrent of Western theology. He sees himself as providing a psychological dimension to a theology that has not had the benefit of depth psychological analysis.

However, I sometimes worry that books such as *Aion* and *Answer to Job* are so difficult that it is hard to know if many are going to benefit from the insight he is striving to bring to the West. If, as he said in the interview, he was planning on being uninhibited and open about his secrets, it is a pity that his insights remain buried beneath arcane scholarship, Gnostic philosophies, and esoteric quotations from Greek and Latin sources. In Jung's mind, he is trying to make his insights more scholarly rather than appear as random assertions from his mind, but the result is not favourable to his thesis. In a letter of April 1953 to a theologian who misunderstands his work on the God within he writes, "I am evidently a bad advocate in my own cause." He is caught in a double bind: the desire to express is almost obliterated by the desire to impress. But impress who? Certainly not us, but perhaps classical scholars whom he imagined might pore over his findings. He does not seem as uninhibited about delivering his message as he claims to have been. He was trying to make his thesis appear congruent with historical sources, but in our minds he is engaged in obfuscation and obscurity.

Aion can't be "read" in the usual way, it has to be interpreted, wrestled with, and it might take more than one reading before the reader can grasp the main points. I am suggesting that there may be some kind of block in Jung's mind preventing his wisdom from being communicated. Perhaps he is suffering from shame and embarrassment at being so out of step with Western knowledge. The Jungian argument about the God within requires a great deal of discernment before any conclusions can be reached. The first stage in this discernment is establishing the crucial difference between ego and Self, and this is why *Aion* begins with apparently simple opening chapters where he discusses the nature of the ego and the Self. These chapters are not difficult, but the connection between them and the dense speculations that follow are hard to figure out.

What inspires *Aion* is a sense of responsibility that Jung feels towards the present historical moment. He sees countless people succumbing to disorientation and mental confusion as they find no purpose or meaning in their lives. In the foreword to *Aion* he says that although much of the book is about the history of the Christ figure in Western culture he is not writing about this topic as a believer or religious advocate, but because he thinks that it is important to understand Christ to grasp the archetypal dominant that has governed the West for 2,000 years.

> My reader should never forget that I am not making a confession of faith or writing a tendentious tract, but am simply considering how certain things could be understood from the standpoint of our modern consciousness—things which I deem it valuable to understand, and which are obviously in danger of being swallowed up in the abyss of incomprehension and oblivion; things, finally, whose understanding would do much to remedy our philosophic disorientation by shedding light on the psychic background and the secret chambers of the soul. (1951, p. x)

If Western culture is in a chaotic state, Jung believes it is nevertheless important to understand the cultural and psychological dynamics that brought us to this point. He continues:

> The essence of this book was built up gradually, in the course of many years, in countless conversations with people of all ages and all walks of life; with people who in the confusion and uprootedness of our society were likely to lose all contact with the meaning of European culture and to fall into that state of suggestibility which is the occasion and cause of the Utopian mass-psychoses of our time. (Ibid.)

We live in a time in which the destruction of the old is more apparent than the birth of the new. Jung believed that we fare better if we understand why things are as they are. Edward Edinger argues that in *Aion*, Jung is trying to develop a new myth of the value of individual

THE INDIVIDUATION OF GOD   183

consciousness, to alleviate the loss and suffering of those who are in a mythless state. Edinger says: "A new myth can regenerate a society, and Jung's myth offers Western civilization a sound container to hold the precious life-essence of meaning which has been spilled during the breaking of the vessels of traditional religion" (1984, p. 9).

Edinger argues that the meaning of myth is not understood. It holds the psyche intact and prevents it from shattering in times of suffering and difficulty. Myth allows us to hold the tension of whatever it is that is trying to destroy our integrity.

> The loss of a containing myth is the root cause of our current indi-
> vidual and social distress, and nothing less than the discovery of
> a new central myth will solve the problems for the individual and
> society. (Ibid.)

When a foundational myth like Christianity is shattered, meaning drains away and "… in its place, primitive and atavistic contents are reactivated." In other words, civilisation regresses to an inferior state before it progresses to a new myth. Edinger again:

> Differentiated values disappear and are replaced by the elemental
> motivations of power and pleasure, or else the individual is
> exposed to emptiness and despair. With the loss of awareness of a
> transpersonal reality (God), the inner and outer anarchies of com-
> peting personal desires take over. (Ibid.)

Slouching towards Bethlehem

The loss of a foundational myth brings about an apocalyptic situation which is imagined by the poet W. B. Yeats in his poem "The Second Coming" (1919).

> Turning and turning in the widening gyre
> The falcon cannot hear the falconer;
> Things fall apart; the centre cannot hold;
> Mere anarchy is loosed upon the world.
> The blood-dimmed tide is loosed, and everywhere
> The ceremony of innocence is drowned;
> The best lack all conviction, while the worst
> Are full of passionate intensity.

Surely some revelation is at hand;
Surely the Second Coming is at hand.

The Second Coming! Hardly are those words out
When a vast image out of Spiritus Mundi
Troubles my sight: somewhere in the sands of the desert
A shape with lion body and the head of a man
A gaze blank and pitiless as the sun,
Is moving its slow thighs, while all about it
Reel shadows of the indignant desert birds.
The darkness drops again; but now I know
That twenty centuries of stony sleep
Were vexed to nightmare by a rocking cradle,

And what rough beast, its hour come round at last,
Slouches towards Bethlehem to be born? (1919, p. 184)

This poem is a summation of everything that Jung is speaking about in terms of the apocalyptic situation of humanity. As far as I know, Yeats and Jung never met and did not influence each other, but both arrived independently at the same cosmological insights, and both in response to the Armageddon of the First World War.

Like Jung, Yeats imagined the passing of the ages as a passage through great expanses of time ("Turning and turning in the widening gyre"), the human ego loses contact with the creator ("The falcon cannot hear the falconer"), and as a result social chaos ensues and life loses its coherence ("Things fall apart, the centre cannot hold"). After the passing of a great myth, there is an atavistic regression to the elemental motivations of pleasure and power and the blind forces of instinct are "loosed upon the world". The innocence of human life is lost, and people of integrity lose heart, while the worst of humanity tends to thrive in the chaotic conditions: "The best lack all conviction, while the worst/Are full of passionate intensity."

"Surely some revelation is at hand" mirrors Jung's anticipation of a new age of the spirit, after the collapse of Christianity. However, it is just here that the expectation of the dawning of a new age turns bleak and dark. As he imagines a Second Coming, Yeats is disturbed by "a vast image out of Spiritus Mundi" (the spirit of the world), which "troubles [his] sight". A figure embodying the Anti-Christ is seen emerging from the cosmic plane. It has the shape of a lion body and the head of a man, which is almost identical to the picture in the frontispiece of *Aion*, which shows a second-century sculpture of the Mithraic god Aion, also a mixture of lion and human features.

The end of the Christian era does not bring the anticipated Second Coming, but on the contrary the birth of the Anti-Christ, as foreshadowed in the Book of Revelation. This same psychospiritual situation is what obsesses Jung in *Aion*, because he argues that the decline of Christianity releases the polar opposite of Christ, the Anti-Christ. The post-Christian age falls into its opposite, which Jung refers to by the Greek term *enantiodromia*, which literally means, "running counter to" the previous morality. Jung writes:

> Christian tradition from the outset is not only saturated with Persian and Jewish ideas about the beginning and end of time, but is filled with intimations of a kind of enantiodromian reversal of dominants. I mean by this the dilemma of Christ and Antichrist. (1951, p. x)

These two great minds, visionary poet and depth psychologist come up with exactly the same prophetic pessimism about the changing of the gods. This reminds me of the 1960s and '70s which I lived through as a young man: many felt that the collapse of Christianity was a good thing, leading to a welcome release of constraints on the human instincts, especially sexuality, but what was released was not just the joy of instinct, but the terror of what was suppressed throughout 2,000 years of Christian morality. This piled-up realm of evil, as Yeats says, which was asleep for twenty centuries, was "vexed to nightmare by a rocking cradle". The allusion is to the manger of Bethlehem, which, by way of an enantiodromian reversal, no longer holds the baby Jesus but this daemonic figure of collective evil. The rough beast, "its hour come around at last", now "slouches towards Bethlehem to be born".

Once again the genius of Yeats and that of Jung converge on the same insight: that the evil principle that Christianity tried to contain and suppress for so long, has burst forth with renewed vitality, and not only demands expression but asks to be recognised as sacred, holy. It wants to be born in Bethlehem, in the same way that the principle of good, the baby Jesus was inducted into the world in the Christmas story. Our age is Christmas in reverse: the dark forces awaken and will eventually demand to be seen as an aspect of the Godhead, which is a central argument of Jung's *Answer to Job*. The popular joke about a "dog in a manger" captures the spirit of this insight. What is left out of the Christian world-picture will try to destroy everything unless it is given more serious attention, credence, and substance. Jung's argument in *Answer to Job* is that the Christian understanding of evil as the so-called *privatio boni*, a term used in Catholic theology referring to the "deprivation of good", is no longer sufficient for our modern circumstances, and does not do justice to our exposure to devastating amounts of evil through the catastrophes of two world wars and continuing wars after them.

One can see from this brief survey of Yeats's poem why I spent forty years as a university lecturer in English literature while at the same time building a second career in the field of depth psychology. For some years, from 2001 to 2010 I taught short courses at the Jung Institute in Zürich, while spending the rest of the year teaching courses in literature at an Australian university. These are complementary activities, and the one discipline is able to throw light on the other. In some ways, English literature is more succinct and powerful than Jung's turgid essays in depth psychology, but if one can forgive Jung for his prolixity we can see how his ideas give substance and depth to what is otherwise incomprehensible in literature. Needless to say that an important work of reference to me during that time was Jung's Volume 15 of the collected works, *The Spirit in Man, Art and Literature*.

For Jung, God is a complex of opposites, and the religions do not recognise it, because God has been imagined as something all light, without darkness. Jung has a sense of urgency about this, because the upwelling of evil in humanity in modern times is not just a psychological problem, but a global, universal, and spiritual problem. Jung summarises the main argument of *Aion* better in his memoirs, where he writes:

> The complex of opposites (complexio oppositorum) of the God-image thus enters into man, and not as unity, but as conflict, the dark half of the image coming into opposition with the accepted view that God is "Light". This very process is taking place in our own times, albeit scarcely recognized by the official teachers of humanity whose task, supposedly, is to understand such matters. There is the general feeling, to be sure, that we have reached a significant turning point in the ages. (1961a, p. 366)

The beast slouches towards Bethlehem to be born, but this is not recognised as such, and so the evil side is attributed solely to humanity, whereas it is the emergence of something archetypal beyond humanity. But I keep asking this question: why is this so difficult for Jung to articulate? Why does he express this thought repeatedly, but not clearly, but buried in difficult scholarship, such as we find in *Aion*. It is really only until we get to *Memories, Dreams, Reflections*, which is not in the collected works, that Jung comes out and states directly his new myth for humanity. In his official writings it remains camouflaged, hidden, and still secret.

The reality of evil

In *Aion* Jung takes issue with his friend, Catholic theologian Victor White, who accused Jung of being a Manichean dualist in terms of his emphasis on the polar opposites of light and dark (1951, p. 51n.). However, in reply, Jung says it is Victor White and his Catholic tradition that is dualistic, because of its failure to integrate light and dark into a complex whole. He says in *Aion*:

> The reality of evil does not necessarily lead to Manichaean dualism and so does not endanger the unity of the God-image. As a matter of fact, it guarantees that unity on a plane beyond the crucial difference between the Yahwistic and the Christian points of view. Yahweh is notoriously unjust, and injustice is not good. The God of Christianity, on the other hand, is only good. (Ibid., p. 99)

It is not Jung but Christianity that is stuck in dualism, because it cannot view the interaction of the opposites as an interplay of complementary forces.

Individuation, which Jung defines as a reconciliation of opposites in the human personality, is reframed by Jung as a form of divine service, a service to the Godhead. In coming to terms with the opposites of human nature, the individual is assisting the Godhead (a term used by Meister Eckhart) in coming to terms with its inherent conflicts and polarities. As Jung claims in his memoirs:

> The unavoidable internal contradictions in the image of the Creator God can be reconciled in the unity and wholeness of the self, as the

coniunctio oppositorum of the alchemists or as a *unio mystica*. In the experience of the self it is no longer the opposites "God" and "man" that are reconciled, as it was before, but rather the opposites within the God-image itself. That is the meaning of divine service, of the service that man can render to God, that light can emerge from the darkness, that the Creator may become conscious of his creation and man conscious of himself. (1961a, p. 371)

As is often the case, Jung is clearer about his main themes in his memoirs than in his major writings. Here he states plainly that the reconciliation of the opposites in the human psyche is a work that relates theologically to the reconciliation of the opposites in the divinity. Individuation is a two-way process in which the coming together of opposites in humanity is at the same time a representation of the individuation of God. The Creator becomes conscious of its creation as man becomes conscious of itself. The image of the mirror and the concept of mirroring is crucial in this process. In the individuation process God beholds its own unknown face.

It seems almost silly to speak of the *individuation of God*, but that is what Jung is saying is the theological basis of this process, and why individuation is so deeply situated in the human psyche. It is deeply grounded in the human personality because it is grounded in the divine nature; we are all coordinated by the necessity of the Godhead to become conscious of its dualistic nature. By becoming conscious of the warring opposites, the dualistic nature is transcended and a new synthesis is reached. How this effects the Godhead itself is too difficult for me to understand, but we enter a realm at this point in which poetry and scripture replace scientific explanation. Every human psyche is part of the being of God, and yet we don't realise it. We think of ourselves as separate and distinct but we are all in this process together. The billions of human psyches are aspects of the one Universal Mind, and at this point psychology ends and philosophy and cosmology begins.

In the above quote, Jung says that individuation is part of the service that man can render to God, and Edward Edinger picks up the theme in this way:

> The divine opposites that were separated by Christianity into the eternal antagonists, Christ and Satan, are now beginning to be reunited consciously in the vessel of the modern psyche. Each

individual is a unique experiment in the creation of consciousness and the sum total of consciousness created by each individual in his lifetime is deposited as a permanent addition in the collective treasure of the archetypal psyche. (1984, p. 23)

Words almost fail at this point. To speak of the individual consciousness as a "deposit" in the collective treasure of the archetypal psyche is, I guess, one way of imagining this process, but it is only a hint at the mystery of the way in which an individual life contributes to the larger work of universal consciousness.

I haven't spent much time on the astrological dimension of Jung's *Aion* because it is not a great interest of mine. But I do want to say a few words about his astrological predictions. Jung originally argued that the Aquarian age began in 1940, under the influence of one of his associates, Rebekka Biegel, a Jewish professional astronomer. She had said that in 1940 the equinoctial point aligned with the midpoint between the last star of Pisces and the first star of Aquarius. However, late in his career he changed his mind, and said the dates of the end of one era and beginning of another are "indefinite" and "arbitrary".

Nevertheless, he was always certain that the start of the Aquarian era would be occasioned by upheaval, chaos, and violence, which was a far cry from the ideology promulgated by the New Age movement of the 1960s, which claimed Jung as a source of their inspiration. The New Age believed that the new aeon would be marked by an increase of love and harmony, an idea taken up by the San Francisco "summer of love" in 1969, as well as the Australian Aquarius Festival in Nimbin in 1973. Jung was not an optimist; he always hoped for the best but feared the worst. Like many of us who are getting older, he feared for the world facing our children and grandchildren, because he was not cheerful about the future. Shortly before his death, he wrote to a correspondent:

Transitions between the aeons always seem to have been melancholy and despairing times, as for instance the collapse of the Old Kingdom in Egypt between Taurus and Aries, or the melancholy of the Augustinian age between Aries and Pisces. And now we are moving into Aquarius …. And we are only at the beginning of this apocalyptic development! Already I am a great-grandfather twice over and see those distant generations growing up who long after we are gone will spend their lives in that darkness. (1955)

Jung saw the approaching Aquarian aeon as no panacea, and following the predictions of Nostradamus, he said it would lead to a rough time, at least at the start, during the changing of the epochs. Astrologer and psychoanalyst Liz Greene wrote:

> Jung did not assume that the union of the opposites would be a smooth passage into a higher and more loving stage of spiritual consciousness, as did the Theosophists and the New Age proponents of the late twentieth century. He foresaw "a new advance in human development", but he viewed the transition into the Aquarian aeon as a dangerous time, fraught with the potential for human self-destruction. (2017, p. 156)

Since Jung viewed the Aquarian aeon as an epoch when individuals would need to interiorise the god-image, he did not anticipate a new avatar for the new epoch who would manifest externally as a saviour figure. He declined to adopt Rudolf Steiner's belief in a Second Coming of Jesus, or Annie Besant's hope of a new World Teacher.

It seems that Jung understood himself to be an individual vessel for the psychodynamics of the new aeon, and the work he pursued on his own integration was work on behalf of a collective that he feared was already beginning to struggle blindly and destructively with the same dilemmas: the rediscovery of the soul; the acknowledgement of good and evil as inner potencies; the terrible responsibility that comes with that acknowledgement; and the recognition of a central interior self, which alone can be supposed to integrate the opposites.

Endnotes

1. This was originally written at the request of the Jung Society of Melbourne, for a public lecture on 25 May, 2023, under the title, "Jung's Myth for Our Time: Ongoing Incarnation".
2. These comments on *Aion* were made to Margaret Ostrowski-Sachs in a private conversation, which she recorded; Margaret Ostrowski-Sachs, *From Conversations with C. G. Jung* (1971, p. 68). Quoted in Edward Edinger and Deborah Wesley, *The Aion Lectures: Exploring the Self in C. G. Jung's Aion* (1996, p. 13).

3. Chiliasm (pronounced kil-iasm) or millennialism is the belief that a golden age or paradise will occur on earth prior to the Last Judgement and future eternal state of the world to come. The etymology comes from the Greek *khilias*, meaning 1,000 years.
4. Jung, Letter to Walter Robert Corti, September 12, 1929. In: *C. G. Jung Letters, Vol. I, 1906–1950*, ed., Gerhard Adler (1973, p. 69).
5. Note that a study of Eckhart's life and work is entitled *Dangerous Mystic: Meister Eckhart's Path to the God Within*, by Joel Harrington (2018).

CHAPTER 9

Returning religion to its symbolic roots[1]

Taking it seriously does not mean taking it literally.

—Jung (1916, § 184)

Over the last 200 years, there has been a concerted effort to read the Bible in symbolic or metaphorical terms, instead of literally. Jung brings a vast knowledge to bear on the project of deliteralising religion and returning it to its base in symbol. Like progressive thinkers, he was frustrated by the way in which religious tradition had turned metaphors into supposed "historical" facts, but unlike them he did not want to throw the metaphors out but had the patience to interpret them anew. Like conservatives, he respected what had been handed down by tradition, and found meaning in the creeds and dogmas. But unlike conservatives he interpreted creeds symbolically, and never accepted the face value of religious statements.

Jung's message is that we have unnecessarily discounted myth and need to develop a new appreciation of its revelatory power. The truth-bearing capacity of metaphor is where we locate the values of the soul. He believed "An archetypal content expresses itself, first and foremost, in metaphors" (1940, § 267). He argued that the well-being of the soul depends on our ability to turn from our obsession with facts and find respect for the non-literal. Jung took risks with truth and tried to relate religious statements to the psyche. He felt truth must never remain static but had to be updated. He put the situation paradoxically: "Eternal truth needs a human language that alters with the spirit of the times" (1946, § 396). He was prophetic to the extent that he saw the spirit of tradition languishing, and argued that it needed to be liberated from its theological imprisonment.

The Jewish idea of *midrash* is one that most readily comes to mind when trying to convey what Jung was doing. Midrash is the art of reinterpreting truth for new and rising generations which are at odds with conventional expressions of religious truth. Successive generations are in danger of losing touch with their heritage, and midrash was the term for reinterpreting the legacy so it remains contemporary and relevant. Jung wasn't Jewish, but he was a midrashic scholar in this sense, devoting decades of research to the task of digging up the treasure in religious traditions that modernity had rejected. As a young man he wanted to become an archaeologist and, in a sense, he fulfilled that dream in another field, becoming an excavator of the soul. He claimed that myths were too valuable to allow them to die or be disposed of by modernity.

We must "dream the myth onwards and give it a modern dress", he said (1940, § 271). Myth must be taken up in a redemptive spirit and interpreted in new and appropriate ways. Unlike Rudolf Bultmann, whose programme of demythologising led to the abandonment of the symbolic (1941, in Ogden, 1984), Jung believed that demythologising should give way to remythologising. Remythologising is not just pretending that the old myths can live again in the old ways. Remythologising is allowing myths to live again by taking them out of their obsolete contexts and linking them to psychological or spiritual meanings.

Reworking the past

For Jung symbols are permanent and we should not expect to get rid of them or surpass them. But the way they are interpreted will constantly change. The theological monopoly on religious symbols has to be broken, so we might experience them in new ways. All aspects of faith need to be removed from their prescientific dress and translated into terms that can be understood. This involves, above all, drawing attention to the need for a metaphorical reading of scripture and dogmas. The modern mind has to be introduced to a new way of reading, a new "hermeneutics", based on *mythos*. If this modality has been lost by scientific advancement, we should make a special effort to recover it. Jung was not convinced that this re-education would come from religious traditions, since they are mired in the bog of literalism. He believed this would be the momentous contribution of depth psychology or psychoanalysis.

In 1910 Jung had written with excitement to Freud that the true task of psychoanalysis was not to explore the unconscious within a materialist or reductive frame, but to engage in the revival of religion by locating the mystery in the souls of human beings.

> I imagine a far finer and more comprehensive task for psychoanalysis than alliance with an ethical fraternity. I think we must give it time to infiltrate into people from many centres, to revivify among intellectuals a feeling for symbol and myth, ever so gently to transform Christ back into the soothsaying god of the vine, which he was, and in this way absorb those ecstatic instinctual forces of Christianity for the one purpose of making the cult and the sacred myth what they once were—a drunken feast of joy where man regained the ethos and holiness of an animal.

Paul Bishop reads this as Jung's desire to "transform Christ into Dionysus" (2008, p. 40), but in my view this is a misreading. The reference to the god of the vine is a reference to the gospel of John, which was Jung's favourite gospel. Jung was thinking of these words: "I am the vine and you are the branches ..." (John 15:5). The link is not to the Greek god of revelry and intoxication but to the Johannine image of Jesus as the wine-producing god of spirit. Bishop associates Jung with Greek mythology instead of the Christian mythos. It is typical of academics today to privilege the Greco-Roman world above the Hebraic-Christian world. But Jung was anchored in both worlds, not one or the other.

Jung goes on to tell Freud that there is an untapped resource in religion, which he felt was a key to unleashing the passions which psychoanalysis sought to release in the modern person. Jung bemoans the fact that religion had, for inexplicable reasons, turned from its ecstatic impulses towards an all-too-prevalent and boring moralism, and for this reason religion had become a "Misery Institute" (1910). He felt that "infinite rapture and wantonness lie dormant in our religion, waiting to be led back to their true destination" (ibid.).

But the sober and rational Freud was in no mood to play a redemptive role in the return of Christianity. Freud must have been offended by Jung's reference to "our" religion, since Freud was a Jew, albeit a secular one, and in his enthusiasm Jung appears to have overlooked this. Even if Freud were religious, which he was not, he would not have shared Jung's passion for the redemption of Jesus. Freud was of the persuasion that God was dead, and we were better off as a result (1927c). Nor was Jung's enthusiasm for reviving Christianity shared by others in the predominantly Jewish psychoanalytic circle, which served to alienate him from his fellow investigators and precipitate his excommunication from the fold.

Jung's interest in religion made him appear unacceptably conservative to his colleagues, and although his interest in "spirituality" is of interest in our time, in his own day it was seen as eccentric and regressive. Above all, it was seen as unscientific to harbour enthusiasms for discredited systems of belief. Jung was attacked from both sides: the sciences saw him as too religious, and the religious saw him as not religious enough, since they claimed he was "reducing" revelation to "mere" psychology. The charge of *psychologism* was often made against Jung, but it was misguided.

Jung had no intention of reducing religion to psychology, with its explanations for all phenomena. His interest was in linking religion to a new depth psychology that took the unconscious into account. The unconscious for Jung was not merely a Freudian rubbish dump for impulses that had been suppressed. It was a dimension of mind that was surrounded on all sides by mystery, and Jung was so impressed by the spiritual potentials of the *psyche* that he sometimes avoided this clinical term to speak of the *soul*.

The term "soul" had long been discredited by science and philosophy, but Jung took it upon himself to bring it back into scientific discourse, a burden which was almost too great for him to bear, since he drew to himself the same criticism that science had already dished out to the religious ideas of soul and spirit. He was almost a martyr to his cause and his reputation is only now beginning to improve, since the values by which he was attacked are now themselves under attack in a postmodern and post-secular world.[2]

Jung felt Christianity was a great myth, sorely in need of revision and development. He believed myths have to be nurtured and adapted to changing cultural conditions, so they remain relevant and culturally embedded. Without this adaptation the myth would languish and with it the spirit of the people whose lives have been shaped by the mythos. In "Late Thoughts", Jung turned to reflections on Christianity and its critical condition:

> [Humanity] sickens from the lack of a myth commensurate with the situation. The Christian nations have come to a sorry pass; their Christianity slumbers and has neglected to develop its myth further in the course of the centuries. Those who gave expression to the dark stirrings of growth in mythic ideas were refused a hearing …. People … do not realise that a myth is dead if it no longer lives and grows. Our myth has become mute, and gives no answers. The fault lies not in it as it is set down in the Scriptures, but solely in us, who have not developed it further, who, rather, have suppressed any such attempts. The original version of the myth offers ample points of departure and possibilities of development. (1961a, p. 364)

The myth as evident in the scriptures is not at fault; rather, the Christian West is at fault for refusing to develop the myth further. Jung felt that the myth was crying out for the further development of the archetype of the feminine and of the role of evil or what he called the "shadow".[3] In some respects these themes were taken up by alchemy, esotericism, and artists and writers. But the official holders of the myth, the churches, were interested only in suppressing attempts to develop the myth further, and now the Christian West is suffering the price of this suppression. The myth is dying for want of development.

It is dying because the holders of the myth did not realise it was myth. They saw it as absolute revelation, theology, and dogma. They turned it into logos, and deprived the narrative of its mythical ground. The literalisation of the narrative was central to this process. It was uprooted from its ground, and ever since it has been languishing. Church traditions did not realise it was what Jung called a *mythologem*, that is, a myth which needs to be extended and developed over time.

He saw the mythologem as like a vital organ of the body, and if the organ is not exercised, nourished, and replenished, it withers and dies.

It is ironic that those who attempt to preserve Christianity in its literal form, who oppose any creative adaptation or new interpretation that might link it with a new era, are its executioners. They are killing the myth with rationality. The best thing that could be done for religion is to take it away from the theologians and bishops who want to mummify it, and hand it over to poets, visionaries, and philosophers who might breathe new life into it.

The therapeutic function of myth

Jung saw religions as therapeutic systems that help regulate the mental life of the community. When these systems break down the psyche is attacked by nonrational forces which are unable to be controlled. Psychic forces previously held in symbolic containers are "let loose" upon unsuspecting humanity. Such forces, no longer honoured by culture or the individual, turn against the human ego that refuses to honour them. In ancient Greek times, this would have been understood as the vengeance of the defiled Olympian gods. In the Hebrew Bible it would be interpreted as the wrath of an angered Yahweh. We cannot personify it that way anymore, but we can view it in terms of the compensatory functioning of the unconscious: when ignored it rises up in protest. In our time there is no living mythos or religion to placate these forces, and just because we have stopped believing in religion does not mean they suddenly go away.

We live in a secular age that knows nothing about God or gods, and is embarrassed by such archaic discourse. We have lost wisdom and occupy ourselves with knowledge and information. We are unprepared for the assault of psychic forces and our consciousness has no way of understanding what is happening. Hence ours is an age of anxiety and distress, because the deepest parts of the self are not being satisfied. Jung famously said "the gods have become diseases" (1929b, § 54), by which he meant that archetypal forces express themselves negatively in a culture that ignores them. Jung is decisive on this matter: we either cultivate faith consciously or disintegrate under the sway of unruly forces. Christianity is at a loss to understand his argument, since it has an idealised understanding of God as a source of love. How could a God of Love turn against us in this fashion? The Jewish idea that Yahweh can turn against his people has been expunged, making the Christian West even less likely to read the situation correctly. I have written a book on this topic (2011) and will leave it for now.

Spirit requires mythos, and a culture without a mythos has no way of regulating the forces that hold sway in the unconscious. The task of religion is to "link us back" to the mythic domain and placate the forces beyond rationality:

> What is the use of a religion without a *mythos*, since religion means, if anything at all, precisely that function which links us back to the eternal myth? (1952a, § 647)

Religion, he reminds us, derives from the Latin *religio*, to "link back". "This original form of *religio* ('linking back') is the essence, the working basis of all religious life even today, and always will be, whatever future form this life may take" (1940, § 271). What religion links us back to is the sacred, the holy, and that which is beyond awareness:

> Religion is a vital link with psychic processes independent of and beyond consciousness, in the dark hinterland of the psyche. (Ibid., § 261)

We can only know this reality indirectly, through metaphor and symbol. It is not that metaphors try to obscure or distort the real, but they bring out its deeper aspect. As Jung put it: "The archetype does not proceed from physical facts, but describes how the psyche experiences the physical fact" (ibid., § 260). This is why metaphor is indispensable; it describes how the soul experiences a fact. This is the perspective we have lost, which is why metaphors are incorrectly said to hide truth, while historical facts reveal it.

We have confused the nature of the real by trusting too much in logos. It is an overdose of logos that has made us unreceptive to the sacred and its symbolic language. Religion and myth perform the vital function of reconnecting consciousness to its source, to a life independent of itself:

> If this link-up does not take place, a kind of rootless consciousness comes into being no longer oriented to the past, a consciousness which succumbs helplessly to all manner of suggestions and, in practice, is susceptible to psychic epidemics. (Ibid., § 267)

To lose our myths and stories is to lose our well-being. Without them, we become rudderless, lacking purpose and direction. We become strangers to ourselves, and suffer from this alienation. If governments understood how much our health depended on the cultivation of a symbolic life, they might put more emphasis into exploring the connections between mind and body, psyche and society, attitude and well-being.

Mystery without literalism

The best place to discover what Jung had to say about literalism in scripture is his five-page introduction to *Answer to Job*.[4] Perhaps the title of this piece, "Lectori Benevolo", or "To the Kind Reader", is a form of propitiatory magic, because Jung is aware that many of his readers will be far from kind. He opens his introduction to *Job* by admitting that he runs the risk of being "torn to pieces by the two parties who are in mortal conflict about [religion]" (1952a, § 553). He is referring to believers and non-believers. The first take the statements of scripture literally, and the second assume they are illusory. The conflict between them "is due to the strange supposition that a thing is true only if it presents itself as a physical fact". He explains:

> Some people believe it to be physically true that Christ was born as the son of a virgin, while others deny this as a physical impossibility. Everyone can see that there is no logical solution to this conflict and that one would do better not to get involved in such sterile disputes. Both are right and both are wrong. Yet they could easily reach agreement if only they dropped the word "physical." "Physical" is not the only criterion of truth: there are also *psychic* truths which can neither be explained nor proved nor contested in any physical way … Beliefs of this kind are psychic facts which cannot be contested and need no proof. (Ibid., § 553)

He goes on to present his clearest case about the nature of religious truth:

> Religious statements are of this type. They refer without exception to things that cannot be established as physical facts. If they did not do this, they would inevitably fall into the category of the natural sciences. Taken as referring to anything physical, they make no sense whatever, and science would dismiss them as non-experienceable. They would be mere miracles, which are sufficiently

exposed to doubt as it is, and yet they could not demonstrate the reality of the spirit or *meaning* that underlies them, because meaning is something that always demonstrates itself and is experienced on its own merits. (Ibid., § 554)

Our concept of truth is defective if we believe that only physical facts are true. Jung is aware that the typical believer is unable to comprehend this point of view, since the religious institutions have conditioned followers to believe that something is true only if it happened as a fact in time and space. Jung becomes impatient with religious institutions, and asks whether they are generating more ignorance than awareness. If they are not enabling people to enter into the spirit of a critical spirituality, but merely into a credulous or blind faith, Jung doubts that such traditions deserve to continue into the future. He is unsentimental about this possibility, and seals the fate of such traditions by indicating that they are fraudulent. Ironically, then, in a breathtaking reversal of conventional opinion, religions are only true if they declare their mythic nature, and false if they pose as history or fact.

I feel a certain tension in his work as he casts judgement on religion. He wants to slough off its infantile traits, yet he wants to preserve what is good and noble in Christianity. He says that a literal understanding of the miracles is not needed to get the message of the gospels. That message comes through in the moral and spiritual values that are apparent in Christ's ministry. We don't need supernatural acts to demonstrate the worth of his ministry:

> The spirit and meaning of Christ are present and perceptible to us even without the aid of miracles. Miracles appeal only to the understanding of those who cannot perceive the meaning. They are mere substitutes for the not understood reality of the spirit. This is not to say that the living presence of the spirit is not occasionally accompanied by marvellous physical happenings. I only wish to emphasize that these happenings can neither replace nor bring about an understanding of the spirit, which is the one essential thing. (Ibid., § 554)

Regardless of whether miracles are literally true or not, they cannot "bring about an understanding of the spirit". The mere existence of miracles does nothing to change the consciousness of the reader of scripture; it does nothing to bring the believer into a relationship with spirit. It satisfies the primitive human desire for a sign, but that, according to scripture, is unholy and unreliable. In Matthew we are told that "It is an evil and unfaithful generation that asks for a sign!" (Matthew 16:4),[5] and thus the gospels confirm Jung's argument that miracles do not bring a person into a relationship with spirit. Only faith can do that, or what today we might call "intuition". Miracles excite the need in us for supernatural displays, the same kind of delight that we gain when, for instance, looking at acts performed by a stage magician. Yet none of this concerns the reality of the spirit, but merely that part of us that seeks the spectacular.

Jung is at pains to convince his readers that psychic facts are not nothing, and cannot be dispensed with lightly. He knows his argument has to contend with the age-old prejudice about what constitutes "reality", and that is why he keeps trying to approach the reality of the psyche from different angles:

> The fact that religious statements frequently conflict with the observed physical phenomena proves that in contrast to physical perception the spirit is autonomous, and that psychic experience is to a certain extent independent of physical data. The psyche is an autonomous factor, and religious statements are psychic confessions which in the last resort are based on unconscious, i.e., on transcendental, processes. These processes are not accessible to physical perception but demonstrate their existence through the confessions of the psyche. The resultant statements are filtered through the medium of human consciousness: that is to say, they are given visible forms which in their turn are subject to manifold influences from within and without. (1952a, § 555)

The psyche, like spirit, is a "transcendental" factor, and as such there are no ways of accessing the psychic process apart from symbolic images. The metaphors of the psyche are not "invented" arbitrarily by gospel writers or poets, but are impressed on their consciousness by the creative imagination. As Jung says later in this piece:

> Ideas of this kind are never invented, but enter the field of inner perception as finished products, for instance in dreams. They are spontaneous phenomena which are not subject to our will, and

we are therefore justified in ascribing to them a certain autonomy. They are to be regarded not only as objects but as subjects with laws of their own. (Ibid., § 557)

Here Jung seems to be exaggerating to make a point. I don't think religious ideas enter the minds of scripture writers as "finished products" from a cosmic source. Surely those ideas are suggested to such writers by tradition, training, and cultural factors. I doubt such ideas come to writers "finished", as if they were taking divine dictation. But I can't see Jung's argument damaged by suggesting, for instance, that apostles and scribes are inspired by seed-ideas and images, and that such materials have to be worked on and shaped by the conscious mind before they find final expression. To be "inspired by God", or to write the "word of God" need not mean that one is divested of one's human faculties and shaping devices.

Respect for a God unknown

Jung raises an argument about the unknowable nature of God and spirit. He points to one of his central preoccupations in all his writings: whether our metaphorical expressions of the sacred have any bearing on the sacred itself:

> Whenever we speak of religious contents we move in a world of images that point to something ineffable. We do not know how clear or unclear these images, metaphors, and concepts are in respect of their transcendental object. If, for instance, we say "God," we give expression to an image or verbal concept which has undergone many changes in the course of time. We are, however, unable to say with any degree of certainty—unless it be by faith—whether these changes affect only the images and concepts, or the Unspeakable itself. After all, we can imagine God as an eternally flowing current of vital energy that endlessly changes shape just as easily as we can imagine him as an eternally unmoved, unchangeable essence. (Ibid., § 555)

According to Jung, all statements about God are provisional. Despite what religions claim about their own revelations, Jung insists that such revelations are not absolute, and he introduces a note of relativity into all discussions of a religious nature. This is what makes many religious people nervous. He is saying that the so-called Word of God is not definite, beyond challenge, or eternally valid, but that it is simply the "best possible expression of something as yet unknown" (1921, § 817). The consolation for the religious is that it is our best chance at knowing God, but Jung believes it is not our only chance, and nor is it beyond reproach. He is a relativist when it comes to such phenomena; no single revelation is binding but all have relative significance. Jung's relativity does not, however, extend to uncertainty about the existence of God. He assures us:

> There is no doubt that there is something behind these images that transcends consciousness and operates in such a way that the statements do not vary limitlessly and chaotically, but clearly all relate to a few basic principles or archetypes. (1952a, § 555)

This is an important point, lost on his religious critics. He is relativistic only in terms of our knowing, not in terms of the existence of the objects of our knowing. In this way, Jung demonstrates his indebtedness to the philosopher Kant, who was the first to make distinctions between what we can know and the objects to which our knowings point. But these observations point much further back than Kant. Jung derives much of his religious vision from Meister Eckhart, whose late medieval philosophy represents a negative theology (*via negativa*). Eckhart believed we need discourse about God, but must accept and understand that our discourse does not describe the Godhead itself, which remains beyond all human description and cannot be finally or fully known.

Jung is aware that most believers, some of whom would include his readers, are not sophisticated. It is asking a lot of believers to think in terms of a philosophical difference between religious statements and the objects to which they point. He says "The naïve-minded person has never separated [religious symbols] from their unknowable metaphysical background" (ibid., § 558). Such people "instantly equate the image with the transcendental x to which it points" (ibid.). Nietzsche referred to this as "word magic", but the technical term is hypostatisation, treating something conceptual as if it were real. Religious traditions encourage such thinking, because it shores up their status and serves to strengthen the faith of their following. In my experience, however, it only alienates followers, especially those who understand that the relation of signifier to signified is arbitrary at best. As Jung puts it, a religious image "does not posit" the transcendental object to which it points (ibid.). In this regard, he seemed to foreshadow the philosophy of Derrida, who emphasised this same disjunction.

The Assumption of Mary

In *Answer to Job* Jung gives a specific example of his symbolic approach when applied to a dogmatic assertion. The bodily assumption of the Virgin Mary into heaven, or *assumptio mariae*, was proclaimed as dogma by Pope Pius XII in 1950. Jung became excited by this new dogma, as it seemed to him that a developmental process was operating within the church. The masculine religion of Christianity, he felt, was changing into something more complete, and moving towards a more androgynous position. Hitherto Christianity was in danger of being "nothing but a *man's religion*, which allows no metaphysical representation of woman" (ibid., § 753). The dominance of the Father and the Son, he felt, was now being compensated by the rise of the feminine:

> The feminine, like the masculine, demands an equally personal representation. The dogmatizing of the Assumption does not, however, according to the dogmatic view, mean that Mary has attained the status of a goddess, although, as mistress of heaven and mediatrix, she is functioning on a par with Christ, the king and mediator. At any rate her position satisfies the need of the archetype. The new dogma expresses a renewed hope for the fulfilment of that yearning for peace which stirs deep down in the soul, and for a resolution of the threatening tension between the opposites.[6] (Ibid., § 754)

Jung spoke of the dogma as an expression of "divine intervention arising in the collective unconscious" (ibid.), to compensate for the one-sided masculinity of religion. He argued that only Catholic sacramentalism and mystical spirituality could allow Christianity to summon the imagination to connect with the spirit of the time. He applauds Catholicism for having the courage to believe that, "with the assistance of the Holy Ghost, the dogma can progressively develop and unfold" (ibid., § 655). He is delighted that the Catholic church is able to respond to the "popular movement" in which "the visions of Mary have been increasing in number over the last few decades" (ibid., § 748). He wrote:

> The motive and content of the popular movement which contrib-
> uted to the Pope's decision solemnly to declare the new dogma con-
> sist not in the birth of a new god, but in the continuing incarnation
> of God which began with Christ. (Ibid., § 749)

Contrary to Protestant commentators of the day, Jung argued that the dogma of the Assumption was validated by the desire of the Holy Spirit to express itself more fulsomely in a new time. Protestant theologians, as well as "English archbishops", were scandalised by the Vatican's superciliousness and arrogance (Duggan, 1989). It seemed to them that the Vatican was being conceited and self-interested, bowing to public pressure to include a feminine dimension of the divine. To Protestant clergy, the Vatican was inventing a dogma out of thin air, without scrip-tural foundation or precedent.

Although Protestant by birth, Jung often attacked the Protestant position, arguing that it had lost touch with the spirit which makes con-tinuing revelation possible. The aging and cantankerous Jung flew into a rage, pronouncing:

> The failure to understand that God has eternally wanted to
> become man, and for that purpose continually incarnates through
> the Holy Ghost in the temporal sphere, is an alarming symptom
> and can only mean that the Protestant standpoint has lost ground
> by not understanding the signs of the times and by ignoring the
> continued operation of the Holy Ghost. It is obviously out of
> touch with the tremendous archetypal happenings in the psyche
> of the individual and the masses, and with the symbols which
> are intended to compensate the truly apocalyptic world situation
> today. (Ibid., § 749)

This vigorous defence of the Catholic position, however, overlooks a crucial fact. At risk of appearing to offer a crass pun, Jung and Rome are working from different "assumptions". The Vatican views the Assumption literally, and Jung sees it symbolically. Rome's dogma is about a physical miracle, and its constitution states that the Virgin Mary "having completed the course of her earthly life, was assumed body and soul into heavenly glory".[7] Jung does not believe in a physical assumption, any more than any other Protestant of his time. His mind was modern and not prone to superstition. Rome would find his support cynical, undermining, or sacrilegious. To this extent, Jung's championing of the Catholic cause can appear misleading and disingenuous.

Significantly, although he tries to bury it, his conscience cannot allow him to overlook this problem. There is an important footnote, which reads:

> The papal rejection of psychological symbolism may be explained by the fact that the Pope is primarily concerned with the reality of metaphysical happenings. Owing to the undervaluation of the psyche that everywhere prevails, every attempt at adequate psychological understanding is immediately suspected of psychologism. It is understandable that dogma must be protected from this danger. If, in physics, one seeks to explain the nature of light, nobody expects that as a result there will be no light. But in the case of psychology everybody believes that what it explains is explained away. However, I cannot expect that my particular deviationist point of view could be known in any competent quarter. (Ibid., § 749, fn. 2)

Why is this relegated to a footnote when it should be incorporated into his main text? The answer is that Jung is so carried away by his reading of the papal bull that he does not want to detract from it by pointing to its shocking literalism. In the footnote is the sobering voice of reason, which is trying to understand the Assumption in symbolic terms. Jung is part of the Protestant community that he harangues and berates, although in his essay he wants to side with the Catholic cause, since it shows evidence of what he calls dreaming the myth onward. But he is unable to support Catholic literalism and cannot protect the dogma from the doubt of rational thought.

Jung's consciousness is Protestant, despite his sentimental attachment to Catholicism. He is caught in the knot of his complex nature: his soul wants to be Catholic, but his mind remains Protestant and cannot believe what has been pronounced in such a superstitious manner. Later in *Answer to Job* his passion for Rome subsides, and he becomes cool-headed about the dogma and its assertion of a physically impossible fact:

> It does not matter at all that a physically impossible fact is asserted, because all religious assertions are physical impossibilities. If they were not so, they would, as I said earlier, necessarily be treated in the text books of natural science. But religious statements without exception have to do with the reality of the *psyche* and not with the reality of *physis*. (Ibid., § 752)

This heralds the return of the Jung we know: an astute and fierce critic of Christian literalism. His thinking about the reality of the psyche represents an attempt to hold the tension between Catholic soul and Protestant mind. He wants the nourishment of soul and the honesty of clear thinking, and for him these come together in the symbol, something which is spiritually but not literally true. The living symbol represents the synthesis that can unite our ancient hunger for myth and our desire for scientific understanding.

But Jung's thinking, which insists on the psychic but not physical reality of religious assertions, cannot be supported by Protestantism or Catholicism. To that extent his outlook remains "a deviationist point of view", as he says, not able to be incorporated into mainstream religious thinking. The "reality" of the symbol is the key to the future religious consciousness, but due to the "undervaluation of the psyche that everywhere prevails" Christianity is unable to follow Jung's lead.

For all their espoused differences, Catholic and Protestant theologies are expressions of the same Western psyche that has undervalued the symbol, leading the former to hypostatise the symbol as fact, and the latter to freeze the sacred in an historical revelation that has no "mystical" presence in today's world. Catholicism degenerates into sacrosanct unintelligibility, and Protestantism into social work. Jung's suggestion that dogmas are "psychologically true" is cold comfort to religious traditions that have emphasised historical and concrete thinking.

The elevation of the symbolic

To Jung, all the major ideas of religion were part of an archaic mythological system which had to be reinterpreted for a new consciousness. They represented childhood or infantile ways of imagining God.

Not only was the idea of God out of date, but the entire story of Christian faith was mythological and had to be translated into a new language. The virgin birth, the resurrection, the second coming were symbols of the life of the spirit. The time had arrived, Jung believed, for us to take on the enormous task of reinterpreting all religious truths. He wrote in 1952, after the proclamation of the assumption of Mary:

> This is a favourable opportunity for [modern man] to ask himself, for a change, what is the meaning not only of the new dogma [the *Assumptio Mariae*] but of all more or less dogmatic assertions over and above their literal concretism…. He should bend to the great task of reinterpreting all the Christian traditions. If it is a question of truths which are anchored deep in the soul—and no one with the slightest insight can doubt this fact—then the solution of this task must be possible. (Ibid., § 754)

He was performing a deconstructive task similar to that found in post-modern philosophy, decades ahead of schedule. The religious symbols did not point to historical events in time or metaphysical objects in space. They pointed to a different kind of reality, to events in the soul. He was constantly trying to define, and redefine, the meaning of the symbol.

Equally, he reflected on the reality to which the symbols point. In "Psychology and Literature" he said, "The true symbol is an expression for something real but unknown" (1930b, § 148). "What most people overlook or seem unable to understand", he said, "is that I regard the psyche as real." "They seem to believe only in physical facts" (1952a, § 751). "Most people" in the West seemed to have, or suffer from, a constricted view of reality. The symbol can be psychologically and spiritually real, pointing to events that take place repeatedly and eternally in the soul.

> By a "symbol" … I do not mean an allegory pointing to something all too familiar, but the expression of something profoundly alive in the soul. (1930b, § 159)

The assumption is that events "alive in the soul" are taking place all the time. Jung tried to get religious people to understand his view of symbolism. But it is difficult, if not impossible, to convince a religious tradition that has been based on assumptions of "historical fact" that its core elements may not have happened as fact. The gospel writers were poets who were amplifying the meaning of events by supplying images which brought out the deeper dimension of what took place. These images are not illusions, but truths that reveal the depth dimension of events. The error is not in the images, not in the scriptures, but in how we interpret them.

We might see similar category errors in our response to dreams. A person or figure in a dream does not necessarily refer to the person I know in external social reality. It refers to a psychic or internal reality of the mind, and to view the dream as a message or fact about someone in real life is to misconstrue the dream's meaning. For Jung, Christianity has been operating in a childish mode for centuries, and it need not continue in this mode, since it now has the knowledge at its disposal to introduce a new understanding of truth.

The symbol is not just a consolation prize for those who have been disenchanted by the knowledge that dogmatic events are not historical facts. The symbol is itself the royal road to the sacred. It is "the best possible description of a relatively unknown fact" (1921, § 814), "an expression for something that cannot be characterized in any other or better way" (ibid., § 816). Moreover, "Whether a thing is a symbol or not depends on the attitude of the observing consciousness" (ibid., § 818). So here is a conundrum: unless we maintain reverence for the images, they do not transport us to the places to which they point. This is why the loss of literalism can be disastrous for some: when the literal spell is broken, there is nothing left. Images can only function as symbols of transformation if we give them value, if our imaginations allow them to resonate. Many a believer feels let down, deflated, and inclined to go into reverse, claiming that he or she has been duped. Therefore, we have to work with diligence on educating the imagination and restoring sacredness to symbolic images.

Early Christian thought

As an important addendum to this chapter, I now wish to explore the intellectual climate of third century Christianity, before the religion was transported to the West and based in Rome. It is clear that while Christianity remained grounded in the Middle East and Egypt, the faith was regarded as a symbolic system pointing to transcendental realities that cannot be known or accessed directly, but only indirectly through symbol and metaphor. That is, the earliest incarnation of Christianity corresponded entirely with Jung's understanding of religion, which in our time, after centuries of literal thinking and dogmatic theology, has become synonymous with claims to historical/literal understanding.

In his preface to *The Roots of Christian Mysticism*, Jean-Claude Barreau remarks: "Christianity is in the first place an Oriental religion, and it is a mystical religion" (1982, p. 7). Westerners do not have to travel to the Far East to find the mystical dimension that many seek today; it is already present in Christianity, but buried beneath mountains of misreadings and misrepresentations. There is an Eastern, Oriental core to this tradition, and it is the task of future generations to uncover it. We have to admit that we know very little about mystical Christianity, and our current knowledge of its core dimension is hopelessly inadequate.

Return to Alexandria

One way to uncover the true Christianity is to return to Alexandria and the early church before the Roman appropriation of this religion. The early Church Fathers wrote insightfully and profoundly about the mystical content of Christianity (Cattoi, 2018).

In the third century CE, Origen and Clement of the Alexandrian school practised a mythopoetic approach to the scriptures, and drew out the mystical dimension that later generations would ignore or cover up. Origen (184–253) has been hailed as "the greatest genius the early church ever produced". I will focus on his work because he was eloquent on our present theme: "All language that we use, that even Christ could use, of the world beyond the veil, is necessarily mythical, figurative" (McGuckin, 2004, p. 25).

He used the image of the veil in a different sense; not only as the divide between physical and metaphysical, but as applied to biblical language: "Scripture", he says, "contains very many things that are to be spiritually understood, and employs the letter as a kind of veil in treating of profound and mystical subjects" (Origen, "On First Principles", in Kirby, 2019).

Origen distinguished the Bible as it appears to the common reader from how it appears to those who understand its literary and symbolic form. "The mass of men will necessarily accept the symbol for the idea [that it represents], and this will make large numbers 'superstitious'" (Origen, in Crombie, p. 184). Perhaps this might sound too elitist for our taste today, where every street corner preacher believes that the Bible contains common sense and "gospel truth", by which is meant, literal truth. However tactless this might seem today, Origen was simply claiming that to understand the Bible properly involves an understanding of its literary genre, which is not known to those who have not been educated in the art of scripture. Such understanding does not come automatically, but requires tutoring. The egalitarian ethos of popular Christianity would continue to baulk at this call for an educated approach.

Mistaking symbols for realities creates a credulous attitude, where images become idols, or rather, symbols become superstitions. But Origen generously concedes that even taking the symbols and myths at their face value might have some merit: "It is enough if their superstition is such as to lead them in the right direction" (ibid.). Although the Church Fathers recognised there was a hierarchy in the readership of scripture, and simple approaches were not regarded as yielding the deepest meaning, they were sufficiently gracious in their outlook as to award value to superficial approaches. Again, today this sounds patronising, but it may still be true.

Origen held that "Innumerable passages in both Testaments have no sense at all except as allegories" (ibid., p. 175). He posed the question that many want to pose today: If there are passages of the New Testament that "in their literal sense are not true", why are they in scripture at all? To this he replied, emphatically: "Though in one sense untrue, they are in another the highest, the only valuable truth" (p. 176). "The letter is the external garb, often sordid and torn, but the king's daughter is all glorious within" (p. 177).

Origen, a Platonist as well as a Christian, was providing a Platonic defence of the Greek *mythos*, the language of sacred story. In its external sense untrue, mythos nevertheless expresses "the highest, the only valuable truth". This reminds me of a story reported by Robert Johnson, a Jungian writer who had a wonderful gift for making complex subjects appear simple. Apparently an American school teacher asked her class, "What is a myth?" A young boy raised his hand and replied: "A myth is something that is true on the inside, but not true on the outside" (1983, p. 2). In such unerring simplicity, the school boy rediscovered the sophisticated logic of Origen, from 1,700 years ago.

In his interpretation of John, the least historical of the gospels, Origen says that John "contains many statements which are not literally true, but must be read spiritually and mystically" (Origen, "Commentary on John", in Kirby, 2019). This would be violently rejected by fundamentalists today who believe that the Good News is clear, direct, and accessible to all. Origen is arguing that the Bible asks its readers to become initiates of a new level of meaning, the meaning towards which the symbols point. The contents are fingers pointing to the moon; they are not the moon.

In "On First Principles", Origen argues that our wrestling with the implausibility of scripture is a positive stimulus to search for its true meaning:

> The exact reader must search the Scriptures and carefully ascertain in how far the literal meaning is true, and in how far impossible; and so far as he can, trace out, by means of similar statements, the meaning everywhere scattered through Scripture of that which cannot be understood in a literal signification. (Origen, "On First Principles", in Kirby, 2019)

He is arguing that the symbolic mode of scripture is designed to generate a puzzlement that inspires us to go on a journey of reflection.

The important point, according to Origen, is not to discard a scriptural passage that cannot be understood in literal terms: "If the connection taken literally is impossible", this may urge us to discover the true meaning of the story, because "the sense preferred is not impossible." "For with respect to Holy Scripture, our opinion is that the whole of it has a spiritual, but not the whole a bodily meaning, because the bodily meaning is in many places proved to be impossible" (ibid.).

In this way, Origen anticipates the problems of the "rationalising intellect" that Jung speaks about in his warnings to those intellectuals who tend to discard what they fail to understand:

> The really dangerous people are not the great heretics and unbelievers, but the swarm of petty thinkers, the rationalizing intellectuals, who suddenly discover how irrational all religious dogmas are. Anything not understood is given short shrift, and the highest

values of symbolic truth are irretrievably lost. What can a rational-
ist do with the dogma of the Virgin Birth or with Christ's sacrificial
death, or the Trinity? (1912a, § 339)

The mysteries of scripture can too easily be trashed or dismissed by the
"petty thinkers" who cannot deal with the symbolic truths that are out
of their reach.

Origen is critical of the way in which scripture writers create
confusion by presenting spiritual ideas and symbols *as if they were
historical facts*. He comments:

> They tack on to their writing, with language apparently implying
> things of sense, things made manifest to them in a purely intel-
> lectual way. I do not condemn them if they even sometimes dealt
> freely with things which to the eye of history happened differently,
> and changed them so as to subserve the mystical aims they had in
> view. (Origen, "Commentary on John", in Kirby, 2019)

Mythos, in Origen's view, was always the dominant mode of the
gospels.

He argued persuasively that the reason the four gospels cannot be
harmonised is because they were not historically accurate depictions of
Jesus's life in the first place, but mythic interpretations of it. The writers
"proposed to speak the truth where it was possible both materially and
spiritually, and where this was not possible it was their intention to prefer the spiritual to the material. The spiritual truth was often preserved,
as one might say, in the material falsehood" (ibid.). This surely sums
up the problem that many scripture scholars have faced. They search in
vain for the "historical Jesus", in texts which are, according to Origen,
by definition not historically accented.

The claim that scripture contains "material falsehood" is a strong
one that would not have been tolerated after Christianity became the
official religion of the Roman Empire.[8] Anyone who dared to make
such an assertion from about 380 CE onward would have been put to
the stake, but in the mid third century, it was not only tolerated but
condoned. Among Origen's staunch supporters during his lifetime
were Ambrose, Athanasius of Alexandria, Theoctistus of Caesarea, and
Bishop Alexander of Jerusalem. He won international fame as a teacher
and preacher, and was admired for the clarity of his writings.

A stark indication of the differences between this early Christian culture and Christianity under Roman law is evident in the fact that in 543 CE Emperor Justinian condemned Origen as a heretic and ordered all his writings to be burned. As a result, only a tiny fraction of his works have survived. His emphasis on the allegorical or symbolic interpretation of scripture was regarded as offensive to the established church. The Second Council of Constantinople in 553 confirmed Justinian's judgement, and cited Origen's interpretation as unacceptable to a church determined to emphasise the historical inerrancy of scripture.

This excursion into early Christian thought has shown that the Christian Testament, like the Jewish Testament before it, is written in a symbolic language that requires effort to unravel and education to appreciate. As with Jewish writings, *midrash* is required, which means that the text is obscure until we learn to understand its language, and its symbols have to be interpreted anew for each generation. They have no fixed meaning, but point to mysteries that each age will have to discern for itself. The gospel truth, or "good news", can never be simple, but has to be rediscovered and made known to an ever-changing consciousness.

Above all, the supernatural appearances of the Bible give way, when properly understood, to a symbolic language that makes us aware that spirit has to be conceived not as a magical force sent from heavens above, but a natural force present in the deepest core of our reality. In the Middle East, this was basic to the understanding of religion, and thus we can say that to read the Bible literally, and take its symbols as facts, is really a gentile conspiracy begun when it was uprooted from its native ground and appropriated by Rome.

If theologians today find the symbolic method eccentric or against the grain, it is because they have forgotten, suppressed, or lost the mystical roots of their tradition. The West turned a Middle Eastern religion into something more to its liking, because the West favoured a literal interpretation that accorded with its limited sense of truth. Some believers find this approach distressing and unacceptable, seeing it as undermining religion. But reading religious stories as symbols and metaphors restores their dignity as carriers of wisdom. Those who deliteralise are not thanked for their efforts and not understood as engaging in a redemptive task in which religion is saved from a literalism that is destroying it.

In recent times, a new school of mythopoetic thinkers has tried to return our understanding to the thinking of the Alexandrian tradition.

C. G. Jung was my first inspiration in this work of reclaiming the original point of view. After Jung, I was encouraged by anthropologists, literary scholars, and historians such as Northrop Frye, Matthew Arnold, Karen Armstrong, and Joseph Campbell. One of the most insightful explorers of this terrain, banned by his Catholic church as a heretic, is theologian Eugen Drewermann, who wrote:

> The scriptural myths never speak about anything alien or distant from us: ultimately they always deal with our own existence, insofar as it opens itself to the divine. (1994, p. 33)

Religion is about us, or more precisely, the mystery of the spirit in which we dwell and live and have our being. It is not just about special, gifted people of the ancient past who were subject to supernatural forces and an interventionist God. Religion is about the potential for holiness within ourselves and our lived experience, if we can find the symbolic key to unlock the code and enter into the kingdom of spirit. If some people continue to complain that this sounds like a religion for the elite, they are belittling the need for education in our experience of the sacred order. In this regard, we might want to adapt the words of Jesus to Nicodemus, who failed to understand Jesus's teaching: "What, art thou a teacher of Israel, and do not know these things?" (John 3:10).

Endnotes

1. Originally presented as, "Jung, Psyche, Symbol", a talk for The Guild of Pastoral Psychology, Oxford University, Worcester College, UK, August 2016; revised as "Returning Religion to its Symbolic Roots", September 2023.
2. The contemporary relevance of Jung's thought is further discussed in my section, "Jung's psychology and the future", in "General Introduction" of Tacey, ed., *The Jung Reader* (2012, 14ff.).
3. I have written a book on these developments; see Tacey, *The Darkening Spirit: Jung, Spirituality, Religion* (2013).
4. This can be found as chapter 10 in Tacey, ed., *The Jung Reader* (2012, pp. 253–256).
5. *The Holy Bible, The Jerusalem Bible* (Garden City, NY: Doubleday, 1966).
6. Jung, ibid, § 754.

7. Pius XII, in his Apostolic Constitution, 'Munificentissimus Deus: Defining the Dogma of the Assumption', par. 44, Vatican, November 1, 1950. Located at: http://vatican.va/holy_father/pius_xii/apost_constitutions/documents/hf_p-xii_apc_19501101_munificentissimus-deus_en.html

8. This took place in stages: in 313 CE Emperor Constantine accepted Christianity and believers were no longer executed; in 380 CE Emperor Theodosius made Christianity the Empire's state religion.

CHAPTER 10

Spirituality and healing[1]

The fact is that the approach to the numinous is the real therapy.
—Jung (1945b, p. 377)

Wholeness and the holy

Healing occurs in the psyche when the conscious mind makes receptive and respectful contact with the unconscious. Healing occurs when each element of the psyche is encouraged to accept the invitation to become conscious. Healing arises from reconnecting parts that belong together, but have been separated due to personal limitations or environmental and developmental factors. Suffering derives from the experience of brokenness. Healing is synonymous with making whole, or overcoming divisions and rifts in the psyche. When previously warring elements are united, this puts an end to neurosis and the individual can function more proficiently. Increased consciousness broadens the scope of personality, lifts repressions, and allows buried elements of personality to act positively rather than negatively.

Jung's emphasis on wholeness runs counter to the position of James Hillman's archetypal psychology, which has been influenced by postmodernism and proclaims a psychological outlook based on diversity and plurality (1975). In my view, Hillman misreads Jung on this point. Jung is not advocating a wholeness that stifles the many psychic elements and part-personalities. Jung encourages diversity and plurality at every turn, but argues that, paradoxically, we must have a unifying principle that compensates for this plurality, and gathers the parts into a working relationship. Hillman reads Jung's idea of wholeness with jaundiced eyes, and mistakes his unity for uniformity. Hillman argues that Jung's wholeness is moribund, drab, and out of date, whereas his own emphasis on plurality is contemporary and in league with postmodernity. This is one of the many features of Jung's work that is misconstrued by those seeking to create a post-Jungian psychology.

Becoming whole is not only a psychological undertaking, but a spiritual enterprise. It is no accident that "whole" and "holy" not only sound similar but have the same etymological roots. The English word "holy" dates back to the Old English *halig*, deriving from *hal*, which means whole, uninjured, sound, complete. To achieve wholeness is to achieve a degree of holiness. Jung said, "Healing may be called a religious problem" (1932, § 523). Why should this be? Well, contact with the unconscious brings more than we bargained for. In the unconscious there are many elements, not just complexes and traumatic traits but also links to the Self or Atman, the spiritual centre of the psyche. When conscious and unconscious are brought together, so are the profane and the sacred. A third thing is born, the Self, which is greater than the sum of its parts, conscious and unconscious.

But the Self or Atman is not lost or buried like other elements of the unconscious, because it was never conscious in the first place. It is like a sacred centre that only rises to the horizon of possibility as consciousness allows it to ascend from the depths. The Self is like a submerged continent that only comes to the surface when conditions allow it to rise. Note that we have to say, "the Self is like this", or "the Self is like that", because it is a transcendental entity that cannot be known directly or described in precise terms. But as we bring the unconscious into consciousness, up comes more than we thought likely or even possible. This is the mystery of individuation and why I keep saying individuation is not only psychological but spiritual as well. The Self surfaces along with our lost or forgotten parts, and in this way our psychological and spiritual work go hand in hand.

Our connection with the Self can be interrupted by the ego, especially if the ego has become defensive or overly rational in its orientation.

A highly intellectual attitude, and a rigid demand for proof or reason, can kill off the life of the spirit and prevent us from experiencing its healing field. In some ways it is odd for a strongly developed intellect like Jung's to warn us against the dangers of the intellect, but this is what he does. In his view intellectualism is responsible for the proliferation of neuroses, as he writes in "The Soul and Death":

> Anyone who cherishes a rationalistic opinion … has isolated himself psychologically and stands opposed to his own basic human nature. This contains a fundamental truth about all neuroses, for nervous disorders consist primarily in an alienation from one's instincts, a splitting off of consciousness from certain basic facts of the psyche. Hence rationalistic opinions come unexpectedly close to neurotic symptoms. Like these, they consist in distorted thinking, which takes the place of psychologically correct thinking. The latter kind of thinking always retains its connection with the heart, with the depths of the psyche, the tap-root. (1934d, § 808)

The intellect has failed us not only because it is narrow and limited, but because we have relied too heavily on it. It makes a great instrument but a bad master.

Our education system places too much emphasis on intellect, which is unreliable and likely to convince us that God and gods do not exist, that all that exists is what we can see, that rationality can define reality— all toxic and dangerous when it comes to care of the soul. We think of ourselves as clever to have rejected the ancient world of beliefs and superstitions, but when we are landed with a neurosis for throwing out what is essential to the psyche we need to revise our views. No mystery can heal us if we condemn and denounce the mystery.

The numinous and healing

In a remarkable letter to P. W. Martin of London, Jung wrote, in English:

> It always seemed to me as if the real milestones were certain symbolic events characterized by a strong emotional tone. You are quite right, the main interest of my work is not concerned with the treatment of neuroses but rather with the approach to the numinous. But the fact is that the approach to the numinous is the real therapy

and inasmuch as you attain to the numinous experience you are released from the curse of pathology. Even the very disease takes on a numinous character. (1973, p. 377)

Who is P. W. Martin? He is known to us today as the author of the groundbreaking *Experiment in Depth*, a comparative study of Jung, Toynbee, and T. S. Eliot. Jung says in his letter that the real therapy is not the doctor's words or technique, not what he or she knows or what is conveyed to the patient through speech. It is not the medication or prescribed drugs, not chatting about problems, but this more mysterious and subtle factor: contact with the numinous. The numinous is a "field" as I understand it, and it is a field that interacts with us all the time, if we could see. The transference to the analyst is effective only insofar as it conveys a sense of the numinous to the patient, in other words, insofar as it activates the internal healing capacity.

The problem with the theory of the healing power of the numinous is that it is scientifically unproved, invisible, and subtle. Most people don't believe it and science itself cannot understand it. Jung is willing to support it nevertheless, based on his experience as a psychotherapist. He borrowed the term *numinous* from Rudolf Otto, who coined it in 1923: "Omen has given us 'ominous'", says Otto, "and there is no reason why *numen* should not give rise to the word 'numinous'" (1917, p. 7). "Numinous" is widely used today, but few realise its etymological connection with the sacred. The Latin *numen* refers to the nod or might of a deity, and numinous thus refers to the power of an *other* whom one might encounter in intuitive, reflective, or critical moments (see Tacey & Casement, 2006). Otto and Jung believe that the modern person living outside religion, and not only the traditional person living within a religion, can experience the numinous.

Healing is ultimately self-healing, although most of us have no way of knowing it. The "Self" that heals is not the common self, but something more mysterious which is nevertheless part of our interiority. The healing process begins in earnest not when the patient has followed the cues of the analyst, but when the patient has sensed the presence of an *other* at the core of his or her being. The idea of an objective spiritual presence at the core of our subjectivity is new to Western medicine, which tends to externalise the healing process, seeing it as the result of one's encounter with the doctor, or the result of medical interventions.

The inward healing presence is, alas, often absent in Western religions as well, where it is sometimes felt that only the saint or the monastic, and not the everyday person, has access to living spirit. If ordinary people claim this kind of experience they are treated with suspicion, or regarded as witches, blasphemers, or frauds. In the West we have downplayed the healing resources of the body-mind-spirit, which is why so many of us are at the mercy of the external forces of medicine.

Let me say that we are not talking about miraculous cures through the spirit. Such might happen, but if they do occur, it is due to the workings of the divine, and not due to our asking for it. On this point, I have argued with colleagues in the healing profession, including psychiatrists interested in spirituality, who seem more concerned with cure than healing. But I am otherwise inclined: to me, healing is more important, and by healing I mean a reconciliation within a person to the suffering that has befallen him or her, not necessarily a getting rid of the symptoms. Healing may lead to cure, but it may not. If the illness is still confined to the mental domain, there is more chance of a cure through contact with the numinous. However, if a neurosis has been somatised, there could be less chance of a recovery, since once the body has somatised the illness, working with it through the mind or spirit might be less effective.

But how does this work? How does contact with the numinous bring about healing? In this regard, I work with my intuition. I am interested in metaphor and its powerful effects. I like the metaphor that has emerged over the last hundred years from theoretical physics, about waves and particles, and I would like to apply this metaphor to healing and recovery from illness. In physics and chemistry this is called *wave-particle duality*. To apply this metaphor to healing through the numinous is something I have developed over years, inspired by Jung's notion that the ego moves like a ship on an unseen, unknown ocean.

The wave-particle paradox

Many of us imagine the human self to be a discrete entity, solid and known. But this could be an illusion of our making, albeit a useful illusion, that allows us to act efficiently in the world. Researchers of the unconscious have found that the self has no definite boundaries, and that at its inner depths it trails off into mystery and the unknown.

To borrow the metaphor from physics, what we had previously thought of as a solid entity may turn out to be a wave of infinite extension.

Quantum physics discovered that the smallest elements of matter behave in one moment as particles and in another as waves. As particles, they are discrete and separate, and can be "split" to release energy, as in the atomic explosion. As waves, they behave less like bits of matter and more like bands of light or energy, reaching out to eternity. They cannot be confined or boxed in, but participate in an ocean of being.

This suggests a certain paradoxical instability at the heart of matter. Matter looks stable to the common eye, but from the perspective of microphysics, the world is fluid, uncertain, and even bizarrely so. Einstein argued that all particles have a wave nature, and vice versa. Heisenberg, Max Planck, and others refined and changed the theory. Needless to say, this discovery shattered the prevailing views of Newtonian physics, and its ramifications are still being felt today. As Brian Greene put it in *The Elegant Universe*, "Matter has been dematerialized" (1999, p. 104).

What has happened in physics has occurred in the parallel movement of Jung's analytical psychology. This is more than coincidence, because while he was a Swiss citizen and based in Zurich, Albert Einstein befriended Jung and they had many discussions about the nature of reality (Cambray, 2009). Apparently they went down to Bollingen with bottles of red wine and enjoyed many such discussions. Einstein was discovering relativity in physics and Jung was discovering it in psychology. Like matter, the self is only relatively stable. At its depths, it can lose its solid formation and appear as a wave or a fluid process. The notion of applying the *wave-particle duality* to psychology is mine, not Jung's, but I think the metaphor holds if we think in terms of the healing experience of the numinous. As with the concept of matter in physics, I think we live simultaneously as waves and particles as psychological beings.

As particles, we are distinct, physical, and discrete, each with our own personality and make-up. As waves, we are not so individual. We are similar to each other at this level, and participate in the cosmos in pre-determined ways. As waves, we are spiritual beings, fluid, open-ended, and connected to other waves. We are especially receptive to archetypal currents that course through us, which Jung identified as universal and collective. In his terms, the particle is the ego or conscious self, and the wave is the infinite expanse of the unconscious. In "The Meaning of

Psychology for Modern Man" (1934c), Jung compared the ego to a vessel on an expansive ocean: "Despite our individual consciousness the psyche unquestionably continues to exist as the collective unconscious, the sea upon which the ego rides like a ship" (1934c, § 285).

In another essay, Jung says, "The suprapersonal or collective unconscious is like an all-pervasive, omnipresent, omniscient spirit." It represents "an extension of man beyond himself; it means death for his personal being and rebirth in a new dimension as literally enacted in certain of the ancient mysteries" (1918, § 13). Establishing a wave-like connection is what we today call *spirituality*, namely, the capacity to feel connected to the cosmos and the entirety of life, giving rise to psychological rebirth.

The healing effect of waves

My contention is that as we experience ourselves as waves, this has a healing effect on consciousness. When this connection is restored, we overcome ego-bound existence and anxiety, and feel ourselves to be part of a larger whole. The ego's concerns and worries are dropped and we feel renewed. It is burdensome to be confined to the ego and its limited world. As Freud correctly observed, the ego is the *seat of anxiety*, and when we move outside the ego our anxiety—which is productive of disease and neurosis—falls away.

It seems that we are not designed to dwell all our lives in the ego and its limited world. This has long been known to human wisdom, which is why ritual and liturgy played such a huge role in people's lives in the past. The task of ritual and liturgy is to lead us out from the ego to embrace the larger realities that encompass and transcend it. Today we are more likely to seek out this experience of transcendence in a variety of secular ways, including music, drugs, sexuality, relationship, contact with nature, and awe and wonder.

There is a core dimension in us that is not about material causation and mechanics, but about the cosmos at large. I do not see this point of view as "romantic" or far-fetched, but realistic. There is a hidden dimension of our lives that is real and needs attention, especially in times of illness and despair. From a spiritual point of view, mental illness might be described as alienation from our source. Religions have long known this, and that is why the core rituals of religions are about *communion*, that is, binding back to the divine.

But in a non-religious time, we still need to have the experience of communion, which restores the soul and vivifies the spirit. When we transcend ego boundaries in rituals, psychotherapy, art, or meditation we return to the ocean of being and are restored. Jung felt that our meddling intellect gets in the way of our need for experiences of transcendence. We deny ourselves this release, and sometimes even feel embarrassed if we discover our need for such experiences. Our embarrassment derives from our identification with the encapsulated ego, and denial of the waves that undergird the ego, our little ship.

The tranquillity that we experience as we walk beside the ocean, or the calm that descends as we look across a landscape, or move through a ferny gully, is related to the experience of the particle returning to the wave. The therapeutic effect of music or dance, which takes us outside the ego into "waves" of sound and movement, is expressive of the joy experienced as we enter the wave. The word *ecstasy*, from the Greek *ek-stasis*, meaning to be "outside the self", points to the pleasurable experience of transcendence. The wave-like effect is what all religions seek in their rituals.

It is possible to see the relation between particle and wave in the experiences of the devotees of Dionysus. In many ways, Dionysus is the god who invites us to return to the source and immerse ourselves in the ocean of being. As Zurich analyst Verena Kast writes of the Dionysian festivals of ancient Greece:

> Those seized by Dionysus broke out of the conventional order to become part of a cosmic order; human beings became one with nature, social rank was obliterated, rivalries ceased. Torn out of their isolation, individuals experienced prophecy and a momentary connection with the transpersonal Self. (1991, p. 6)

In these ancient festivals, the ego personality was momentarily eclipsed by a different order of being, or as Kast puts it: "The devotees of the god experienced the Self through momentary forgetfulness of self" (ibid., p. 6). The Dionysian spirit is ecstatic and brings release from the burden of egoism.

In liturgy, prayer, and ceremony, the isolated self is eclipsed and we participate in a relationship with forces beyond ourselves. Religions build communities in ways that secular society never can, because they reach beyond the façade of individuality and draw from the depths our longing to connect to our "home", as Wordsworth called it. But it is hard to find our way home in a secular society, which has no respect for our spiritual needs, and can only offer us religious substitutes, addictions, food, or drugs to satisfy our craving.

The struggle to reach the waves

There is little doubt that, with the absence of formal pathways of transcendence, a major way to spiritual experience is suffering. This is the typically modern way to move beyond the ego. Suffering is the enforced way to break open the ego and move into the waves. If we cannot return to God through the cultural doorway of *mythos*, there is only the path through *pathos*. With culture committed to the ego rather than spirit, nature gets its revenge. Mental suffering is often the trigger to a religious conversion or a spiritual point of view.

When life proceeds normally, and the task of social adjustment is successful, there may never arise the need or opportunity to find a relationship to a spiritual core. But when the normal self has been ruptured, the only option, apart from running to others for help, is to seek reunion with the wave-like dimension at our core. By so doing, we turn to what is most profound in ourselves, and ask it, implore it, to close our wounds and grant us life.

This is why many recovery programmes, and methods of dealing with addictions, alcoholism, drug dependence, eating disorders, depression, and anxiety, as well as techniques to deal with grief and trauma, find themselves moving into the spiritual domain, of which the AA movement is paradigmatic (Morgan & Jordan, 1999). Our society produces, and encourages, the myth of the atomised, discrete, self-sufficient, and autonomous ego, and that is the source of illness in our world. The socially adapted and healthy ego is not interested in humbling itself before the divine. It thinks of this as something antiquated, even perverse. It does not make sense from the ego's point of view. Alas, that is why the ego must suffer, because it cannot come to the sacred any other way.

In normal life, and in going about our business, we live a "particle" existence. We behave like separate and autonomous entities, each concerned with his or her own self-interest or a small family group. Beyond these narrow circles, there is no interest in the cosmos at large or with God as an agent in our lives. But as waves, we seek connection to that which is beyond the ego. We extend beyond the particular, breaking its boundaries, and reach out for eternity and the stars.

Thomas Berry wrote that ecological healing occurs when the world is no longer experienced as a collection of objects, but a communion of subjects (1988, p. 2). This is the formula that underpins the creation of community and it is the formula at the heart of the ecological vision. This is also the formula for psychological healing. Healing occurs when we no longer experience ourselves as isolated particles in a world of objects, but when we experience ourselves as waves merging and interacting with other subjects.

I have never attended rave parties or trance dances, but I imagine that this is the allure of such activities. The jailhouse of the ego needs to be opened now and then. The self may not realise its true nature, which releases bliss, until it experiences itself in relation to a larger subject. The self "comes home" to itself when it glimpses the *other* who is its origin. Longing is fulfilled when we recover our belonging.

Security in the mystery

Spirituality works towards healing by engendering a sense of security. The world of the ego, our atomised existence, is buffeted by the forces of change and subject to vulnerability and contingency. The particle self lives in the cycle of birth-death-rebirth, in the midst of coming to be and passing away. Our wave-like existence does not participate in this world, and exists as it were in the realm of the unborn, the realm prior to manifestation. When we contact our wave-like reality we feel detached from the tragedy of life and removed from the vulnerabilities that bring insecurity and anxiety. The particle self may try to find its security in the incarnate realm, by creating allegiances, traditions, networks, insurances, loyalties, plans, and constitutions. But the world of manifestation is inherently unreliable and the things of this world do not assuage our need for a deeper spiritual security.

This is why the great spiritual teachings of all times have advised us not to look for security in the changing world. Rather, we are encouraged to look beyond the world (Christ) or beyond the normal categories of thought (Buddha), to find our true belonging and stable ground. Buddha insists that to attempt to find happiness in the normal world is self-defeating and a category error. We must, he said, work with diligence on our enlightenment, because happiness can only be found once we have broken through the attachments of this world and discovered a connection to the eternal mind. Christ said his kingdom is "not of this world", and urged those who would be influenced by his teachings to direct their attentions to the eternal, not the temporal. "Do not store up for yourselves treasures on earth, where moth and rust destroy them, and where thieves break in and steal" (Matthew 6: 19). The Christian West did not to take his advice, but decided to live primarily on the material level and seek satisfaction at this plane.

The deep security of the spiritual traditions is difficult to attain and involves effort and dedication. It involves the cultivation of trust, spiritual confidence, and faith, an ability to let go of the ego and its anxieties and allow oneself to be embraced and held by a mystery. In Buddhism, the mystery is the supreme consciousness and eternal mind, and in Judaeo-Christianity it is God the father, to whom one hands over one's life, as well as one's troubles and anxieties. All stress and tension are buried in the unfathomable depths of God, and this enables the ego to live free from debilitating stress or incapacitating anxiety. The existential writings of Søren Kirkegaard are especially illuminating on this point.

To experience the healing power of spirituality, the individual has to "fall in love" with the mysterious Other. In religious language, we need to experience a conversion. The psyche realises its depth when it sees that an Other loves it. In the same way that the newborn infant realises his or her identity in the arms of a loving parent, the psyche realises its spiritual, wave-like potential only when it is drawn towards a loving spiritual reality that is perceived as larger than itself. Without the sense that love comes from the Other, I doubt that the soul could summon the confidence and trust to embark on the spiritual journey, or take the leap of faith into reality. In this sense, the soul is by definition incomplete, and striving for a new wholeness or integration is written into its constitution. It finds its completion on recognising its at-one-ment with its creator. As Augustine wrote, in the words immortalised by Johann Sebastian Bach, "Our hearts are ever restless, until they find their rest in thee" (c. 398: 346).

The oceanic feeling

We are emerging from an historical period in which our search for connection to the wave-like dimension has been represented as pathological or deluded. Modern society has invited us to seek security in the material world and this has amounted to a shift in the direction of civilisation. We seek material security, but we do not find it and cannot find it, since the search is self-defeating. But the longing for real—that is, spiritual—security is innate and this search continues despite the contrary impulses of society. Without true security we fall prey to nervous disorders, obsessions, and desires. It seems that if we fail to care for the needs of the soul, we pay a price at individual and collective levels.

Freud wrote about the wave-like experience in negative terms. He called it the "oceanic feeling", but with a sneer. Unlike Jung, he feared the waves and saw them as tempestuous and dangerous. It is fascinating that Freud wrote his 1914 polemical tirade against Jung under the Latin epigraph, *fluctuat nec mergitur*, "tossed by waves, it does not sink" (1914d, p. 7). For him, only the particle is the true identity and place of stability. The wave in Freud's polemic is associated with Jung, and is constructed as the hostile opponent of the heroic particle. The Freudian particle has to bravely strive against the destructive Jungian wave to survive.

Freud was opposed to all forms of spirituality, referring to them as illusory and escapist. In his book *The Future of an Illusion*, he attempted to discredit all religion, reducing it to mere wish fulfilment (1927c). But his mystical friend, Romain Rolland, a Nobel Prize winning author who had studied in the East, protested at Freud's treatment of religion, claiming that he had not understood the true source of religious sentiment, which was a "sensation of eternity", or "oceanic feeling". Rolland refuted Freud's reduction of religion to wish fulfilment, arguing that the "oceanic feeling" was enjoyed and sought after by "millions of people" around the world. Freud responded saying he had no personal connection to an "oceanic feeling"; he had not experienced it at all. He was far more respectful and polite towards the mystical Rolland than he was to the mystical Jung. Perhaps Rolland mattered less, so he could afford to be more magnanimous.

Due to his respect for Rolland, Freud decided to investigate the sensation of eternity, and made some connections with it in *Civilization and Its Discontents* (1930a, p. 64). He described the solidity and seeming permanence of the ego in the average person. Then he explored the idea that the child starts out in an oceanic state, a sea of sensation and emotion with no boundaries. Children cannot tell themselves from their mother, or any other outside object. The development of the ego over time can be seen as the sharpening and clarifying of boundaries and limits. The task of the adult is to keep those boundaries intact, and not fall into the state of what Rolland called "something limitless, unbounded". Freud conceded that "there is only one state" in which the loosening of ego boundaries cannot be "stigmatized as pathological", and that is the state of love:

> At the height of being in love the boundary between ego and object threatens to melt away. Against all the evidence of his senses, a man who is in love declares that "I" and "you" are one, and is prepared to behave as if it were a fact. (Ibid., p. 66)

Apart from this exception, Freud believed the oceanic feeling was negative for ego development, and characterised the feeling that neurotic patients experience in states of regression. Freud distrusted the wave-like dimension of the psyche, and saw our longing for it as a symptom of our desire for incest, for returning to the womb. In the regressed state, we huddle in the womb like an embryo, buoyed up by waves of amniotic fluid. He felt we should aim at all times to "maintain clear and sharp lines of demarcation" and identify ourselves with our solid and separate egos. Interest in the oceanic state was suspect and all concern with altered states of consciousness was treated with disapproval by the pioneer of psychoanalysis.

Swimming or drowning

Freud believed that in states of mental disorder, the suffering person can be lost to the world of form and definition, and dropped into a chaos of undifferentiated life. "Pathology has made us acquainted with a great number of states in which the boundary lines between the ego and the external world become uncertain or in which they are actually drawn incorrectly" (ibid., p. 66). This is why psychotic patients report that they are often "at sea" and cannot distinguish the outlines of objects, such as chairs or tables, because their perception is blurred, and everything appears to be in a swirling chaos. Psychosis plunges us into an oceanic void which precedes form, where everything is intermixed with everything else, and nothing can be perceived as separate from the chaotic stream.

Jung would call this the descent into the underworld, or the *nekyia* into the teeming life of the collective unconscious. This is clearly not a state of cosmic consciousness, although it does share with spiritual experience the overriding sense that "all things are one", that every-thing is connected and nothing is separate. However, in psychosis this is far from a pleasant or elevating experience. It is deeply destructive and the ego seems to drown in the ocean of being, and is not swept along blissfully by its current, as in the states of transcendental meditation or spiritual rebirth described by the Indian sages.

This is a vital point of difference that we need to make clear. What the mystic or guru experiences as a state of bliss can be experienced by the psychotic as a nightmare of disintegration. The waves of preconscious existence can be destructive, like a tsunami or tidal wave, but they can also bring healing if we relate to them in the right way. The ocean of being is the same ocean in madness as it is in transcendence, but the difference between awakening and psychosis depends on the nature of the consciousness that encounters it. Here we might refer to a relevant passage in Campbell's *Myths to Live By*:

> The difference [between the mystic and the schizophrenic] is equiv-alent to that between a diver who can swim and one who cannot. The mystic, endowed with native talents for this sort of thing and following, stage by stage, the instructions of a master, enters the waters and finds he can swim; whereas the schizophrenic, unpre-pared, unguided, and ungifted, has fallen or has intentionally plunged, and is drowning. Can he be saved? If a line is thrown to him, will he grab it? ... What I am saying is that our schizophrenic patient is actually experiencing inadvertently that same beatific ocean deep within that the yogi and saint are ever striving to enjoy; except that, whereas they are swimming in it, he is drowning. (1972, pp. 215–216, 226)

Joseph Campbell was basing his observations on Jung's research, although he does not always acknowledge his sources. Jung begins his chapter on the Self in *Aion* with a series of warnings. If the ego "lacks any critical approach to the unconscious ... it is easily overpowered and becomes identical with the contents that have been assimilated" (1951, § 23). He says it is a "psychic catastrophe when the ego is assimi-lated by the self" (ibid., § 24). Jung insists that the ego must find a "right relation" to the unconscious, and this involves, first of all, the ego pre-serving its integrity in face of the ocean of being that constitutes the collective unconscious.

If the ego is not properly formed, if it has been damaged by trauma, or eclipsed by devastating inner or outer experiences, it is not in a fit state to make contact with the ocean of being. When the ocean comes towards it, the ego will drown, because it needs to hold its integrity before the onslaught of the unconscious. If it can't hold its integrity, it is lost in the water, and becomes a subhuman fish swimming in the sea, or more fatally, dissolves in the ocean like an aspirin dropped in a tumbler of water. In states of psychotic depression or anxiety, dreams will indicate that the ego has been submerged under a wave, or lost to some distant galaxy or star. The metaphors will constantly change, but the message will be the same: an eternal force has obliterated the temporal personality. This becomes problematical if the sufferer is a follower of a cult or creed which views such self-obliteration as a spiritual achievement.

Classic symptoms of psychic dissolution are inflation, depression, paranoia, mania, catatonia, and bipolar disorder. In each of these states, the ego has been eclipsed and replaced by archetypal contents that substitute for the personality. In severe cases of psychosis, this involves identifying oneself with an archetypal power or figure, in which the person claims to be Jesus, Caesar, or Napoleon. Whatever the chosen figure, it is apparent that the ego has been annulled by the unconscious, which has wiped out the human element and replaced it with a primordial content that exerts a destructive impact.

Pathological spirituality

The negative effects of the ocean are not only found in psychotics who have entered into dangerous states. Some risk-taking adventurers in search of mystical experiences can end up with the same disorders, as can those who engage in recreational drugs or binge drinking, or who experiment with hallucinogenics and altered states of consciousness. They can find themselves in deep water and unable to survive. There are people who misread Buddhism, Jung, Vedanta, the Upanishads, and Christian or Jewish mystical writings, and adopt a foolhardy attitude in their quest for a spiritual journey. They do not appear to be deliberately misreading these writings; rather, under the influence of a powerful complex, the misreading is involuntary and unintentional.

They misread spiritual writings with a view to extinguishing their ego in the unconscious, rather than adopting a responsible attitude.

They say their goal is enlightenment or wholeness, but interpret this to mean loss of ego in the ocean of being. Typically, this is a Western misreading of Eastern spiritual goals. Such people are on a path of regression, and in this sense Freud was right to suspect mental illness at the core of some attempts at spiritual experience. Where Freud went wrong was in universalising this tendency, and refusing to see that some spiritual experience is authentic. Obviously, discernment is needed to tell the difference between pathological and authentic spirituality.

Today, with much ignorance and sentimentality attached to the spiritual domain, it is relatively easy to pass off pathology as spirituality. This is one reason why, in previous times, religious traditions insisted that every spiritual journey should be monitored by a director, who might be able to save us from the possibility of delusion or regression. But in the deregulated arena of today's experience, everyone considers him- or herself a master of the Way, and many do not submit to genuine teachers, who admittedly, are hard to find. Instead, those who are hopelessly lost in the spiritual arena are themselves likely to pose as teachers, which gives a bad name to spirituality in society.

We can easily confuse a mental disorder with an experience of the spirit. Some claim to be tired of living as egos, and are impelled towards a new or bigger life. Where they go wrong is in assuming that the ego can be thrown aside, and a new self taken on, like a new garment. If the ego is ditched in this way, they do not become wise, mystical, or spiritual, but rather monsters of egotism and madness, as many stories of the lives of recent gurus attest. If the ego is not brought into a conscious relation to the archetypal figures, it is replaced by them, and this causes inflation, arrogance, and megalomania. Strictly speaking, it is not their ego that has become huge, but an archetypal figure that has seized control. The ego has been annulled, and it is the archetypal personality which gives the impression of "egotism" by virtue of its arrogant display.

In therapy—if they seek it, and don't assume that they are wiser than the therapist—such people need to be returned to their ordinary personality, which some might see as boring and not "spiritual" enough. Analysts can have trouble with such clients, who might consider the analyst's attempt to ground them as an attack on their spiritual nature. They might see therapy as a form of brainwashing, a way of forcing adaptation to social norms. But therapy will show that the ego is smashed up in the unconscious, despite the fact that some around them complain of their "egotism".

Such victims might claim they have sacrificed their ego for the sake of a higher life in the Self. They have flung themselves into the unconscious and relied on the Self or Atman to save them. However, the Self is not always able to save. What we encounter first in the unconscious are wild and primordial forces, aptly represented in myths and legends as dragons, monsters, and demons. The Self may only come into being once the ego and the unconscious have interacted with each other and a dialogue has been established. The popular myth of the all-saving Atman can be destructive if people imagine they can abandon themselves to the unconscious without having to do any work to achieve psychic balance. We need a healthy respect for the unconscious and its ability to devastate. If we don't have this respect, we are devoured by the archetypes and forced to lead a less than human life. There is a great difference between psychic disintegration and individuation.

The balance between particle and wave

When I was a university student in the 1970s, many young people in my peer group were experimenting with their receptivity to the wave, which in those days was called "cosmic consciousness". However, it occurred to me on more than one occasion that a more appropriate term might be cosmic *unconsciousness*. Often the wave they tried to ride was their last. One thing I noticed was a tendency towards dangerous or unhealthy relations with the "cosmos". The notion that one can trust the wave and give in to its healing powers has to be compensated for by a dose of reality.

The "soft" idea of letting go and surrendering to the other has to be balanced by the "hard" idea of making sure the ego is in a fit state to let go, or that others are around to provide backup and support. The ego can only give itself over to the unconscious if it has the right attitude, and if it does not secretly wish to destroy itself. I saw several friends destroy themselves by drugs, meditation, and sexual excess. It seemed that they harboured a death wish, although they said they were hungering for the embrace of the cosmos. I was not convinced, and had read enough Freud to make me aware that the death wish can operate in an autonomous way, and may disguise itself as a desire for altered states.

According to Freud, everyone harbours a death wish, and we have to be careful how this might manifest. If the ocean proves destructive it may not be the fault of the ocean, as it were. We have to face the destructiveness of our nature, and ask whether we went to the ocean in the first place to drown ourselves. Today there is a popular hatred of the ego, partly as a response to society's obsession with the ego. Too many of us are prepared to give the ego away at a moment's notice, to sacrifice it for a higher cause. It is as if, below our egotism, there is a repulsion towards the ego and a desire to see it smashed. We have to monitor this in ourselves, and make sure this anarchic streak is not what we are calling "spirituality".

The psychologist Ken Wilber has explored the differences between spirituality and self-destruction in *Up from Eden* (1986) and *The Atman Project* (1980). Wilber points out that a negative attachment to the unconscious can disguise itself as spiritual experience, and we are seeing borderline personality disorders misrepresented as mystical conditions in which the ego is supposedly "transcended". Wilber argues that spirituality cannot be allowed to stand in for, or take the place of, psychological development. Spirituality is about adjustment to the needs of the spirit, and the normalising project is about adjustment to society. Both are important.

Wilber points out that it is typical for some of us, especially those dazzled by New Age ideas, to confuse failed development of the ego with transcendence. The higher and lower levels of development have a feature in common: in both, the *nonegoic* is the dominant element. In the authentic spiritual state, the ego is transcended by a higher order of integration, in which the ego learns to serve and nurture the entire personality. However, in the case of pathology, the ego has not been fully "born" into the world. Wilber's thesis is that we are often unable to tell the difference between spiritual development and infantile regression, and to the inexperienced eye the transcendence of ego and the pre-egoic condition look the same. Wilber calls this the "Pre/Trans Fallacy", by which he means we confuse the pre-rational with the trans-rational (1980, p. 58). Many cannot tell them apart, which is why a pathological person can parade as a spiritual guru and get away with it. But those of us who despise the ego have to be made aware that it has an important role to play and needs to be treated with respect.

Finding a right relation to the unconscious is finding the middle path. On the one hand, the normal ego is inclined to deny the reality of the ocean—what ocean, I don't see one? This leads to debunking positions such as rationalism, cynicism, intellectualism, scientism, all of which are attempts to convince oneself that the unconscious does not exist. On the other hand, we must avoid drowning in the ocean due to an ostensible love of the cosmos. This leads to false humility, depression, melancholia, catatonia, and bipolar disorder. The corollary of this is where the ego attempts to swallow the ocean in an act of assimilation. This leads to hubris, triumphalism, identification with archetypal figures, inflation, and mania. A right relation to the ocean can be found when we respect the otherness of the ocean and the integrity of the ego, and attempt to get them into dialogue. This dialogue is what many experience symbolically as they engage in surfing, bodyboarding, and other water sports.

We have to learn to live with the ocean, and not allow it to overwhelm us. If we learn to attune ourselves to the waves, we can allow ourselves experiences of unity, and these can have positive effects on our state of mind, nervous system, immune system, and mental condition. The numinous can heal the body and psyche, but we have to enable this to happen. By experiencing the more-than-human, we are released from our ego-bound state, and returned to a deeper sense of humanity. Ironically it is contact with the non-human, the beyond, that makes us human, and allows us to be restored so we can live another day and meet the challenges before us. For its part, the wave does not set about to extinguish the particle. The gods do not set out to destroy their creations. Eternity has a need for the particle, because without it it has no way of entering time or incarnating into reality.

Endnote

1. A much earlier version of this paper appeared as "Spirituality and Healing" in *Ata: Journal of Psychotherapy Aotearoa New Zealand*, 20(1), 2016: 19–33. The article is based on an invited keynote speech given to the Annual Conference of the New Zealand Association of Psychotherapy, held in Napier, April 20–23, 2016.

CHAPTER 11

Towards a future religion[1]

J ung is a fierce critic of mainstream religion, but he was always alert to the possibility of a future religion that might replace it. He sensed that another religion was on the rise, but it was still too early to determine what this religion would look like. He argued that psychologists have a moral obligation to be mindful of religion. In his essay on the dogma of the trinity he wrote:

> In proposing to approach the central symbols of Christianity, I realize that I am trespassing on territory that must seem very far removed from psychology. Everything to do with religion, everything it is and asserts, touches the human soul so closely that psychology least of all can afford to overlook it. (1942a, § 172)

We live in a time in which traditional religion is in rapid and irreversible decline. Ours is a time in which personal spirituality is rising as rapidly as religion is declining. Arguably, Jung gave impetus to this cultural shift with his emphasis on the resacralisation of the individual and the spiritual renewal of patients.

The shift of focus to religion

At first the spirituality of whole societies, which is what religion is, did not interest him, as it fell outside his clinical interests. But as Jung grew older, he became just as interested in religion as he was in personal experience of the divine or the numinous. This is because Jung began to realise the limitations of personal spirituality; while it might renew the individual, it would not renew society or the larger community.

He began to realise that the spiritual renewal of the whole of society was more vital than the resacralisation of the individual. This shift of interest to the whole of society is evident in all his last works, including *Man and His Symbols*, *The Undiscovered Self*, and *Memories, Dreams, Reflections*. He made this shift for several reasons. We are not separate individuals but each of us forms a unit in the fabric of society as a whole. If only the individual found renewal but not society, there is every possibility that human society might falter and collapse, unless a common thread of spirit or commitment was woven into its fabric.

When there is no bulwark against evil, society stands vulnerable and exposed. Moreover, it is hard to imagine that individual spirituality could be passed on to others and thus it could not inform the institutions that educate young people and help them grow into responsible citizens. Although not a sociologist, Jung developed a deep conscience about society as a whole, and about the need for society to work towards a common vision or shared meaning that could be passed on to young and future generations.

After a duration of 2,000 years, the Christian religion could no longer provide a satisfactory platform for shaping, educating, and humanising the rising generations. In particular, it seemed to be incapable of controlling the outbreak of evil in human nature, and had nothing to say to the darkness that had accumulated in the psyche and exploded in catastrophic world wars. It was ridiculous to declare evil a sin and hope it would go away. Jung regarded this as a form of magical thinking. The Lord's prayer that asked God to "protect us from evil" was ineffectual and had done nothing to stem the tide of evil in psyche or society.

The problem with Christianity, said Jung, was that it had "no imagination for evil", apart from clichés about Satan and the Devil lurking in the world. Modern people had long realised that Satan and Devil did not exist, but what did exist was the evil which these figures personified in an archaic mythological system. As a psychologist, Jung was interested in finding ways to release and expose this evil in human experience. He advocated a homeopathic approach: use some evil to banish major evil. The Christian ban against evil allowed it to proliferate and intensify, due to its secret life in the unconscious. Banishing evil makes it worse, now that we know about the reality of the unconscious, and what happens to repressed contents. Evil is a propensity of the personality and requires serious acknowledgement. The Christian moral outlook is too narrow to allow evil to be expressed, and the repression of evil adds fuel to the fire. This morality is harmful and a new ethic is needed to integrate the reality of evil.

Jung also argued that evil was not confined to the human realm, but that the evil once expressed in Satan and Devil was a split off, dissociated component of God's nature. This shocked the Christian world so much that even those theologians who had formerly been supportive of Jung and his findings were quick to withdraw their support and declare him mad. Jung sympathised with the view of the alchemists and gnostics, who recognised the presence of evil in the divine nature. He had also seriously considered the theology of Hinduism, and felt, along with the Hindus, that God had a complex ambivalent nature: God was both Brahma the creator and Shiva the destroyer (Zimmer, 1972). This was too much for Christians to cope with, and Father Victor White, who had championed Jung's work for some time, had to pull away. The impression that theologians had was that Jung's image of God had nothing to do with the Christian religion. However, it would be more difficult to claim that his image of the divine had nothing to do with Judaism, since the Hebrew God, Yahweh, was ambivalent, capricious, and wrathful.

Increasing dissonance between Christianity and modernity

Jung believed the lack of congruence between Christianity and modernity would increase in time, causing widespread malaise, anxiety, disorientation. Thus Jung set himself the task of trying to understand what had gone wrong with Christianity, and what might be required to build a new religious vision for the future. Whether this new religious vision would be recognisably "Christian" was uncertain. Jung would build his new vision using the materials of the past, but some aspects of Christianity, especially its long-standing dependence on dogma, doctrine, and belief, would be thrown out due to the modern demand for experience. Jung ranged widely across all religious traditions, ancient and modern, southern and northern European, Eastern and Western, in an effort to build a religious platform that might form the basis of a viable and credible religion of the future.

Central to Jung's project was the understanding that while religion is in decline, we need to distinguish religion as such from the traditional forms that have operated under its name. Religion would endure, he was confident of that, even though its current expressions were disappearing. His vision of archetypes was similar: there would always be archetypes, but archetypal images would come and go, as the requirements of humanity changed. So although ours is a time in which religion has dated, Jung wished to remind us that this did not mean that religion itself was finished. It would go on, and be reshaped as civilisation changed to accommodate new images of the divine. While Jung maintained his clinical focus to the end, there was this larger vision about where the present was pointing, and what moral and spiritual foundations would form the basis of a future society.

He could see that plurality and diversity were looming, and local beliefs and closed systems would be challenged and changed by contact with new ideas and beliefs. Jung travelled extensively, to North and East Africa, to India, the United States, and throughout Europe, to see what was happening in all corners of the world. The future would be multicultural, multiracial, and pluralistic, and the new world view would be impacted by this multiplicity. This would not lead to confusion and chaos, because he thought the psyche would be integrating and sifting all these elements, in an attempt to create a global vision that would accommodate differences. Jung's vision was biased towards wholeness and unity, but his was not a unity that would impose restrictions and limitations. He looked towards a unity that was not synonymous with uniformity.

Jung's psychology of modern society hinged on a paradox which sometimes appeared to be a contradiction: we need religion but cannot have it in its present forms. It is a paradox that has been echoed many times since Jung explored this problem. Many postmodern philosophers and sociologists have explored this same conundrum (Gadamer, 1998, p. 207). They have also said we need religion, and there is urgency in it, but no matter how often we make this call, we are blocked by the realisation that we cannot return to its traditional expressions.

Steeped as traditional religions are in superstition, supernaturalism, miracles, and impossible events, they do not match our consciousness.

We need a new expression of the religious impulse, and one that does not fly in the face of what we know about the world. As yet, this new religious form has not developed; at least, not in the West. Perhaps it is currently in the making. As we will see, Jung believed we are in the process of developing a new religion, which was of great interest to him. He knew we could not survive as a civilisation with individualistic spirituality, where everyone constructs their own brand of personal religion. The social world encourages this disunity, with fragmentation and individualism rampant in society.

The need for religion

The soul needs religion as a source of nourishment and culture. Without religion, the soul can lose its way, become lost in materialism and worldliness, or afflicted by neuroses and illness. The soul might shrivel up and die of isolation. It is not natural for the soul to be self-enclosed and walled up within the individual—this is a modern condition, promoted by "personal therapies" with no cultural responsibility. The soul longs for connection to spiritual forces beyond it. The idea of the soul as a "possession" of the individual is a recent idea, and one foreign to its nature. The soul might be defined as that impersonal force which links us with meaning, strives for community, and seeks connection with nature and ultimate reality. It is not personal but ancestral, while at the same time experienced as the core of our individuality.

Yet Western religion in its present forms is not helpful to the modern soul and does not assist its quest. The soul seeks wholeness but religion continues to strive for perfection, which is why religion has no answer to darkness and evil. The soul struggles to integrate the feminine in psyche and society, but Western religions remain patriarchal, despite a few changes initiated by feminist theology. Religions are products of society and not critical enough of society in prophetic witness of the spirit. The soul longs for poetry, myth, metaphor, and imagination, but the religions remain literal and historical. The soul needs religious experience, an encounter with the numinous, but religion is unable to provide it, preferring dogma, doctrine, and creed. The soul wants intrinsic, inward religion and tradition offers extrinsic, external religion.

The tension between these incommensurables, the soul and its needs and the traditions and their need for self-preservation, produces a tension so great that our religious and spiritual lives are in crisis.

It is difficult for many to tell right from wrong, true from false. As a civilisation we are confused, because if the soul wants one thing, and religion another, which way do we go, and in whom do we trust? A therapeutic ethic initiated by Freud, Jung, and their followers has replaced the religious ethic of the West, but beyond the world of the clinic and consulting room, there is no institutional representation of the new ethic. The best book on this crisis is Erich Neumann's *Depth Psychology and a New Ethic* (1949b).

Jung's ancestral roots

A question needs to be asked: Why does Jung bother with Christianity, given that he thinks it is so out of date as to be harmful to the soul and its needs? He writes: "The living spirit grows and even outgrows its earlier forms of expression" (1932, § 538). The earlier forms of expression, he argues, are organically connected to the new forms that are in the process of emerging. Jung presents another paradox of psychological life: if we cut ourselves off from the past, we become alienated from the life-energy or "rhizome" (as he calls it) that flows through our psychic lives.

Therefore Jung never advocates getting rid of the past but calls for the past to be reshaped and transformed. We need to keep in touch with our ancestral roots, but this has to be done in a way that does not alienate us from the present. Thus psychospiritual life, for Jung, consists in avoiding total immersion in the past or in the present. He suggests we try to move between them, leading a creative life between past and present.

Jung emphasises the importance of remaining connected to the archetypal powers of the psyche:

> The archetype ... throws a bridge between present-day consciousness, always in danger of losing its roots, and the natural, unconscious, instinctive wholeness of primeval times. Through this mediation the uniqueness, peculiarity, and one-sidedness of our present individual consciousness are linked up again with its natural roots. (1940, § 293)

It is the responsibility of every epoch to "translate" the archetypes into terms that are acceptable to the contemporary mind. If we lose this connection, the mind withers because it cannot be sundered from its roots without consequences. If this vital link is lost, consciousness languishes, and we find ourselves, as a civilisation, losing direction and purpose. The Jews have long known of this need to remain connected to the past, yet update and translate its expressions. This hermeneutical practice of reinterpretation is called *midrash*.

Jung's insight is that contemporary times are confused and dislocated because consciousness has moved far away from its archetypal roots, and this has occurred too quickly, removing us from the rhizome that feeds the soul. Von Franz puts it well when she says: "Jung was convinced that we are in a period of cultural decline today and that the survival or disappearance of our culture depends on a renewal of our archetypal myth" (1975, p. 183).

Jung does not attend to the transformation of Christianity because he is nostalgically attached to the religion of his childhood. Nor does he engage in such work because he feels that religious institutions require his support. He engages in this work because he believes we need to be reconnected to the archetypal roots of our civilisation, and thus "bound back" (*religio*) to the forces that sustain life.

This desire for connection to the past gives rise to a conservative element in his thinking, and he admits there is always a danger that consciousness will sink back into the past, as in a fundamentalist regression. But the word Von Franz uses is apt: Jung seeks a *renewal* of our archetypal myth, but this does not mean revival. Renewal involves transformation, as past and present come together in a creative synthesis. Revival produces an atavistic reversion to the past.

Reworking the vision

Jung's experience of Christianity is full of strange happenings and enigmas that cannot be understood as a continuation of tradition. His religion is of an unusual kind: his God lets fly a giant turd which crushes the Basel cathedral. This God reappears in a dream as a ritual phallus in an underground chamber. Jung wants to add a fourth member to the Trinity, but cannot make up his mind if the missing fourth is the feminine, as in Mary, Sophia, or Eve, or evil, as in Satan, Devil, or Lucifer. This is an anomaly in his major work, *Answer to Job*. It is arguably his greatest spiritual achievement, but to understand this prophetic work is extremely difficult. The reader is never sure what his "missing fourth" is.

It seems that Jung wants to add not only a fourth, the feminine, but also a fifth, the principle of evil. He cannot squeeze evil and the feminine into the same category, or turn the Trinity into a post-Christian quaternity. He talks of fashioning a quaternity, but in reality he points towards a quincunx, an image of the divine composed of five elements. But whatever we imagine Jung to be doing, he is working with a Christian base and trying to modify and change what he sees as the imbalances in the traditional model.

If we ask what archetypal figure is inspiring Jung's work, what do we answer? His spirit is fluid, mercurial, unconventional, heterodox, mythopoetic. It seems to have more in common with the Greek Hermes or Latin Mercurius than with Jesus. This theme has been taken up by Marie-Louise von Franz (1975) and Murray Stein (1983). Hermes has an element of the devil in him; he is a shape-shifter, good and evil. He is more ambivalent than anything that might answer to the description of "Christian". Jung's spirit finds significance where religious convention says it should not exist. He finds gods in diseases, spiritual meaning in neuroses, and divine grace in psychological healing. There is something baffling and complex about his vision, and I am sure that Jung himself would argue that it is the Self, archetype of wholeness, that drives him on his search.

Jung wanted to present a psychology of life integration, free from any attachment to formal religious language or ideology. He wanted his religiousness to be seen as natural and innate, rather than as supernatural or as an object of belief. To him the psyche was *naturally* religious, and he hoped, perhaps naïvely, that an unprejudiced scientific investigator would arrive at the same conclusion, after considering the facts that had been assembled by his psychology. This is why Jung kept claiming he was an empiricist, much to the astonishment of the scientific world. He was interested in what Neville Symington (2006) called "natural" religion rather than "revealed" religion. Jung's hope was that natural religion would emerge under the unprejudiced eye of science. It was not something that had to be added by an ecclesiastical tradition; it was already present in the psyche.

Religion as a resource for individuation

Jung wanted to explore religions as resources for spiritual growth, but did not want to see society dominated by religions. He did not like the idea of religion being imposed on people from above, and to that extent he seemed to be modern and secular in his point of view. For Jung, religious authority is best kept at the margins of society. At the centre of society, in commanding or dictatorial roles, religions would act as oppressive and tyrannical forces which the individual would have to fight against to embark on individuation. True to his Swiss German ancestry, Jung likes to think of society as a secular and democratic order, with religions on the edge or periphery, offering guidelines and directives for the symbolic life. But Jung wants the modern person to have the freedom to choose from a range of religious options. There is no absolute way for him; all religions are relative attempts of expressing the inexpressible. The only binding feature is that the individual must be true to him- or herself.

If the symbolic life is driven by deep impulses and inspired by fate, any capitulation to an external religious order for the sake of smoothing the way will bring suffering. An individuation process that is willed by fate is not going to be satisfied by an appropriation of a symbolic order for the sake of fitting in. If, for instance, one's inner life is driven by feminine archetypes and one adopts a patriarchal religion, or if the inner life is gnostic or mythopoetic and one adopts a literal or rational system, there will be difficulty as the soul collides with its adopted beliefs. One must accept suffering as part of what individuation means. Even if the world says you are wrong, one has to keep following the guiding star.

But it is important that cultures, religions, and arts provide a rich and diverse array of images, symbols, myths, and imaginative options— otherwise it would be impossible to know how to read the interior life. We can only respond to the psychic field if we are exposed to a range of symbolisms found in history and culture. This forms the basis of the clinical technique of amplification: interpreting symbolic materials by relating them to larger contexts of meaning. Each of us has to become a hermeneut and engage in amplification to understand the interior sources of meaning. There is no such thing as a sacred truth which is objectively given; everything we know and live by has to be interpreted and contextualised.

Although the secular order has impoverished the master narratives and left us without any dominant religious system, it has at least freed us from the tyranny of any single ideology. This means that those of us who have the courage of our convictions are able to follow the promptings of the inner voice and weave a web of meaning in whichever way we see fit. However, those without courage are not going to thrive spiritually in the secular order. They will never know where to turn for guidance, since society will show no direction and only an array of competing and contradictory systems. The modern condition suits those who have resilience and courage, otherwise there might be no spiritual life at all.

Return to society as an aspect of healing

In his late work Jung felt that healing involves not only the connection of the mind with soul, but a connection of the individual with society. How is the individual who has experienced a neurosis or mental illness to heal him- or herself if he or she remains alienated by virtue of an idiosyncratic experience of the unconscious? Jung asked this question more than fifty years ago, and it is even more important today.

Could every individual develop a spiritual intelligence and achieve a personal relation to the sacred? Jung began to doubt this, and in the later phase of his thinking, he shifted from being existential and individualistic, to being historical and traditional. Perhaps this is what happens when one's thinking shifts from ego to Self. Instead of "my" soul and "my" salvation, we begin to think of the soul of the world and the salvation of humanity. Jung's tone becomes darker, gloomier, more reflective. He realises the individual cannot merely "use" religion or "borrow" its symbols, but must build on it and add something to it.

Religion becomes more important, and more substantial, than a resource for personal spirituality. By 1932 Jung was already heading in this direction:

> Modern thought has unfortunately overlooked the fact that man has never yet been able single-handed to hold his own against the powers of darkness, that is, of the unconscious. Man has always stood in need of the spiritual help which his particular religion held out to him. (1932, § 531)

Without religion, the soul is handicapped and muted. Symbolism is not born out of the soul like a ready-made, pristine inheritance from within, but symbolic formation depends to a high degree on the individual's exposure to the social and cultural order. The soul without culture is impoverished, thin, and inarticulate; it hardly knows how to express its own longings. The idea of the soul as a self-sufficient entity which can function independently of culture and society is a product of individualism. Jung came close to individualism in his early think-ing, and the religions often charge him with this attitude. But I believe he saw beyond individualism and recognised the value of culture and tradition.

In his foreword to Victor White's *God and the Unconscious*, Jung wrote:

> If the patient is able to rediscover himself ... [by discovering] a healing, living quality which can make him whole ... then the question of reconciling his individual realization—or whatever one may choose to call the new insight or life-giving experience—with the collectively valid opinions and beliefs becomes a matter of vital importance. That which is only individual has an isolating effect, and the sick person will never be healed by becoming a mere indi-vidualist. He would still be neurotically unrelated and estranged from his social group. (1952b, § 452)

This is a side of Jung's work that few know. Scholars often complain that Jung gave little thought to the worldly dimension of our lives, and associate him with the "individualism" that he criticises in this passage. They imagine he is giving unconditional support to private experience, and that he cares nothing for how this squares with society and culture. But Jung goes on to say that:

> In view of the extraordinary importance of these so-called universal truths [of religion], a rapprochement between individual realiza-tions and social convictions becomes an urgent necessity. And just as the sick person in his individual distinctiveness must find a *modus vivendi* with society, so it will be a no less urgent task for him to compare the insights he has won through exploring the uncon-scious with the universal truths, and to bring them into mutual relationship. (Ibid.)

In the next paragraph he writes: "A great part of my life's work has been devoted to this endeavour." Indeed, one might say that the quarrel between individual experience and religious tradition is one of the cen-tral tensions of Jung's life and work. At first it seems that he favoured experience above tradition, and this is the "Jung" who is remembered by posterity. But as he got older, the role of tradition assumed greater importance.

Perhaps it could be said that the soul develops through three stages. First is the depth connection to the interiority of the person and the unconscious. This stage is personalistic, interior, reflective. Second there is the vertical connection to the transcendent and the life of the divine. This stage is spiritual, adventurous, questing, striving. Today many of us end our journey at this stage, thinking that we have reached the goal. But there is a third stage: a horizontal reconnection with society, culture, and community. It is not enough to win the boon from the unconscious and squander it on personal concerns. The boon must be shared and brought into community. In the same way that Arnold van Gennep (1960) outlined the three stages of initiatory process: separation from others, initiation into mystery, and return to the world, so these stages are still relevant today, even though we are often encouraged to believe that the spiritual journey is a purely personal matter.

The vertical connection to the transcendent must be complemented by a horizontal reconnection with the world, and spiritual experience is not complete until one finds a way back to others. This could be the saving grace, the connection that protects us not only from being lost in the unconscious but from being subject to the possibility of mental illness. We make the journey back not only for the sake of others, but for our own mental health.

Building on tradition

This is one reason why Jung kept coming back to his natal faith. He kept returning to it to find out what had gone wrong and how it could be fixed. The final chapter of his memoirs, "Late Thoughts", begins with the words: "What is remarkable about Christianity is ..." (1961a, p. 359). He was obsessed with it, and could not let it go. Despite his earlier dismissive attitude to his natal faith, he wanted to play a role in breathing new life into religion, in saving it from itself. He was not a priest, and could never be one. But he was burdened with the prophetic spirit and he wanted to discover a way to "dream the myth onwards".

Freudians have suggested that Jung wanted to destroy Christianity, as the religious heritage of his father. His Oedipal rage against his father's faith is demonstrated, they assert, in the childhood vision of the giant turd which destroyed the cathedral (Hodin, 1972; Rieff, 1966). This confirms, for them, his "anal aggressivity" towards his father, whom he wanted to destroy, just as he wanted to "destroy" Freud soon after. But this Oedipal filter is inappropriate and distances us from the reality. Instead of wanting to murder the father, Jung sought to redeem the father by going beyond him. In a sense, everything Jung did was an attempt to show that his father's faith had the potential to be renewed, but not in the old forms in which it was held.

He found the substance of Christianity in the discarded mystical traditions, such as alchemy and hermeticism, in which archetypal motifs could be related to the lived experiences of the soul. Jung showed, above all, that an outworn religion had an inner life which had yet to be explored. He did not wish to terminate the Christian myth, but to "dream the myth onwards" (1940, § 271), by reconnecting it with its lost mystical roots. As early as the 1950s, Freudian scholar David Bakan identified one of the key sources of Jung's psychology. He argued, and I would agree, that Jung's work arose "from a clearly mystical tradition within Christianity" (1958, p. 58).

Rather than wanting to destroy his father's house, a more apt metaphor is that he wanted to rebuild it and add more space. It had collapsed of its own accord, and Jung had observed this collapse as a boy. In his work *Aion*, he argued that the structure of Christianity could be altered and made more spacious than the current practitioners of faith allow. But he was aware of the destructiveness of those who purport to maintain the faith and protect it from change:

> The advocates of Christianity squander their energies in the mere preservation of what has come down to them, with no thought of building on to their house and making it roomier. Stagnation in these matters is threatened in the long run with a lethal end. (1951, § 170)

Ironically, the conservatives are destroying what they are claiming to preserve, by not allowing it to grow. Jung sees tradition as a living thing, whereas what conservatives call "tradition" is actually "convention", a stultifying dogma. The tradition wants to outgrow the conventions that are killing it. The priests safeguard the conventions, and the prophets and poets try to allow the tradition to grow. Yet they are the ones who are called the destroyers.

Jung makes it clear that the Christian religion requires a new interpretation, and the absence of revitalisation is proving detrimental:

> This is not to say that Christianity is finished. I am, on the contrary, convinced that it is not Christianity, but our conception and interpretation of it, that has become antiquated in face of the present

world situation. The Christian symbol is a living thing that carries in itself the seeds of further development. It can go on developing; it depends only on us, whether we can make up our minds to meditate again, and more thoroughly, on the Christian premises. (1957a, § 542)

This is not the reflection of an Oedipus trying to destroy his father's house. Rather, what we find is a son who wants to engage in what the Jewish tradition calls *midrash*, namely, the "making new" of ancient truths by translating them into modern terms. My colleague at La Trobe University, John Carroll, wrote: "*Midrash*, the Hebrew tradition called it, the process of each age taking up the ancient, sacred stories and retelling them in a way that spoke to the new times. Every living culture is inwardly driven to *midrash*" (2001, p. 13). We could say the same of Jung: he was driven to *midrash*, and felt this to be a task that Christianity had shirked.

In *Memories, Dreams, Reflections* Jung wrote:

> The Christian myth remained unassailably vital for a millennium, until the first signs of a further transformation of consciousness began appearing in the eleventh century. From then on, the symptoms of unrest and doubt increased, until at the end of the second millennium the outlines of a universal catastrophe became apparent, at first in the form of a threat to consciousness .... Christianity slumbers and has neglected to develop its myth further in the course of the centuries. Those who gave expression to the dark stirrings of growth in mythic ideas were refused a hearing; Joachim of Flora, Meister Eckhart and Jacob Boehme have remained obscurantists for the majority .... Our myth has become mute, and gives no answers. (1961a, pp. 360–364)

Jung believes that the tradition has tried to grow, but these attempts have been crushed by authorities. Growth has tried to take place since the eleventh and twelfth centuries, but to no avail. The authorities claim they are doing the right thing by stamping out "heresies", but they are killing the truth. Here one is reminded of a famous saying of the artist Picasso: "Tradition is having a baby, not wearing your father's hat." Conservatives wear their father's hat, and think they are being faithful, but tradition longs for new life. Its spirit calls for renewal, but conservatives are only interested in revival. The new growth involves divesting the faith of some conventions, and putting the old hat aside, but this is perceived as a malicious attack. It is the inability to see the spirit of tradition, as distinct from its form, that brings about this blindness.

The possibility of a new religious vision

Jung worked tirelessly on the project of rebuilding the Christian religion, and trying to add various new "rooms" to its structure. But at times he despaired for the future of Christianity. He was not confident that a religion that idealised the past could read the signs of our time, especially if the new spirit seemed "unholy", insofar as it is open to the principle of darkness. Hence Jung cries out:

> Where are the answers to the spiritual needs and troubles of a new epoch? And where the knowledge to deal with the psychological problems raised by the development of modern consciousness? (1946, § 396)

It was this despair that made him fear for the future of the West, and along with his prophetic aspect came a note of gloom, as he worried about where the saving grace would come from. His late works, *Man and His Symbols* and *The Undiscovered Self: Present and Future*, are permeated with a pessimism that competes with his more positive, upbeat voice about the possibilities of the human species. In a filmed interview Jung said, "The world today hangs by a thin thread, and that thread is the psyche of man" (1957b, p. 17).

With his respect for history and the world of the past, Jung was not predisposed to reflect on the idea of an entirely new religion. He had condemned the theosophists for suggesting that a new religious system based on Hinduism could be grafted onto the West. He upset Rudolf Steiner and his anthroposophical movement for the same reason. He was critical of Westerners who had abandoned Western religions, only to appropriate the symbols and philosophies of the East:

> Why, then, should the West not assimilate Eastern forms? ... Shall we be able to put on, like a new suit of clothes, ready-made symbols grown on foreign soil, saturated with foreign blood, spoken in a foreign tongue, nourished by a foreign culture [and] interwoven with foreign history? (1934a, § 25–27)

Using architectural imagery again, Jung spoke of the disrespect and thoughtlessness which is expressed by those who rush into foreign temples:

> We are, surely, the rightful heirs of Christian symbolism, but some-how we have squandered this heritage. We have let the house our fathers built fall into decay, and now we try to break into Oriental palaces that our fathers never knew. (Ibid., § 28)

One can see the respect that Jung held for "the house our fathers built", and in this mood he is certainly no Oedipus wishing to tear it down.

In public, Jung was reluctant to make pronouncements about a new religion. In his talk to the London Guild of Pastoral Psychology he said, "I am not going to found a new religion, and I know nothing about a future religion" (1939b, § 633). After delivering the Terry Lectures at Yale, Jung said:

> People sometimes call me a religious leader. I am not that. I have no message, no mission; I attempt only to understand. We are philoso-phers in the old sense of the word, lovers of wisdom. That avoids the sometimes questionable company of those who offer a religion. (1937, p. 109)

As if fending off his prophetic role, Jung said to the London Guild:

> But I do not care for a historic future at all, not at all; I am not con-cerned with it. I am only concerned with the fulfilment of that will which is in every individual. My history is only the history of those individuals who are going to fulfil their hypotheses. (1939b, § 639)

This strikes me as a lie, to avoid facing the unpleasantness of his pro-phetic calling. He does care, very much, about the historic future, and as he said in the Victor White text, "A great part of my life's work has been devoted to the endeavour [of connecting individual lives with the historical traditions]" (1952b, § 453). Jung was resistant to his prophetic role because he knew that it came with the burden of hubris, and he always tried to squash it, at least in public. He felt the tragic fate of Nietzsche as something close to his own calling, and he did not want Nietzsche's madness as his own.

In private, however, Jung appears to have been more open to the prophetic element. Max Zeller, one of his first generation followers, asked Jung for a parting word or blessing when he left Zurich in 1949. Zeller, a Jew from Berlin, was moving to the United States to commence a new life and clinical practice. He asked: "What am I doing as an analyst? With the overwhelming problems in the world, to see twenty or twenty-five patients, that's nothing. What are we doing, all of us?" (1975, p. 1). Before leaving for Los Angeles, Zeller had a dream that he discussed with Jung:

> A temple of vast dimensions was in the process of being built. As far as I could see ahead, behind, right and left there were incredible numbers of people building on gigantic pillars. I, too, was building on a pillar. The whole building process was in its very first beginnings, but the foundation was already there, the rest of the building was starting to go up, and I and many others were working on it. (Ibid., p. 1)

In response to this, Jung said:

> "Yes, you know, that is the temple we all build on. We don't know the people because, believe me, they build in India and China and in Russia and all over the world. That is the new religion. You know how long it will take until it is built?"
> I said, "How should I know? Do you know?" He said, "I know." I asked how long it will take. He said, "About six hundred years."
> "Where do you know this from?" I asked. He said, "From dreams. From other people's dreams and from my own. This new religion will come together as far as we can see." (Ibid., p. 2)

Zeller said he could now take leave of his mentor and move to North America, knowing what analysis is about, and what larger social process it is addressing. But there has been remarkably little discussion in Jungian circles about this matter, or on the nature and direction of a so-called new religion.

Perhaps Zeller's dream is responding to Jung's architectural metaphor, namely, that the house of religion is too small and needs to be rebuilt. This dream might be seen as a creative answer to Jung's childhood vision of God's house being destroyed by the turd. The soul needs a dwelling place or *temenos* for its reality, and the gods need a sacred abode where the soul and the gods can commune. However, Jung's specific concern about Christianity is eclipsed in this dream of the Jewish Zeller. The universality of the dream, and the fact that it involved "incredible numbers of people", indicates that the new sacred awareness must include and transcend specific and local traditions. Jung relishes this aspect, it seems, and by emphasising India, Russia, and China he is thinking of a universal religious awareness, rather than a specific religious tradition.

Endnote

1. This is based on a talk given as part of a lecture series to the Moscow Association for Analytical Psychology on May 21, 2021. A later version was delivered as a lecture for the Jung Society of South Australia, October 1, 2021.

REFERENCES

Abraham, K. (1909). Dreams and myths: A study in folk psychology. In: H. C. Abraham (Ed.), *Clinical Papers and Essays on Psychoanalysis*. London: Hogarth, 1955.

Adler, G. (Ed.) (1976). *C. G. Jung Letters, Vol. 2*. Princeton, NJ: Princeton University Press.

Auden, W. H. (1939). In Memory of Ernst Toller. In: *Another Time*, from *Collected Poems*. New York: Random House, 2007.

Bakan, D. (1958). *Sigmund Freud and the Jewish Mystical Tradition*. Boston, MA: Beacon.

Barreau, J.-C. (1982). Preface to Olivier Clément. In: *The Roots of Christian Mysticism*. London: New City, 2015.

Bates, D. (1938). *The Passing of the Aborigines*, 2nd edn. London: John Murray, 1966.

Berry, T. (1988). *The Dream of the Earth*. San Francisco, CA: Sierra Club.

Berry, T., & Swimme, B. (1992). *The Universe Story*. New York: Harper San Francisco.

Bishop, P. (2008). *Analytical Psychology and German Classical Aesthetics: Goethe, Schiller, and Jung, Vol. 1, The Development of the Personality*. London: Routledge.

Bishop, P. (2009). *Analytical Psychology and German Classical Aesthetics: Goethe, Schiller, and Jung*, 2 vols. London: Routledge.

Black, D. (Ed.) (2006). *Psychoanalysis and Religion in the 21st Century: Competitors or Collaborators?* London: Routledge.

Blake, W. (1793). *The Marriage of Heaven and Hell.* In: A. Kazin (Ed.), *The Portable Blake.* New York: Viking, 1975.

Bleuler, E. (1910). *Dementia Praecox: or, The Group of Schizophrenias.* J. Zinkin (Ed.). New York: International Universities Press, 1950.

Bly, R. (1990). *Iron John: A Book About Men.* Reading, MA: Addison-Wesley.

Bultmann, R. (1941). New Testament and mythology: The problem of demy-thologizing the New Testament proclamation. In: S. M. Ogden (Ed.), *New Testament and Mythology and Other Basic Writings.* Philadelphia, PA: Fortress, 1984.

Cambray, J. (2009). *Synchronicity: Nature and Psyche in an Interconnected Universe.* College Station, TX: Texas A & M University Press.

Campbell, J. (1972). *Myths to Live By.* New York: Viking.

Capra, F. (1995). *Toward a Transpersonal Ecology.* New York: State University of New York Press.

Caputo, J. (1997). *The Prayers and Tears of Jacques Derrida: Religion without Religion.* Bloomington, IN: Indiana University Press.

Carrette, J. R., & King, R. (2005). *Selling Spirituality: The Silent Takeover of Religion.* London: Routledge.

Carroll, J. (2001). *The Western Dreaming.* Sydney, Australia: HarperCollins.

Cattoi, T. (2018). Rescuing Alexandria: Depth psychology and the return of tropological exegesis. In: T. Cattoi & D. M. Odorisio (Eds.), *Depth Psychology and Mysticism.* London: Palgrave Macmillan.

Cattoi, T., & Odorisio, D. M. (Eds.) (2018). *Depth Psychology and Mysticism.* London: Palgrave Macmillan.

Cobb, M., Puchalski, C., & Rumbold, B. (Eds.) (2012). *The Oxford Textbook of Spirituality in Healthcare.* Oxford: Oxford University Press.

Collins, A., & Molchanov, E. (Eds.) (2013). *Jung and India, Spring 90: A Journal of Archetype and Culture.* New Orleans, LA: Spring Journal.

Delio, I. (2023). *The Not-Yet God: Carl Jung, Teilhard de Chardin and the Relational Whole.* Maryknoll, NY: Orbis.

Derrida, J. (1996). Faith and knowledge: The two sources of "religion" at the limits of reason alone. In: J. Derrida & G. Vattimo (Eds.), *Religion.* Redwood City, CA: Stanford University Press, 1998.

Derrida, J., & Vattimo, G. (Eds.) (1998). *Religion.* Stanford, CA: Stanford University Press.

De Souza, M., Francis, L., O'Higgins-Norman, J., & Scott, D. (Eds.) (2009). *International Handbook of Education for Spirituality, Care and Wellbeing.* Heidelberg, Germany: Springer.

Dillard, A. (1984). *Teaching a Stone to Talk.* London: Picador.

Drewermann, E. (1994). *Discovering the God Child Within: A Spiritual Psychology of the Infancy of Jesus.* New York: Crossroad.

Duggan, P. E. (1989). *The Assumption Dogma: Some Reactions and Ecumenical Implications in the Thought of English-Speaking Theologians.* Cleveland, OH: Emerson.

Edinger, E. F. (1984). *The Creation of Consciousness: Jung's Myth for Modern Man.* Toronto, Canada: Inner City.

Edinger, E. F., & Wesley, D. (1996). *The Aion Lectures: Exploring the Self in C. G. Jung's Aion.* Toronto, Canada: Inner City.

Eliade, M. (1969). *The Quest: History and Meaning in Religion.* Chicago, IL: University of Chicago Press.

Eliot, T. S. (1922). The Waste Land. In: *Collected Poems 1929–1962.* London: Faber and Faber, 1974.

Evans, R. I. (1979). *Jung on Elementary Psychology.* London: Routledge & Kegan Paul.

Fan, L., & Whitehead, J. D. (2005). Spirituality in a modern Chinese metropolis. In: D. A. Palmer (Ed.), *Chinese Religious Life.* Oxford: Oxford University Press, 2011.

Flannery, T. (2002). *The Future Eaters: An Ecological History of the Australasian Lands and People.* New York: Grove.

Frost, R. (1947). Directive. In: M. Ferguson, M. J. Salter, & J. Stallworthy (Eds.), *The Norton Anthology of Poetry,* fifth edn. New York: W. W. Norton, 2005.

Foucault, M. (1984). The ethic of the care of the self as a practice of freedom. In: J. Bernauer & D. Rasmussen (Eds.), *The Final Foucault.* Cambridge, MA: MIT Press, 1991.

Freud, S. (1900a). *The Interpretation of Dreams. S. E., 4.* London: Hogarth.

Freud, S. (1914d). On the history of the psychoanalytic movement. *S. E., 14.* London: Hogarth.

Freud, S. (1927c). *The Future of an Illusion. S. E., 21.* London: Hogarth.

Freud, S. (1930a). *Civilization and Its Discontents. S. E., 21.* London: Hogarth.

Gadamer, H.-G. (1998). Dialogues in Capri. In: J. Derrida & G. Vattimo (Eds.), *Religion.* Stanford, CA: Stanford University Press.

Gauthier, F. (2023). Spirituality and wellbeing as a global phenomenon. Paper delivered at the Spirituality, Wellbeing and Risks international conference, at Deakin University, Melbourne, June 22.

Gebser, J. (1949). *The Ever-Present Origin.* Athens, OH: Ohio University Press, 1986.

Girard, R. (1972). *Violence and the Sacred.* London: Continuum, 2005.

Greene, B. (1999). *The Elegant Universe.* New York: Vintage.

Greene, Liz (2017). "The way of what is to come": Jung's vision of the Aquarian age. In: M. Stein & T. Arzt (Eds.), *Jung's Red Book for Our Time: Searching for Soul under Postmodern Conditions, Vol. 1.* Asheville, NC: Chiron.

Grieves, V. (2009). *Aboriginal Spirituality: Aboriginal Philosophy: The Basis of Aboriginal Social and Emotional Wellbeing*. Discussion Paper No. 9. Darwin, Australia: Cooperative Research Centre for Aboriginal Health). http://crcah.org.au/publications/downloads/DP9-Aboriginal-Spirituality.pdf. Date last accessed: 20 December 2023.

Habel, N. (2002). Ecojustice hermeneutics: Reflections and challenges. In: N. Habel & V. Balabanski (Eds.), *The Earth Story in the New Testament* (pp. 3–4). London: Bloomsbury Academic.

Habel, N. (2009). *An Inconvenient Text: Is a Green Reading of the Bible Possible?* Adelaide, Australia: ATF.

Habel, N., & Balabanski, V. (Eds.) (2002). *The Earth Story in the New Testament*. London: Bloomsbury Academic.

Habermas, J. (2010). *An Awareness of What Is Missing: Faith and Reason in a Post-Secular Age*. New York: Polity.

Harrington, J. (2018). *Dangerous Mystic: Meister Eckhart's Path to the God Within*. New York: Penguin.

Hauke, C. (2000). *Jung and the Postmodern*. London: Routledge.

Hay, D. (2006). *Something There: The Biology of the Human Spirit*. London: Darton, Longman & Todd.

Heidegger, M. (1936). What Are Poets For? In: A. Hofstadter (Ed. & Trans.), *Poetry, Language, Thought*. New York: Harper & Row, 1971.

Henderson, J. (1990). *Shadow and Self*. Asheville, NC: Chiron.

Heschel, A. J. (1976). *Man Is Not Alone: A Philosophy of Religion*. New York: Farrar, Straus and Giroux.

Hillman, J. (1975). *Re-Visioning Psychology*. New York: Harper & Row.

Hillman, J., & Ventura, M. (1992). *We've Had a Hundred Years of Psychotherapy and the World's Getting Worse*. San Francisco, CA: HarperCollins.

Hodin, J. P. (1972). *Modern Art and the Modern Mind*. Cleveland, OH: Press of Case Western Reserve University.

Hölderlin, F. (1801). Bread and Wine. In: *Poems of Friedrich Hölderlin*. J. Mitchell (Trans.). San Francisco, CA: Ithuriel's Spear, 2004.

Hölderlin, F. (1802). Patmos, v. 3–4. Quoted in Bambach, C., Does the saving power grow? *Research in Phenomenology*, 46(3) (July 2016): 473.

Huss, B. (2014). Spirituality: The emergence of a new cultural category and its challenge to the religious and the secular. *Journal of Contemporary Religion*, 29(1): 47.

Jacobs, G. (2003). *The Ancestral Mind*. New York: Viking.

Johnson, R. A. (1983). *We: Understanding the Psychology of Romantic Love*. New York: Harper One, 2009.

Johnson, R. A. (1986). *Inner Work: Using Dreams and Active Imagination for Personal Growth*. San Francisco, CA: Harper & Row.

Jung, C. G. (1910). Letter to Freud. In: W. McGuire (Ed.), *The Freud/Jung Letters*. London: Hogarth, 1974.

All Jung listings showing *CW* are from *The Collected Works of C. G. Jung* in 20 volumes. London: Routledge, 1967.

Jung, C. G. (1912a). *Symbols of Transformation. CW, 5*, § 339.

Jung, C. G. (1912b). Two Kinds of Thinking. *CW, 5*, § 38, 138.

Jung, C. G. (1916). The Transcendent Function. *CW, 8*, § 184.

Jung, C. G. (1918). The Role of the Unconscious. *CW, 10*, § 13, 17, 18.

Jung, C. G. (1921). Definitions. In: *Psychological Types, CW, 6*, § 814, 816–818.

Jung, C. G. (1927). Mind and Earth. *CW, 10*, § 52–54, 59, 84, 94, 97, 98, 103.

Jung, C. G. (1928). Analytical Psychology and "Weltanschauung". *CW, 8*, § 717.

Jung, C. G. (1929a). Freud and Jung: Contrasts. *CW, 4*, § 780.

Jung, C. G. (1929b). Commentary on "The Secret of the Golden Flower". *CW, 13*, § 54.

Jung, C. G. (1929c, September 12). Letter to Walter Robert Corti. In: G. Adler (Ed.), *C. G. Jung Letters, Vol. I, 1906–1950.* London: Routledge & Kegan Paul, 1973.

Jung, C. G. (1930a). The Complications of American Psychology. *CW, 10*, § 962, 969, 979, 980.

Jung, C. G. (1930b). Psychology and Literature. *CW, 15*, § 148, 159.

Jung, C. G. (1931a). The Spiritual Problem of Modern Man. *CW, 10*, § 148–196.

Jung, C. G. (1931b). The Structure of the Psyche. *CW, 8*, § 283.

Jung, C. G. (1931c). Archaic Man. *CW, 10*, § 105, 104–147.

Jung, C. G. (1931d). The Stages of Life. *CW, 8*, § 749–795.

Jung, C. G. (1931e). Dream-Analysis in Its Practical Application. *CW, 16*, § 320, 332, 352.

Jung, C. G. (1932). Psychotherapists or the Clergy. *CW, 11*, § 507, 509, 514, 523, 528, 529, 531, 538.

Jung, C. G. (1933). *Modern Man in Search of a Soul.* London: Routledge, 2004.

Jung, C. G. (1934a). Archetypes of the Collective Unconscious. *CW, 9, 1*, § 25–28, 32–33, 40, 50.

Jung, C. G. (1934b). The State of Psychotherapy Today. *CW, 10*, § 367, 591.

Jung, C. G. (1934c). The Meaning of Psychology for Modern Man. Lecture given in Cologne. *CW, 10*, § 285, 328, 304.

Jung, C. G. (1934d). The Soul and Death, *CW, 8*, § 808.

Jung, C. G. (1936). The Two Million-Year-Old Man. In: W. McGuire & R. F. C. Hull (Eds.), *C. G. Jung Speaking.* London: Picador, 1980.

Jung, C. G. (1937). Is Analytical Psychology a Religion? In: W. McGuire & R. F. C. Hull (Eds.), *C. G. Jung Speaking: Interviews and Encounters* (pp. 108–109). London: Picador, 1980.

Jung, C. G. (1938). *Psychology and Religion* (the Terry Lectures). *CW, 11*, § 51–53, 100, 141, 148.

Jung, C. G. (1939a). Psychological Commentary on *The Tibetan Book of the Great Liberation. CW, 11*, § 773.

Jung, C. G. (1939b). The Symbolic Life. *CW, 18*, § 608, 632–633, 639, 682.

Jung, C. G. (1939c). The Meaning of Individuation. In: *The Integration of the Personality*. London: Kegan Paul, 1940.

Jung, C. G. (1940). The Psychology of the Child Archetype. *CW*, *9*, 1, § 260, 261, 267, 271, 293.

Jung, C. G. (1942a). A Psychological Approach to the Dogma of the Trinity. *CW*, *11*, § 172, 233.

Jung, C. G. (1942b). Transformation Symbolism in the Mass. *CW*, *11*, § 400.

Jung, C. G. (1943). The Spirit Mercurius. *CW*, *13*, § 301.

Jung, C. G. (1945a). The Philosophical Tree. *CW*, *13*, § 335.

Jung, C. G. (1945b). Letter to P. W. Martin. In: G. Adler (Ed.), *C. G. Jung Letters, Vol. 1*. Princeton, NJ: Princeton University Press, 1973.

Jung, C. G. (1946). The Psychology of the Transference. *CW*, *16*, § 396.

Jung, C. G. (1951). *Aion. CW*, *9*, part 2, § 23, 24, 67, 170, 301, 303.

Jung, C. G. (1952a). *Answer to Job. CW*, 11, § 553–555, 557, 558, 575, 617, 647, 655, 693, 748, 749, 751–754.

Jung, C. G. (1952b). Foreword to White, V., *God and the Unconscious. CW* 11, § 452, 453. New York: Henry Regnery.

Jung, C. G. (1953, April 30). Letter to Dr. Dorothee Hoch. In: G. Adler (Ed.), *C. G. Jung Letters, Vol. II, 1951–1961*. London: Routledge & Kegan Paul, 1976.

Jung, C. G. (1955, February 25). Letter to Adolph Keller. In: G. Adler (Ed.), *C. G. Jung Letters, Vol. II, 1951–1961*. London: Routledge & Kegan Paul, 1976.

Jung, C. G. (1955–56). *Mysterium Coniunctionis. CW*, *14*, § 503.

Jung, C. G. (1957a). The Undiscovered Self. *CW*, *10*, § 542.

Jung, C. G. (1957b). Conversations with Carl Jung. In: R. I. Evans, *Jung on Elementary Psychology*. London: Routledge & Kegan Paul.

Jung, C. G. (1958, April 19). Letter to F. von Tischendorf. In: G. Adler (Ed.), *C. G. Jung Letters, Vol. 2*. Princeton, NJ: Princeton University Press, 1976.

Jung, C. G. (1961a). *Memories, Dreams, Reflections*. A. Jaffé (Ed.). London: Fontana, 1995.

Jung, C. G. (1961b). Symbols and the Interpretation of Dreams. *CW*, *18*, § 584, 591.

Jung, C. G. (1977). *Jung Speaking: Interviews and Encounters*. W. McGuire & R. F. C. Hull (Eds.). Princeton, NJ: Princeton University Press.

Jung, C. G. (2009). *The Red Book: Liber Novus*. S. Shamdasani (Ed.), M. Kyburz & J. Peck (Trans.). New York: W. W. Norton.

Kalsched, D. (2013). *Trauma and the Soul: A Psycho-Spiritual Approach to Human Development and Its Interruption*. London: Routledge.

Kast, V. (1991). *Joy, Inspiration and Hope*. College Station, TX: Texas A & M University Press.

Kim, J. H. (1996). Sources outside of Europe. In: P. H. van Ness (Ed.), *Spirituality and the Secular Quest*. New York: Crossroad.

Koch, C. (1978). *The Year of Living Dangerously*. London: Michael Joseph.

Levinas, E. (1975). God and philosophy. In: S. Hand (Ed.), *The Levinas Reader*. Oxford: Basil Blackwell, 1989.

Lloyd, G. (1996). *Spinoza and the Ethics*. London: Routledge.

Lohrey, A. (2002). Groundswell: The rise of the greens, *Quarterly Essay, 8*: 1–86.

Lovelock, J. (1979). *Gaia: A New Look at Life on Earth*. Oxford: Oxford University Press.

Mackay, H. (2016). *Beyond Belief: How We Find Meaning, with or without Religion*. Sydney, Australia: Pan Macmillan.

Marchiano, L. (2017). Outbreak: On transgender teens and psychic epidemics. *Psychological Perspectives, 60*(3): 345–366.

Marchiano, L. (2021). Gender detransition: A case study. *Journal of Analytical Psychology, 66*(4): 813.

McCabe, I. (2015). *Carl Jung and Alcoholics Anonymous: The Twelve Steps as a Spiritual Journey of Individuation*. London: Routledge, 2018.

McGrath, S. J. (2012). *The Dark Ground of Spirit: Schelling and the Unconscious*. London: Routledge.

McGuckin, J. A. (2004). *The Westminster Handbook to Origen*. Louisville, KY: Westminster John Knox.

McGuire, W., & Hull, R. F. C. (Eds.) (1980). *C. G. Jung Speaking: Interviews and Encounters* (pp. 108–109). London: Picador.

Meister Eckhart. *Meister Eckhart, Vol. 1*. F. Pfeiffer (Ed.), C. de B. Evans (Trans.). London: John M. Watkins, 1956.

Merton, T. (1961). *New Seeds of Contemplation*. New York: New Directions, 1972.

Moore, T. (1996). *The Education of the Heart*. New York: HarperCollins.

Morgan, O., & Jordan, M. (1999). *Addiction and Spirituality*. St Louis, MO: Chalice.

Neumann, E. (1949a). *The Origins and History of Consciousness*. Princeton, NJ: Princeton University Press, 1973.

Neumann, E. (1949b). *Depth Psychology and a New Ethic*. Boston, MA: Shambhala, 1990.

Neumann, E. (1954). Creative man and transformation. In: *Art and the Creative Unconscious*. Princeton, NJ: Princeton University Press, 1974.

Nietzsche, F. (1887a). *The Genealogy of Morals*. W. Kaufmann (Trans.). New York: Random House, 1989.

Nietzsche, F. (1887b). The madman. In: *The Gay Science* [also translated as *The Joyful Wisdom*], 2nd edn. New York: Frederick Ungar, 1960.

Ogden, S. M. (Ed.) (1984). *New Testament and Mythology and Other Basic Writings*. Philadelphia, PA: Fortress.

Oliver, M. (1999). Winter hours. In: *Upstream: Selected Essays*. New York: Penguin, 2019.

Oord, T. J. (2010). Essential kenosis. In: *The Nature of Love: A Theology*. New York: Chalice.

Origen (c. 220–230). On first principles. In: P. Kirby (Ed.), A. Roberts & J. Donaldson (Trans.), *Early Christian Writings*, June 5, 2019, free online library: http://earlychristianwritings.com/origen.htm

Origen. Commentary on John. In: P. Kirby (Ed.), A. Roberts & J. Donaldson (Trans.), *Early Christian Writings*, June 5, 2019, free online library: http://earlychristianwritings.com/origen.htm

Origen. Against Celsus. In: F. Crombie (Trans.). London: Hamilton & Co, 1899.

Ostrowski-Sachs, M. (1971). *From Conversations with C. G. Jung*. Zürich, Switzerland: Juris Druck.

Otto, R. (1917). *The Idea of the Holy*. J. W. Harvey (Ed.). Oxford: Oxford University Press, 1923.

Poe, E. A. (1849). A dream within a dream. In: R. W. Griswold (Ed.), *The Works of the Late Edgar Allan Poe*. New York: J. S. Redfield, 1850.

Rieff, P. (1966). *The Triumph of the Therapeutic: Uses of Faith After Freud*. New York: Harper & Row.

Roethke, T. (1964). In a Dark Time. In: M. Ferguson, M. J. Salter, & J. Stallworthy (Eds.), *The Norton Anthology of Poetry*, fifth edn. New York: W. W. Norton, 2005.

Roszak, T., Gomes, M. E., & Kanner, A. K. (Eds.) (1995). *Ecopsychology: Restoring the Earth, Healing the Mind*. San Francisco, CA: Sierra Club.

Rudd, K. (2008). Apology to Australia's Indigenous Peoples. http://aph. gov.au/house/Rudd_Speech.pdf (last accessed December 23, 2023).

Sanford, J. (1989). *Dreams: God's Forgotten Language*. New York: Harper One.

Santmire, P. (1985). *The Travail of Nature: The Ambiguous Ecological Promise of Christian Theology*. New York: Fortress, 1991.

Shamdasani, S. (1998). *Cult Fictions: C. G. Jung and the Founding of Analytical Psychology*. London: Routledge.

Shamdasani, S. (2010). *The Making of Modern Psychology: The Dream of a Science*. Cambridge: Cambridge University Press.

Smith, J. (2020). *Religious but Not Religious: Living a Symbolic Life*. Asheville, NC: Chiron.

Somé, M. (1993). *Ritual: Power, Healing, and Community*. Portland, OR: Swan Raven.

Spencer, B., & Gillen, F. (1899). *Native Tribes of Central Australia*. Cambridge: Cambridge University Press, 2010.

St Augustine (397–400). *Confessions*. R. Warner (Trans.). New York: Mentor, 1963.

Stein, M. (1983). *In Midlife: A Jungian Perspective*. Dallas, TX: Spring.

Stein, M. (2013). *Jung's Treatment of Christianity: The Psychotherapy of a Religious Tradition*. Asheville, NC: Chiron.

Stein, M., & Arzt, T. (2017). *Jung's Red Book for Our Time: Searching for Soul under Postmodern Conditions, Vol. 1*. Asheville, NC: Chiron.

Stevens, A. (1982). *Archetypes: A Natural History of the Self*. London: Routledge & Kegan Paul.

Suzuki, D., & McConnell, A. (1997). *The Sacred Balance: Rediscovering Our Place in Nature*. Vancouver, Canada: Greystone.

Symington, N. (2006). Religion: The guarantor of civilization. In: D. Black (Ed.), *Psychoanalysis and Religion in the 21st Century: Competitors or Collaborators?* London: Routledge.

Tacey, D. (1995). *Edge of the Sacred: Transformation in Australia*. Melbourne, Australia: Harper Collins. Republished as *Edge of the Sacred: Jung, Psyche, Earth*. Einsiedeln, Switzerland: Daimon, 2009.

Tacey, D. (1997a). *Remaking Men: Jung, Spirituality and Social Change*. Melbourne, Australia: Viking Penguin.

Tacey, D. (1997b). Rites and wrongs of passage. In: *Remaking Men*. London: Routledge.

Tacey, D. (2001). *Jung and the New Age*. London: Routledge.

Tacey, D. (2003). *The Spirituality Revolution: The Emergence of Contemporary Spirituality*. London: Routledge, 2004.

Tacey, D. (2008). Imagining transcendence at the end of modernity: Jung and Derrida. In: L. Huskinson (Ed.), *Dreaming the Myth Onwards: New Directions in Jungian Therapy and Thought*. London: Routledge.

Tacey, D. (2009). Colonisation in reverse. In: *Edge of the Sacred: Jung, Psyche, Earth*. Einsiedeln, Switzerland: Daimon.

Tacey, D. (2011). *Gods and Diseases: Making Sense of Our Physical and Mental Wellbeing*. London: Routledge, 2012.

Tacey, D. (Ed.) (2012). *The Jung Reader*. London: Routledge.

Tacey, D. (2013). *The Darkening Spirit: Jung, Spirituality, Religion*. London: Routledge.

Tacey, D. (2019). Return of the sacred in an age of terror. In: *The Postsecular Sacred*. London: Routledge, 2020.

Tacey, D., & Casement, A. (Eds.) (2006). *The Idea of the Numinous: Contemporary Jungian and Psychoanalytic Perspectives*. London: Routledge.

Van Gennep, A. (1908). *The Rites of Passage*. Chicago, IL: University of Chicago Press, 1960.

Von Franz, M.-L. (1975). *C. G. Jung: His Myth in Our Time*. Boston, MA: Little, Brown.

Von Franz, M.-L. (2000). *The Problem of the Puer Aeternus*, 3rd edn. Toronto, Canada: Inner City.

Von Franz, M.-L. (2014). *Dreams: A Study of the Dreams of Jung, Descartes, Socrates, and Other Historical Figures*. Boston, MA: Shambhala.

Walker, A. (1997). *Anything We Love, Can Be Saved: A Writer's Activism*. London: Women's Press.

Ward, M. (2011). *The Comfort of Water: A River Pilgrimage*. Melbourne, Australia: Transit Lounge.

Watson, E. L. G. (1946). *But to What Purpose: The Autobiography of a Contemporary* London: Cresset.

Watson, E. L. G. (1990). *Descent of Spirit*. D. Green (Ed.). Sydney, Australia: Primavera.

Weber, M. (1918). Science as a vocation. In: H. H. Gerth & C. Wright Mills (Eds. & Trans.), *From Max Weber: Essays in Sociology*. New York: Oxford University Press, 1946.

Welwood, J. (1984). *Toward a Psychology of Awakening: Buddhism, Psychotherapy, and the Path of Personal and Spiritual Transformation*. Boston, MA: Shambhala, 2000.

White, L. Jr. (1967). The historical roots of our ecological crisis. *Science*, 155(3767): 1203–1207.

White, V. (1952). *God and the Unconscious*. New York: Henry Regnery.

Whitman, W. (1868). A noiseless, patient spider. In: M. Ferguson, M. J. Salter, & J. Stallworthy (Eds.), *The Norton Anthology of Poetry*, fifth edn. New York: W. W. Norton, 2005.

Whitmont, E. C., & Perera, S. (1989). *Dreams: A Portal to the Source*. London: Routledge.

Wilber, K. (1986). *Up From Eden: A Transpersonal View of Human Evolution*. Boston, MA: Shambhala.

Wilber, K. (1980). *The Atman Project: A Transpersonal View of Human Development*. Wheaton, IL: Quest.

Williams, L., Roberts, R., & McIntosh, A. (2012). *Radical Human Ecology: Intercultural and Indigenous Approaches*. Farnham, UK: Ashgate.

Wolff, T. (1934). Structural Forms of the Feminine Psyche. https://cgjung.net/espace/jps/articles/peggy-vermeesch/toni-wolff-structural-forms-feminine-psyche/(last accessed October 28, 2023).

Wordsworth, W. (1798). Lines Composed a Few Miles above Tintern Abbey, On Revisiting the Banks of the Wye during a Tour, July 13, 1798. https://poetryfoundation.org/poems/45527/lines-composed-a-few-miles-above-tintern-abbey-on-revisiting-the-banks-of-the-wye-during-a-tour-july-13-1798 (last accessed October 28, 2023).

Wordsworth, W. (1807). Ode: Intimations of Immortality from Recollections of Early Childhood, lines 58–65.

Wright, J. (1955). At Cooloolah. In: *A Human Pattern: Selected Poems*. Sydney, Australia: Angus & Robertson, 1990.

Yang, F. (2014). What about China? Religious vitality in the most secular and rapidly modernizing society. *Sociology of Religion*, 75(4): 562–578.

Yeats, W. B. (1919). The Second Coming. In: T. Webb (Ed.), *W. B. Yeats: Selected Poetry*. London: Penguin, 1991.

Zeller, M. (1975). *The Dream, The Vision of the Night*. 2nd edn. Boston, MA: Sigo, 1990.

Ziegler, A. (1983). *Archetypal Medicine*. Dallas, TX: Spring.

Zimmer, H. (1972). *Myths and Symbols in Indian Art and Civilization*. Princeton, NJ: Princeton University Press.

INDEX

dissonance between Christianity
and, 241–243
new religious future, 241–243
rejection of belief, 49
Modern Man in Search of a Soul (Jung),
135, 167
modern psyche, 74
crisis of, 243–244
moralism, 195–196
Murray, L., 3
Mysterium Coniunctionis (Jung), 163
mysticism, 2–3
mystical Christianity, 210–211,
211–216
mystical sub-traditions of the
religions, 2
mystical traditions, 251
mystics, 5
and schizophrenia, 232
myth, 194, 212–213
living, 194–198
revitalising Christian myth, 197
therapeutic function of, 198–200
mythologem, 197
mythopoetic men's movement, 80
mythos, 158, 199, 212, 214
revival of, 195
vital role of, 198–200
Myths to Live By (Campbell), 232

Native Tribes of Central Australia
(Spencer and Gillen), 90
"negative capability", 42
Neumann, E., 27, 41, 55, 151, 244
New Jerusalem, 151
new religious consciousness, 48–51
new religious vision, 253–256
new soul religion, 53–56
new spiritual path, 36–38
New World psyche. *See* American
psyche
Nietzsche, F., 55, 66, 67, 68, 72, 204, 254
"night religion", 92–93
non-ordinary reality, 20
Nostradamus, 190
"not-yet" God, 171–172, 177

numinosum, 16
numinous, 221–223

oceanic feeling, 229–231
ocean of consciousness, 235
Oliver, M., 3, 4
the One. *See* the Tao
Origen, 211–216
"orphans of the Real", 20
Otto, R., 5, 222

panentheism, 124–125, 137–138.
See also Self
Paradise Regained, 151
pathological spirituality, 233–235
pathos, 227–228
Perera, S., 155
personal ego, 111
Peterson, J., 164–165
Picasso, 252
Picnic at Hanging Rock (Lindsay), 96
Planck, M., 224
Plato, 134, 161
plerosis, 145–146
Poe, E. A., 176
Pope Francis, 120, 121, 123
Pope John Paul II, 121
post-Christian vision, 32–36
postcolonial reconciliation, 81–86
pre-rational religions, 76
"Pre/Trans Fallacy", 236
priesthood, 37
primal forces, 95–96
primordial mind
activation of, 86–89
and earth, 93–96
primordial spirit, 89–93
privatio boni, 186
The Problem of the Puer Aeternus
(von Franz), 144
progressive voice, 56
psyche. *See* soul
psychic dissolution, 233
psychic epidemic, 164, 165
psychoid, 92
psychological healing, 228

www.ingramcontent.com/pod-product-compliance
Lightning Source LLC
Chambersburg PA
CBHW050632280326
41932CB00015B/2610